Supporting Asian American Students in Multicultural Contexts

LANGUAGE, EDUCATION AND DIVERSITY

Series Editors: **Stephen May**, *University of Auckland, New Zealand*, **Teresa L. McCarty**, *University of California, USA*, **Constant Leung**, *King's College London, UK* and **Serafín M. Coronel-Molina**, *Indiana University Bloomington, USA*

The Language, Education and Diversity series aims to publish work at the intersections of language policy, language teaching and bilingualism/multilingualism, with a particular focus on critical, socially-just alternatives for minoritised students and communities. The series is interdisciplinary, drawing on scholarship from language policy, language education, sociolinguistics, applied linguistics, linguistic anthropology and the sociology of language, including work in raciolinguistics and translingualism. We welcome a variety of methodological approaches, although critical ethnographic accounts are of particular interest.

Topics covered by the series include:

- Bilingual and Multilingual Models of Education
- Indigenous Language Education
- Multicultural Education
- Community-based Education

All books in this series are externally peer-reviewed.

Full details of all the books in this series and of all our other publications can be found on http://www.multilingual-matters.com, or by writing to Multilingual Matters, BLOCK, The Fairfax, Pithay Court, Bristol, BS1 3BN, UK.

LANGUAGE, EDUCATION AND DIVERSITY: 7

Supporting Asian American Students in Multicultural Contexts

Language, Culture, Identity and Power in the US

Chaehyun Lee

MULTILINGUAL MATTERS
Bristol • Jackson

This book is for all educators who
inspire hope and instill a love of learning
for our bi/multi/plurilingual students.

DOI https://doi.org/10.21832/LEE0086
Library of Congress Cataloging in Publication Data
A catalog record for this book is available from the Library of Congress.

Library of Congress Control Number: 2025036720

British Library Cataloguing in Publication Data
A catalogue entry for this book is available from the British Library.

ISBN-13: 978-1-83668-008-6 (hbk)
ISBN-13: 978-1-83668-009-3 (pbk)

Multilingual Matters
UK: BLOCK, The Fairfax, Pithay Court, Bristol, BS1 3BN, UK.
USA: Ingram, Jackson, TN, USA.
Authorised Representative: Easy Access System Europe - Mustamäe tee 50, 10621
Tallinn, Estonia, gpsr.requests@easproject.com.

Website: https://www.multilingual-matters.com
Bluesky: @multi-ling-mat.bsky.social
X: Multi_Ling_MatFacebook: https://www.facebook.com/multilingualmatters
Blog: https://www.channelviewpublications.wordpress.com

The policy of Multilingual Matters/Channel View Publications is to use papers
that are natural, renewable and recyclable products, made from wood grown in
sustainable forests. In the manufacturing process of our books, and to further
support our policy, preference is given to printers that have FSC and PEFC Chain
of Custody certification. The FSC and/or PEFC logos will appear on those books
where full certification has been granted to the printer concerned.

Typeset by Deanta Global Publishing Services, Chennai, India

Contents

Acknowledgments

After more than a decade of teaching about bilingual, biliteracy and multicultural education, I feel indebted to an ever-expanding and growing list of people. My first sincere appreciation goes to my former students at the Korean heritage language schools, who provided rich and invaluable insights into the complex dynamics of teaching and learning. For over 10 years, my students have taught me the gifts of bilingualism that extend far beyond language abilities or communicative skills. I have gained a great deal of understanding and knowledge about life stories and journeys to bi/multilingualism. Thank you all for teaching me the powerful reciprocal nature of learning. Each of you taught me enormously and led me to want to be a better educator and life mentor.

Working on bilingual education has been inspired by my advisor, Dr Georgia Garcia, and other educational scholars, Drs Eurydice Bauer, Sarah McCarthey and Liv Davila from the University of Illinois, Urbana-Champaign, Illinois, as well as Drs Maria Brisk, Patrick Proctor and Anne Homza from Boston College, Boston, Massachusetts, who have supported me in my educational journey. My most profound appreciation goes to my academic and life mentor, Dr Georgia Garcia. I am indebted to her for her guidance, insight, motivation and continuous support. Her inspiring and stimulating work led me to become who I am today, following her educational path.

I also thank my colleagues and friends at Southeastern Oklahoma State University, Oklahoma, Drs Susan Morrison, Maribeth Nottingham, Barbara McClanahan and Stewart Mayers, who provided much-appreciated encouragement and heartfelt support. I owe a debt of gratitude to the university and our Educational Instruction and Leadership (EIL) Department. I appreciate the graciously provided funding and continuous encouragement for my scholarly work.

Finally, I am most grateful to my family, whose love, care and assistance have sustained me throughout the whole process of writing this book. I acknowledge that their unwavering and steadfast support has been crucial in enabling the completion of this book and has always played the most pivotal role in my life.

Foreword

When I was a university professor in bilingual/multicultural education and literacy, I often searched for books that focused on specific minority populations. This is the book on Asian American students that was missing, but that I was hoping to find. Although Asian Americans are one of the fastest-growing minority populations in the US, educators and book publishers rarely emphasize them.

Dr Chaehyun Lee has made an invaluable contribution to the field of education with her book, *Supporting Asian American Students in Multicultural Contexts: Language, Culture, Identity and Power in the US*. In this book, Dr Lee skillfully combines theories and examples from empirical research to explain how and why teachers in all-English classrooms, bilingual/multilingual classrooms and heritage language classrooms should focus on the experiences of Asian American students. She shows the important role that teachers in heritage language classrooms play when they help their Asian American students to identify and confront the discrimination and racism that they experience in US schools. Most importantly, Dr Lee explains how educators can use the heritage language pedagogical approaches with Asian American students in other settings and with students from other diverse backgrounds.

Dr Lee defines and reviews several theories relevant to understanding the academic performance and wellbeing of minority students. I applaud her for dealing with the mental wellbeing of minority students because this topic is usually ignored in the educational literature. Dr Lee specifically reviews the following theoretical concepts and theories and explains how they relate to the improved education of Asian American students and other minority students: heritage languages, Third Spaces, translanguaging, trans-semiotizing, cultural funds of knowledge, transnational and transcultural identity construction, critical border pedagogy, AsianCrit, Critical Race Theory (CRT), critical literacy and raciolinguistics. What I found particularly helpful were pedagogical examples of how Dr Lee and other teachers implemented the theories in their instruction.

A major strength of the book is its focus on Asian American students' responses to the different instructional approaches. For example, Dr Lee illustrates how students responded to her instructional use of multicultural literature and counternarratives. She shows that it is important for teachers to guide their students' thinking and to give them the opportunity to discuss and reveal their thinking. I found her account of fifth-graders' responses to a transnational literacy unit particularly illuminating. In the account, Dr Lee indicates that the fifth graders are second-generation Asian American immigrants who identify as half Korean and half Vietnamese. As teachers, we aren't always aware of our students' multifaceted and transnational backgrounds and how their backgrounds affect their identities and mental wellbeing.

Lastly, I agree with Dr Lee's point that including a focus on Asian American students in US classrooms is just a beginning step. Given the overwhelming dominance of White middle-class and upper-class perspectives and literature in US classrooms, teachers have to counter this dominance by employing critical literacy and counternarratives. Drawing on over 10 years of university and heritage language instruction, Dr Lee shows how educational personnel can implement instructional approaches that emphasize both diversity and equity.

Georgia Earnest García, PhD
Professor Emerita
University of Illinois at Urbana-Champaign
July 28, 2025

Preface

If you are reading this page, you are likely working with school-aged children as classroom teachers, teacher educators, school administrators, literacy specialists, curriculum developers, paraprofessionals, school mentors or pre-service teachers. As our contemporary societies increasingly exhibit cultural and linguistic diversity more than ever before due to factors like globalization, migration and increased intercultural communication, you probably already have or are expected to have students from racially, culturally and linguistically diverse backgrounds in your classrooms, schools and/or communities. However, despite the changing demographics in this highly diverse world, a monolingual mindset remains prevalent and is still a foundational element in US school systems and curricula. Since language education, practices and policies are primarily rooted in monolingual language ideologies, it is acknowledged that the US education system needs to improve and contribute to educational equity and justice, specifically by providing equal access to quality education and implementing inclusive curricula.

This book is designed to empower educators with the teaching methods and strategies needed to foster diverse, inclusive and unbiased classroom environments. This book demonstrates how to effectively adjust and transform your curriculum and instruction to cater to the diverse backgrounds of student populations. Drawing from my years of experience as a critical social justice classroom teacher, teacher educator and educational researcher, I aim to bridge the gap between theoretical knowledge and practical application to generate effective differentiated instruction and adaptive teaching. I delved deeper into the 'why' and 'how' of curriculum transformation, beyond focusing on the 'what' of curriculum development or instructional design, to provide innovative pedagogical frameworks for creating meaningful learning experiences tailored to the diverse needs of students. This book offers a roadmap for educators seeking to foster a more enriching and positive learning community by empowering their students to become critically conscious learners.

Although this book emphasizes the perspectives of Asian Americans by including Asian American students' voices, experiences and (hi)stories to achieve multilingual and multicultural education, educators of other racial, linguistic or cultural groups should apply the pathways to educational transformation, equity, inclusion and justice across all education settings. After reading this book, I hope you will be able to construct an equitable and unbiased learning environment for all students in your classroom, school and community. I hope we can all remember this: if we want to value and create diversity, we must first achieve equity because diversity without equity is not the goal of multiculturalism.

1 Introduction to Understanding the Dynamics of Language, Culture and Power in a Multilingual/Plurilingual World

Multilingualism and Plurilingualism as the New Norms in US Schools

The demographics of the United States (US) have undergone dramatic shifts. According to data from USAFacts (2024), the non-white population in the US has approximately doubled since 1990, increasing from about 24% to over 40% by 2023. Since the percentage of non-Hispanic White groups has decreased from 75% to 58% over the same period, there has been a significant rise in racial and cultural diversity across the country. Accordingly, a growing number of school-aged students in the US school setting are from different racial, ethnic, cultural and linguistic backgrounds, and these student populations are anticipated to increase at a vertiginous rate.

Indeed, according to the National Center for Education Statistics (NCES) (2024), the number of public school students who were White decreased from 51% to 44%. Still, the number of public school students who were Hispanic and Asian increased from 24% to 29% and from 4.8% to 5.5%, respectively, between the fall of 2012 and the fall of 2022. The percentage of school-aged children who are White is projected to continue decreasing, whereas children in each minority ethnic group are anticipated to continue increasing. Thus, schools across the US are becoming increasingly racially, culturally and linguistically diverse (RCLD), and teachers are becoming more likely to encounter RCLD students in their classrooms. Despite the changing demographics in this highly diverse world, monolingualism remains the norm in most US school settings (Watson & Shapiro, 2018).

As opposed to monolingual and monocultural orientations, multilingualism and plurilingualism are considered relatively new phenomena

(Ebrahimi, 2023; Galante & Cruz, 2021) that capture the dynamic, fluid, and flexible linguistic practices and plurality in various social contexts or situations. The terms 'plurilingual' and 'multilingual' were not always distinct. Scholars argue that, unlike the term 'multilingualism', which is generally used in English, 'plurilingualism' (i.e. plurilinguisme in French) is more commonly used in French-speaking countries because French writers use the prefix 'pluri' instead of 'multi' when writing in English (Ebrahimi, 2023). According to the Council of Europe (2001), the Common European Framework of Reference for Languages (CEFR) made a clear distinction between multilingualism and plurilingualism. In the CEFR, multilingualism is described as 'the knowledge of a number of languages or the co-existence of different languages in a given society' (Council of Europe, 2001: 4). As multilingualism describes the coexistence of different languages in the social sphere, it indicates the use of multiple languages on a societal level.

In contrast, plurilingualism denotes the use of multiple languages at the individual level because an individual 'does not keep languages and cultures in strictly separated mental compartments but rather builds up a communicative competence to which all knowledge and experience of language contributes and in which languages interrelate and interact' (Council of Europe, 2001: 4). Thus, unlike multilingualism, which accepts knowledge of many languages and linguistic diversity within a single community, plurilingualism focuses on an individual's interconnected knowledge of multiple languages by emphasizing the development of each speaker's dynamic linguistic repertoire and centering the role of the speaker as a holistic being (Beacco et al., 2016). Accordingly, the multiple languages at the societal level (i.e. multilingualism) do not necessarily correspond to the multiple languages in individuals' plurilingual repertoires (i.e. plurilingualism).

Since plurilingualism is a dynamic and variable competence where an individual's linguistic abilities in different languages can vary depending on the context and language involved, speakers do not compartmentalize their languages in a segregated manner (Ebrahimi, 2023). Rather, plurilingual speakers have 'a single, inter-related, repertoire that they combine with their general competences and various strategies in order to accomplish tasks' (CEFR Section 6.1.3.2) (CEFR, 2001: 30). Thus, plurilingual speakers actively draw on a comprehensive knowledge of their integrated language skills and linguistic understanding to effectively facilitate communication and convey meaning seamlessly.

Leaving Monolingualism Behind: From Monolingual Mindsets to the Multilingual Turn

Although scholars have made a helpful distinction between multilingualism and plurilingualism, translanguaging (see Chapters 3 and 4 of this volume to fully understand translanguaging) is regarded as a common and typical practice among bi/multi/plurilingual speakers because they utilize their entire linguistic repertoires in a dynamic way to make meaning across different contexts (García, 2009; Lee, 2021). Because translanguaging is the natural way people communicate, specialized terminologies (such as multilingualism, plurilingualism or multilingual/plurilingual speakers) are not necessarily needed or used.

However, it is worth noting that the US remains a predominantly monolingual country, where nearly 80% (precisely 78.4%) of the population speaks only English at home, according to the US Census Bureau (2023). As English's dominance in the US has influenced language practices, education and policies, language teaching and learning are largely rooted in monolingual language ideologies (Canagarajah & Liyanage, 2012; Chang-Bacon, 2022; Makalela, 2015; Makoni & Pennycook, 2012; Wiley, 2014; Wiley & García, 2016). Consequently, people (need to) use distinctive terms (i.e. 'multilingualism' and 'plurilingualism' in contrast to 'monolingualism') in this English monolingual environment (the US) to distinguish and characterize different understandings of linguistic tolerance that accepts the existence of language diversity within individuals and society.

Linguistic imperialism, which is the practice of imposing a dominant language (i.e. English) on people who speak other languages, has prioritized and imposed English as the primary language, and it has led to the marginalization and deterioration of many heritage languages spoken by minority groups in the US (Phillipson, 2013). As a result, the US education system has contributed to educational inequality and disparities among the nation's racial and ethnic minorities and continues to fail to support students from those minority groups adequately. As US schools experience a significant demographic transition in the ethnic and racial composition of their student body, it is crucial to adapt and transform teaching methods and curricula to better represent, reflect and cater to the diverse backgrounds of student populations, ensuring inclusivity and unbiased learning experiences for all. It is imperative for educators to go beyond simply recognizing diverse languages and cultures in their classrooms; they must actively challenge the prevailing monolingual perspective by critically examining and reevaluating dominant discourses and practices within their curriculum.

Since monolingual approaches to education provide inequitable opportunities and unfair challenges to RCLD learners, applying a multilingual/plurilingual lens to education is vital (Ebrahimi, 2023; Preece & Marshall, 2020; Veliz & Chen, 2024). Educators need to acknowledge that multilingualism and plurilingualism are common and normal, and that embracing these perspectives can maximize students' potential within the learning environment by leveraging all their linguistic abilities and harnessing the richness of diversity. Specifically, educators must recognize students' heritage languages as valuable resources in educational settings because a collection of heritage languages plays a crucial role in enriching linguistic diversity, preserving cultural traditions, fostering a sense of belonging, and promoting social inclusion (Fishman, 2001; Leeman, 2015; Polinsky, 2011, 2018; Valdes, 2005). It is essential to first learn about what are regarded as heritage languages in the US.

The Classification of Heritage Language in the US

Joshua Fishman (2001), a pioneer of heritage language education in the US, classified heritage languages into three distinct groups: colonial languages, indigenous languages and immigrant languages. Colonial heritage languages refer to the languages (such as Dutch, German, French and Swedish) brought by early European settlers and spoken by the European groups that first colonized the Americas. It may overlap with immigrant heritage languages; for instance, Spanish, which was a colonial heritage language in the past and is now an immigrant heritage language with a vast number of speakers in the US. Indigenous heritage languages refer to the languages spoken by the native peoples of the Americas, such as Navajo and Cherokee. These languages are at risk of endangerment; many of them are now extinct, and very few are spoken by elders and being maintained within communities of speakers. Immigrant heritage languages are languages spoken by immigrants who arrived in the US after it became an independent country. Some examples of immigrant heritage languages include Spanish, Chinese, Korean, Arabic and Russian. Fishman's third categorization of heritage languages (i.e. immigrant heritage languages) is associated with a more recent surge of immigration to the US, and it suitably describes heritage languages and students of these language groups in this book.

Understanding Asian Americans in the US

The Migration Policy Institute reported that Asian immigrants comprised 31% of all immigrants in the US in 2021 (Hanna & Batalova, 2021). According to the Pew Research Center (2021), Asian Americans have been the fastest-growing racial or ethnic group in the US since 2000. The Asian population grew by 81% from about 10.5 million to 18.9 million over the past two decades (from 2000 to 2020), and it was much faster than the growth of other racial and ethnic groups (70% for Hispanics and 20% for Blacks). The Pew Research Center projected that the Asian American population would surpass 46 million by 2055, which is quadruple times greater than their population in 2000. They further predicted that Asian immigrants would outnumber Latinx immigrants by 2055 as Asians are expected to make up 36%, and Hispanics would make up 34% of all US immigrants.

Approximately 22 million Asian Americans in the US currently represent more than 50 different ethnic groups, speaking over 100 languages, and are projected to become the US's largest immigrant group. However, Asian Americans remain largely erased from the school curriculum, and little of their (hi)stories are taught in K-12 US schools. To date, Asian Americans are still regarded as the most invisible figures among ethnic minority groups in US history, modern society and contemporary school curricula (National School Board Association, 2024). In addition, since the sociolinguistic, educational and linguistic anthropology literature primarily had paid attention to African American, Hispanic or Latinx American and Native American groups, Asian Americans have not received the same amount of scholarly attention compared to other racial minority groups in the US (Lê et al., 2026; Reyes & Lo, 2009). Taking this into account, the information in this book offers unique and valuable insights into the experiences of Asian American students, providing educators with the tools to create an inclusive and diverse learning environment by incorporating Asian Americans' voices, stories, perspectives and cultures into their curriculum.

The Aims and Objectives of the Book

Since this book is particularly written with children of Asian immigrant families (i.e. second-generation Korean Americans and multi-ethnic Asian Americans who identified themselves as bi/multilingual and transnational/transcultural individuals), each chapter of this book aims to unpack how Asian American students reside within the complex intersection and dynamics of their linguistic practices, cultural knowledge and all the vibrant factors that contribute to constructing their identities in this increasingly superdiverse (Vertovec, 2007) world. This book includes 10 years of data I have collected at Korean heritage language schools – where children who have the same ancestral ties attend on the weekend to develop their heritage language and cultural knowledge (Fishman, 2001; Valdés, 2001, 2005) – in two different states (Illinois and Texas) when I served as a classroom teacher in first-, second-, third- and fifth-grade classrooms (see Chapter 2 for the role of heritage language schools in the US).

The book provides an in-depth exploration of complex topics, multifarious theories and intricate phenomena, including a postcolonial theory of Third Space, translanguaging, resource pedagogies, such as culturally responsive and sustaining pedagogy, transnationalism, critical border pedagogy, Asian critical (AsianCrit) theory and raciolinguistic ideologies, which are essential for understanding how Asian American students who are bilingual, multicultural and/or transnational navigate the US educational system while carrying a complex blend of linguistic and cultural identities and values. These theoretical perspectives collectively provide a sophisticated lens through which to understand how language, culture, identity and power interact with one another and influence social dynamics. By showcasing solid foundations in the relevant literature and critical analyses of previous scholarship, the book offers readers a comprehensive and robust theoretical foundation for exploring the multifaceted relationship between heritage language learning, cultural value development, identity formation and power relations.

Since this book is written for educators, the respective chapters assist readers (e.g. in-service and pre-service teachers, literacy specialists, school administrators and teacher educators) who work with bi/multilingual students in a variety of school settings to understand their students' language use, literacy development and multifaceted identity construction. This book guides educators in improving their instructional pedagogy to support racially, culturally and linguistically diverse (RCLD) students, including those in various educational programs, such as simultaneous and sequential bilinguals, English learners, heritage language learners, mixed-race or multi-ethnic students, children of immigrant families and transnational students. Thus, educators will gain valuable knowledge and understanding of the best practices to adequately support students from diverse backgrounds by creating inclusive and unbiased classrooms where everyone feels valued and can participate fully, ultimately leading to richer and more meaningful learning experiences for all students.

The Context and Methodology of Studies in This Volume

All the studies in this book took place in two Korean heritage language schools sited in metropolitan cities in two states (Illinois and Texas) in the US. The first school was situated in a university town in Illinois, with a combined population of approximately 200,000. Due to the university town's long-standing history of attracting international students from Korea and its vibrant Korean community, there is a significant presence of Koreans in the area. As many Korean parents pursue master's, doctoral, and/or postdoctoral degrees, the university town has established a heritage Korean language school to serve the needs of Korean parents, who often have children who need to develop their Korean language skills and uphold their cultural heritage. The second school was located in one of the metropolitan cities in Texas where 1.3 million people reside, along with a significant number of the Korean population, making it the largest Korean community in that state. Unlike the university town in Illinois, where only one Korean heritage language school existed, numerous Korean heritage language schools were available in the city in Texas to serve an increasing number of Korean children. Hence, the second school was one of the Korean heritage language schools within the county.

Although the Korean population was growing in the two regions, there were no Korean–English dual language schools or bilingual education programs available in the local school districts in the two states. Many Korean parents who wanted to develop their children's Korean language learning in towns sent their children to Korean heritage language education programs on weekends while teaching them the language of mainstream society (i.e. English) during the weekdays. The community-based heritage language schools were private and non-profit organizations established, funded, and operated by Korean parents and the local community in the towns to teach Korean children about their heritage language and culture by providing formal instruction in Korean at each elementary-grade level.

Most of the enrolled students were second-generation Korean Americans who were born in the US after their parents had immigrated. Some students were born in Korea and moved to the US at a young age with their families. They mostly identified themselves as 1.5 generation, as they grew up primarily in the US. These students self-assessed themselves as fluent English speakers and considered their Korean skills to be less competent than their English skills. Intermittently, newcomers who had recently arrived in the US from Korea enrolled in the schools. In addition, children of mixed race (e.g. a child with a Korean mother and a White Caucasian father) or mixed Asian ethnicity (e.g. a child with a Korean father and a Vietnamese mother) occasionally attended the schools as one of their parents was of Korean descent and had South Korean citizenship. All students attended English-only classrooms during the school week (Mondays through Fridays) and enrolled in Korean heritage language programs on weekends (Saturdays) for three hours in the morning at all grade levels (Kindergarten through Grade 5).

At the time of data collection for the studies in this volume, approximately 10 students (i.e. a maximum of 14 and a minimum of 6) were enrolled in each grade at the schools. There was a similar gender ratio of men and women, with female students slightly outnumbering male students, comprising nearly 60% of the enrolled students. All students in the local classrooms were invited to participate in the study, and both the students and their parents agreed to participate. Parental permission, along with consent letters, was obtained for all students, and student assent letters to participate in the studies were also collected each academic year. Most of the parents were first-generation Korean immigrants who came to the US between their early twenties and early thirties. The other parents came to the US when they were teenagers; thus, some parents were familiar with the American K-12 education system. A few parents came to the US for a short period (for two or three years), for instance, as visiting scholars or expatriates.

Many Korean heritage language schools in the US utilize government-issued textbooks that are also used in all public elementary schools (Grades 1 to 6) in South Korea. Yet, since the textbooks in each grade level are designed for students in Korea, not for students residing in English-speaking countries (i.e. immigrant children, second- or third-generation Korean American children), I understood that students in my classes would learn their heritage language and culture better if they were given class materials that reflect their life experiences and worldviews as Korean Americans. I further acknowledged that my students have had insufficient opportunities to learn about their cultural heritage and values due to the extensive Eurocentric perspective in the American schools they attend during the weekdays. Thus, I prepared socially and culturally relevant, as well as personally meaningful, lessons to provide transformative instruction each academic year by incorporating students' diverse perspectives and lived experiences into the curriculum so that they could feel more engaged, motivated, and empowered in the learning process.

The audio recordings took place during class periods to capture the students' discourses, both oral and written, in the classrooms. The students' literary artifacts (i.e. their art- and writing samples) they created during class sessions were collected. During the data analysis stage, I closely examined the students' classroom discourses, which encompassed both verbal narratives and written communication (i.e. spoken language, dialogic discussions and literary artifacts), as well as the students' accounts from the interview transcripts, to identify themes and patterns that commonly emerged across the data. Since each study in the following chapters is based on a different theoretical framework (e.g. Third Space theory, translanguaging, critical border pedagogy, AsianCrit, raciolinguistic ideologies), I paid attention to the students' classroom discourse data considering the conceptual framework of each study to ensure my analysis aligns with the study's goals and hypotheses. This approach helped me provide a focused lens for interpreting the data and integrating relevant concepts or theories by making real-world connections, thereby maintaining the integrity of my research.

Researcher Positionality and Reflexivity

As a first-generation Korean immigrant who is bilingual in Korean and English and familiar with the beliefs, values and practices of Korean culture from a native perspective, I employed an emic – the insider's – approach over a decade of research. The emic approach prioritizes capturing the beliefs and values of a specific cultural or ethnic group being studied by identifying the social context of a cultural milieu and how members of that group understand and interpret their world (Morris et al., 1999). As a member of the Korean community living in the US, I have gained firsthand insider knowledge and understanding of Korean culture and society (Malinowski, 1922; Morris et al., 1999). Thus, my position as a cultural insider facilitated an understanding of how shared beliefs and values influenced students' personal experiences and learning behaviors in the classroom, thereby enhancing my comprehension of the students' discursive practices, unique backgrounds and lived realities that they brought to the learning environment. In addition, this emic approach enabled me to respond more considerately and appropriately to sensitive issues by understanding the group's norms and values as well as exploring unique insights and lived experiences within specific circumstances and sociocultural dynamics (Banks, 1998). For instance, Asian Americans' storytelling and testimonies provided insight into how my students navigated their dynamic and complex life events, such as maintaining heritage languages, sustaining cultural ties, balancing acculturation and forming their identities, while facing challenges like discrimination and existing inequalities. As the students and I shared the same ethnic and cultural identities, the sense of our shared identity, experiences and knowledge helped us cultivate positive relationships and build trust, security and reciprocity.

However, as an insider researcher, I understood that I could easily accused of inherent bias because I was too close to the participants and familiar with the culture being studied (Merriam *et al.*, 2001; van Heugten, 2004). Scholars have warned that the insider researchers must be conscious and cautious about projecting their own beliefs, experiences and values (van den Hoonaard, 2002) because these interconnected aspects of the insider researchers' identity can easily influence the study methodology, data analyses and overall study results (Bourdieu & Wacquant, 1992; Chavez, 2008; Couture *et al.*, 2012; Mauthner & Doucet, 2003). It has been advised that insider researchers should mitigate their biases by collecting reflective data and documenting personal beliefs or experiences (Drake, 2010; Hellawell, 2006; Mauthner & Doucet, 2003; van Heugten, 2004). Thus, I engaged in reflective journals, memoirs and self-interviews to document my thoughts and feelings throughout the research process, which helped me make my perspective and assumptions transparent and contemplate how these might influence my research.

To avoid biases and mitigate potential biases, I safeguarded myself against relying on earlier observations or investigations from my former classrooms and the understanding I had gained from past studies. I closely examined and subjectively analyzed the students' classroom discourses and a collection of shared artifacts by foregrounding the richness and multiplicity of the students' stories and testimonies (Martinez, 2014, 2018) instead of treating the students in Korean heritage language schools as a monolithic group or presuming their practices and experiences as generic commonalities. I created an inclusive and equitable learning environment to capture the diverse experiences of Asian American students by collecting and valuing a wide range of their voices, practices, stories, experiences and perspectives. I also meticulously scrutinized the students' responses from the interviews to ensure I accurately captured students' understandings and interpretations from the data I collected.

Although self-reflection is crucial for insider researchers to acknowledge their influence on the research process, scholars made a distinction between reflection and reflexivity (Fitzpatrick & May, 2022; Shaw, 2010). Reflexivity in research involves critically examining and judiciously reflecting on researchers' assumptions, beliefs and/or judgments (Couture *et al.*, 2012; Doucet, 2008; May & Caldas, 2023). Reflexivity extends beyond mere reflection, as it requires researchers to confront, question and interrogate their own biases and subjectivities (Wilkinson, 1988; Willig, 2013). Adopting a critically reflexive approach not only identifies but also mitigates potential biases researchers hold, which may significantly impact the research process and outcomes (Guillemin & Gillam, 2004; Kingdon, 2005; McGowan, 2020; Medico & Santiago-Delefosse, 2014). Thus, reflexivity is essential for ensuring the study's credibility and maintaining transparency in qualitative research (Lazard & McAvoy, 2020; Olukotun *et al.*, 2021). Fitzpatrick and May (2022) pointed out that researchers need to reflexively examine their positionality, including ontological, epistemological and cultural preconceptions, because their identity (a personal internal experience, i.e. who they are) and positionality (a broader social and political analysis, i.e. where they are located within society) may shape and influence the research methods and results (Pillow, 2003). Overall, my critical reflexivity in research assists me in revealing my underlying assumptions, including ontological and epistemological ones, and helps me understand 'how [I am] positioned in the research in ways that are complicit with, and reinforcing of, existing hierarchies of power' (Fitzpatrick & May, 2022: 79).

Content in Each Chapter

Chapter 2 provides an overview of the role of heritage language education, highlighting the significance of heritage language learning in the US. The chapter offers an expansive perspective on the Third Space theory, which explores the intersection of various cultures and hybrid identities by transcending traditional boundaries. The chapter illustrates how a Korean heritage language classroom can create a hybrid, transformative and democratic third space that fosters the embrace of students' dynamic discursive practices and navigates their multilayered identities.

Chapter 3 and Chapter 4 focus on the translanguaging paradigm. These two chapters bookend each other, with the former focusing on teachers' translanguaging pedagogy and the latter on students' translanguaging practices, expanding the understanding of bi/multi/plurilingual learners' ability to move fluidly between languages. The chapters demonstrate how teachers' pedagogical translanguaging facilitates students' translanguaging performance by strategically integrating students' diverse linguistic resources, creating a more inclusive and democratic learning environment that enhances participation, comprehension, confidence and overall language learning

As pedagogical interventions and innovations, resource pedagogies or asset-based pedagogies are introduced in Chapter 5. By underscoring theoretical models of culturally responsive or sustaining pedagogy, the chapter emphasizes the importance of incorporating multicultural literature into the school curriculum, thereby facilitating students' understanding of diversity, inclusion and equity, and expanding their worldviews through cultural competence.

Chapter 6 underscores the phenomena of transnationalism and transculturalism in this superdiverse and globalized world. Since the dynamics of transnationalism are understood through the lens of border pedagogy, this chapter covers the concept of critical border pedagogy, which analyzes social, political and historical boundaries between hegemonic ideologies of dominance and minority, as well as the dynamics of power relations within a society. The chapter teaches how transnational literacies can be incorporated into literacy lessons to leverage students' dynamic border-crossing experiences and cultivate their sophisticated and multi-dimensional identities by centering learners' transnational and transcultural funds of knowledge through various literacy practices.

Chapter 7 discusses critical race frameworks – specifically, Critical Race Theory (CRT) and Asian Critical (AsianCrit) theory – that analyze and understand the unique experiences of people from marginalized groups in a racialized society. This chapter focuses on critical literacy and counter-narratives as social justice pedagogical tools to interrogate societal issues and challenge dominant perspectives in disrupting hegemony, stereotypes and racism.

Chapter 8 examines the concept of raciolinguistic ideologies, which explain how race is (co)constructed, reconstructed and deconstructed through and by language. By employing a raciolinguistic approach, this chapter elucidates how individuals' racial, ethnic and national identities impact the lived experiences of their linguistic practices. The chapter specifically examines the ambivalent racial and linguistic positioning of multi-ethnic Asian American students by analyzing their raciosemiotic artifacts, which reveal the (re)construction of their ethno-racial and linguistic identities.

As the final chapter, Chapter 9 addresses the contributions of this book to the fields of multi/plurilingual and multi/pluricultural education by synthesizing key philosophical concepts, theories and perspectives that contemporary educators should be familiar with when working with diverse student populations.

References

Banks, J.A. (1998) The lives and values of researchers: Implications for educating citizens in a multicultural society. *Education Research* 27, 4–17.

Beacco, J., Fleming, M., Goullier, F., Thürmann, E. and Vollmer, H. (2016) *A Handbook for Curriculum Development and Teacher Training. The Language Dimension in All Subjects*. Council of Europe Publishing.

Bourdieu, P. and Wacquant, L.J.C. (1992) *An Invitation to Reflexive Sociology*. University of Chicago Press.

Canagarajah, S. and Liyanage, I. (2012) Lessons from pre-colonial multilingualism. In M. Martin-Jones, A. Blackledge and A. Creese (eds) *The Routledge Handbook of Multilingualism* (pp. 49–65). Routledge.

Chang-Bacon, C.K. (2022) Monolingual language ideologies and the Massachusetts sheltered English immersion endorsement initiative: A critical policy analysis. *Educational Policy* 36 (3), 479–519. https://doi.org/10.1177/0895904820901465.

Chavez, C. (2008) Conceptualizing from the inside: Advantages, complications, and demands on insider positionality. *The Qualitative Report* 13 (3), 474–494.

Council of Europe (CoE) (2001) *Common European Framework of Reference for Languages: Learning, Teaching, Assessment*. Cambridge University Press.

Couture, A.L., Zaidi, A.U. and Maticka-Tyndale, E. (2012) Reflexive accounts: An intersectional approach to exploring the fluidity of insider/outsider status and the researcher's impact on culturally-sensitive post-positivist qualitative research. *Qualitative Sociology Review* 8 (11), 86–105.

Doucet, A. (2008) 'From her side of the gossamer wall(s)': Reflexivity and relational knowing. *Qualitative Sociology* 31 (1), 73–87.

Drake, P. (2010) Grasping at methodological understanding: A cautionary tale from insider research. *International Journal of Research & Method in Education* 33 (1), 85–99.

Ebrahimi, M. (2023) Multilingualism and plurilingualism in teaching the lingua franca: A critical review. *Media and Intercultural Communication: A Multidisciplinary Journal* 1 (2), 97–109. https://doi.org/10.22034/MIC.2023.176626.

Fishman, J. (2001) 300-plus years of heritage language education in the United States. In J.K. Peyton, D.A. Ranard and S. McGinnis (eds) *Heritage Languages in America: Preserving a National Resource* (pp. 81–89). Center for Applied Linguistics & Delta Systems.

Fitzpatrick, K. and May, S. (2022) *Critical Ethnography and Education: Theory, Methodology, and Ethics*. Routledge.

Galante, A. and Cruz, J.W.N.D. (2021) Plurilingual and pluricultural as the new normal: An examination of language use and identity in the multilingual city of Montreal. *Journal of Multilingual and Multicultural Development* 1–16.

García, O. (2009) *Bilingual Education in the 21st Century: A Global Perspective*. Wiley Blackwell.

Guillemin, M. and Gillam, L. (2004) Ethics, reflexivity, and "ethically important moments" in research. *Qualitative Inquiry* 10 (2), 261–280.

Hanna, M. and Batalova, J. (2021, March 10) Immigrants from Asia in the United States. *The Online Journal of the Migration Policy Institute*. https://www.migrationpolicy.org/article/immigrants-asia-united-states-2020.

Hellawell, D. (2006) Inside-out: Analysis of the insider-outsider concept as a heuristic device to develop reflexivity in students doing qualitative research. *Teaching in Higher Education* 11 (4), 483–494.

Kingdon, C. (2005) Reflexivity: Not just a qualitative methodological research tool. *British Journal of Midwifery* 13 (10), 622–627.

Lazard, L. and McAvoy, J. (2020) Doing reflexivity in psychological research: What's the point? What's the practice? *Qualitative Research in Psychology* 17 (2), 159–177.

Lê, K., Tian, Z., Nguyen, A. and Morita-Mullaney, T. (eds) (2026) *Asian Americans in Bilingualism and Bilingual Education: The Long Overdue Voice*. Multilingual Matters.

Lee, C. (2021) *Understanding the Oral and Written Translanguaging Practices of Emergent Bilinguals: Insights from a Korean Heritage Language Classroom in the U.S.* Routledge.

Leeman, J. (2015) Heritage language education and identity in the United States. *Annual Review of Applied Linguistics* 35, 100–119.

Makalela, L. (2015) Moving out of linguistic boxes: The effects of translanguaging strategies for multilingual classrooms. *Language and Education* 29, 200–217.

Makoni, S. and Pennycook, A. (2012) From monological multilingualism to multilingual francas. In M. Martin-Jones, A. Blackledge and A. Creese (eds) *The Routledge Handbook of Multilingualism* (pp. 439–453). Routledge.

Malinowski, B. (1922) *Argonauts of the Western Pacific: An Account of Native Enterprise and Adventure in the Archipelagoes of Melanesian New Guinea.* George Routledge & Sons.

Martinez, A.Y. (2014) A plea for critical race theory counterstory: Stock story versus counterstory dialogues concerning Alejandra's 'fit' in the academy. *Composition Studies* 42 (2), 33–55.

Martinez, A.Y. (2018) The responsibility of privilege: A critical race counterstory conversation. *Peitho Journal* 21 (1), 212–233.

Mauthner, N.S. and Doucet, A. (2003) Reflexive accounts and accounts of reflexivity in qualitative data analysis. *Sociology* 37 (3), 413–431.

May, S. and Caldas, B. (eds) (2023) *Critical Ethnography, Language, Race/ism and Education.* Multilingual Matters.

McGowan, W. (2020) 'If you didn't laugh, you'd cry': Emotional labour, reflexivity and ethics- as-practice in a qualitative field-work context. *Methodological Innovations* 13 (2), https://doi.org/10.1177/2059799120926086.

Medico, D. and Santiago-Delefosse, M. (2014) From reflexivity to resonances: Accounting for interpretation phenomena in qualitative research. *Qualitative Research in Psychology* 11 (4), 350–364.

Merriam, S.B., Johnson-Bailey, J., Lee, M.Y., Kee, Y., Ntseane, G. and Muhamad, M. (2001) Power and positionality: Negotiating insider/outsider status within and across cultures. *International Journal of Lifelong Education* 20 (5), 405–416. https://doi.org/10.1080/02601370120490.

Morris, M., Leung, K., Ames, D. and Lickel, B. (1999) Views from inside and outside: Integrating emic and etic insight about culture and justice judgment. *Academy of Management Review* 24 (4), 781–796.

Olukotun, O., Mkandawire, E., Antilla, J., Alfaifa, F., Weitzel, J., Scheer, V. and Mkandawire-Valhmu, L. (2021) An analysis of reflections on researcher positionality. *Qualitative Report* 26 (5), 1411–1426.

Pew Research Center (2021) Key facts about Asian Americans, a diverse and growing population. https://www.pewresearch.org/short-reads/2021/04/29/key- facts-about-asian-americans/.

Phillipson, R. (2013) *Linguistic Imperialism Continued.* Routledge.

Pillow, W. (2003) Confession, catharsis, or cure? Rethinking the uses of reflexivity as methodological power in qualitative research. *International Journal of Qualitative Studies in Education* 16 (2), 175–196.

Polinsky, M. (2011) Reanalysis in adult heritage language: New evidence in support of attrition. *Studies in Second Language Acquisition* 33 (2), 305–328. https://doi.org/10.1017/S027226311000077x.

Polinsky, M. (2018) *Heritage Languages and their Speakers.* Cambridge University Press.

Preece, S. and Marshall, S. (2020) Plurilingualism, teaching and learning, and Anglophone higher education: An introduction Anglophone universities and linguistic diversity. *Language, Culture and Curriculum* 33 (2), 117–125.

Reyes, A. and Lo, A. (2009) *Beyond Yellow English: Toward a Linguistic Anthropology of Asian Pacific America*. Oxford University Press.

Shaw, R. (2010) Embedding reflexivity within experiential qualitative psychology. *Qualitative Research in Psychology* 7 (3), 233–243.

U.S. Census Bureau (2023, December 7) Most americans speak only english at home or speak English "very well." https://www.census.gov/newsroom/press- releases/2023/language-at-home-acs-5-year.html.

USAFacts (2024) Is the US becoming more diverse? https://usafacts.org/articles/is-the-us -becoming-more-diverse/.

Valdés, G. (2001) Heritage language students: Profiles and possibilities. In J. Peyton, J. Ranard and S. McGinnis (eds) *Heritage Languages in America: Preserving a National Resource* (pp. 37–80). The Center for Applied Linguistics and Delta Systems.

Valdés, G. (2005) Bilingualism, heritage language learners, and SLA research: Opportunities lost or seized? *The Modern Language Journal* 89, 410–426. https://doi. org/10.1111/j.1540-4781.2005.00314.x-.

van den Hoonaard, W.C. (2002) *Walking the Tightrope: Ethical Issues for Qualitative Researchers*. University of Toronto Press.

van Heugten, K. (2004) Managing insider research: Learning from experience. *Qualitative Social Work* 3 (2), 203–219.

Veliz, L. and Chen, J. (2024) Challenging the monolingual mindset: Language teachers' pushback and enactment of critical multilingual language awareness in Australian schools. *Journal of Multilingual and Multicultural Development* 1–16. https://doi.org/ 10.1080/01434632.2024.2352161.

Vertovec, S. (2007) Super-diversity and its implications. *Ethnic and Racial Studies* 30 (6), 1024–1054. https://doi.org/10.1080/01419870701599465.

Watson, M. and Shapiro, R. (2018) Clarifying the multiple dimensions of monolingualism: Keeping our sights on language politics. *Composition Forum* 38. https://www.composition forum.com/issue/38/monolingualism.php.

Wiley, T.G. (2014) Diversity, super-diversity and monolingual language ideology in the United States: Tolerance or intolerance? *Review of Research in Education* 38, 24–55.

Wiley, T.G. and García, O. (2016) Language policy and planning in language education: Legacies, consequences, and possibilities. *Modern Language Journal* 100 (1), 48–63.

Wilkinson, S. (1988) The role of reflexivity in feminist psychology. *Womens Studies International Forum* 11, 493–502.

Willig, C. (2013) *Introducing Qualitative Research in Psychology* (3rd edn). Open University Press.

2 Creating a Transformative Third Space by Embracing Heritage Language and Culture to Promote Multilingualism and Pluriculturalism

During the parent–teacher conference at the Korean heritage language school, Mrs Kim, the mother of a fifth-grade student, Ben, who is introduced in this chapter, and Mrs Choi, the mother of a second-grader, Joy, whom you will meet in Chapter 3, raise their concerns. Although Korean is the language spoken in their home, the mothers worry that their children will lose their heritage language at some stage. Mrs Choi shared that she was more concerned about Joy's English performance in a mainstream school until last year, as Joy used to identify as an English Learner. However, as Joy developed her English language proficiency, Mrs Choi is now concerned about Joy's Korean language learning. Meanwhile, Mrs Kim not only worries about Ben's heritage language attrition but is also concerned about the negative impact of losing their heritage language on his cultural identity conformation and family connections as she understands that heritage language is seen as a link to her child's cultural heritage, strong family relationships and positive identity construction. Both mothers enroll their children in the local heritage language school to prevent their children's heritage language from being lost or attrited.

***

This vignette illustrates the common phenomenon of heritage language attrition among immigrant children of Asian families in the US Responding to immigrant parents' (like the two mothers in the vignettes) concerns about their children's heritage language loss, community-based heritage language schools in the US become vital learning sites that provide heritage language learning opportunities for children of immigrant parents. Yet, second-generation children from immigrant families like Ben and

Joy bring their out-of-school experiences and knowledge into the classroom to shape their evolving identities. Thus, heritage language schools need to be inclusive learning spaces that embrace students' linguistic hybridity and cultural diversity from their lived experiences, cultural understanding and diverse perspectives.

Introduction to the Chapter

By examining various factors that affect immigrant children's heritage language attrition and loss, this chapter provides an in-depth understanding of the role of heritage languages and discusses the significance of heritage language education in promoting the bi/multi/plurilingualism and bi/multi/pluriculturalism of Asian or Asian American students. Then, the chapter presents an expansive perspective on the Third Space (Bhabha, 1994) to elucidate how a Korean heritage language classroom could generate the hybrid, transformative and democratic third space. By illustrating the students' classroom discourses, the chapter demonstrates how the Third Space can become conducive to sustaining students' fluid languaging practices, navigating different aspects of their multilayered identities and embracing dynamic discursive practices.

Immigrant Heritage Languages and Heritage Language Learners in the US

Based on Fishman's (2001) classification of heritage languages into three distinct groups (see Chapter 1), scholars in heritage language studies have contextualized heritage languages in the US (e.g. Montrul, 2008, 2012; Polinsky, 2011, 2018; Valdés, 2005). Valdés (2000, 2001) defined heritage language in the US as a language other than English that a person learns at home, which is associated with their ethnic and cultural background. For Valdés, a heritage language differs from a mother tongue or first language because the latter is acquired from birth in a natural environment and learned during one's critical period, whereas a heritage language is often acquired informally through family, community or cultural immersion.

Montrul's (2023: 400) latest definition describes that heritage language is 'a sociopolitically minority and/or minoritized language acquired as the first or one of the first languages in a bilingual or multilingual context'. Montrul (2008) pointed out that an individual in the immigration context acquires a heritage language as their first language through natural input in the home environment but also learns the majority or societal language as a second language (i.e. English in this context) when starting school in the US. As the majority language becomes dominant and the exposure to one's heritage language reduces, the societal language becomes the individual's dominant or primary language. Thus, individuals' heritage language might have been their first language, but as they develop the majority language while growing up, they differentiate their heritage language from their dominant or primary language (Montrul, 2008).

Unlike Valdés, who distinguished heritage languages from first languages, Montrul (2012, 2023) viewed that learning a heritage language is different from learning a second or foreign language because heritage language learners (re)connect people with their cultural or ethnic roots. In contrast, second or foreign language learning is typically driven by practical needs or personal motivation rather than having a personal connection to the culture. Montrul (2023: 400) stated that heritage languages in the US immigration context are 'typically acquired under conditions of reduced exposure and are often used less than the majority language during late childhood and adolescence'. Thus, heritage language learners are more likely to encounter a gradual loss of proficiency in their heritage language, specifically if they continue to disuse or reduce its use (Schmid, 2010).

For second-generation immigrant children or children of immigrants, no matter whether they are sequential bilinguals who are exposed to their heritage language from birth as a first language or simultaneous bilinguals who are exposed to the two languages (a heritage language and the societal language in a given society) together, the children grow up becoming more comfortable and proficient in the societal language (i.e. English) (Valdés, 2000). According to Polinsky and Kagan (2007), heritage language is best understood as a language continuum model (Valdés, 2000) that ranges from fluent speakers to individuals who barely speak the home language (i.e. the spectrum of heritage language abilities). In other words, heritage language is defined by an individual's upbringing and functional practices in a household where a specific language is spoken. Heritage language learners possess a degree of practical ability in their heritage language, even if it is not their dominant language, because of their exposure to it within their family and cultural connection to it, allowing them to understand and communicate to some extent (Valdés, 2005).

Montrul (2012) indicated that it is difficult to fully develop or master one's heritage language due to insufficient linguistic and instructional input on immigrant heritage languages from the social environment in the US. Montrul then suggested that a sufficient amount and good quality of exposure to a language is a crucial factor in heritage language development. Montrul (2023: 412) described a heritage language as the language 'in between first and second languages' because one's heritage language is acquired primarily through family interactions during infancy within the home setting, so it might not entirely fade away from memory, like a first language. However, insufficient usage can weaken fluency and access to the automatic pathways of language learning, which could lead to incomplete acquisition or attrition, similar to what occurs with a second language.

The Phenomenon of Heritage Language Attrition or Loss in the US

Researchers documented that emergent bilingual students who attended US schools providing English-only instruction were more likely to experience language attrition or loss in their heritage languages (Guardado, 2017; Hinton, 2008; Montrul, 2018; Polinsky, 2011, 2018; Ro & Cheatham, 2009; Shin, 2005; Tse, 2001). According to Montrul (2008, 2010), heritage language loss occurs when an individual's primary language changes to a new or second language when they reside in a new environment or country where their first language is not used (Tse, 1998, 2001; Veltman, 1983). Heritage language attrition is the gradual loss of language skills or a decline in the speakers' ability to thoroughly apply grammatical knowledge of their heritage language (Pires & Rothman, 2009), which is generally caused by both isolation from speakers of that language and the acquisition and use of a new language (Guijarro-Fuentes & Schmitz, 2015). If an individual speaks a new language predominantly and becomes fluent in it, their heritage language can eventually weaken and deteriorate. Heritage language attrition or loss consequently occurs due to insufficient input and incomplete grammatical knowledge when the speaker has switched to the dominant language (Montrul & Bowles, 2009).

According to Schmid (2008), language attrition can be described as a process and as a phenomenon. Schmid identified two feasible scenarios of language attrition: (1) where there is no linguistic input or communication at all after all contact has ceased and (2) where there is overwhelming dominance and constant competition from another language, for instance, as a result of immigration. Thus, language attrition is explained as 'a process of loss, of forgetting, of deterioration' (Schmid, 2008: 10). This process of language attrition is caused by both isolation from speakers of the first or heritage language and the increased use of a second or dominant language. Schmid denotes the two stages of language attrition, which are a pre-attrition stage and an attrited stage (i.e. the complete attrition of a language). The gradual loss of a language leads to the later stage, and this process of language attrition is referred to as the phenomenon of attrition.

An individual's age can be a prediction of language attrition (Montrul, 2018, 2023; Polinsky & Kagan, 2007). Studies have found that young children are more likely to lose their heritage language than older children when the dominant language is introduced because older bilingual children might have fully mastered their heritage language before being exposed to a new language. A heritage language is more likely to be maintained as the primary language for older bilingual learners, whereas younger bilingual children are more susceptible to losing their fluency in it (Montrul, 2018; Polinsky & Kagan, 2007; Schmid, 2010). In this regard, Veltman (1983) viewed young bilingual children in the US as potential linguistic emigrants who have the potential to lose their heritage language. Although children of immigrant families might be exposed to their heritage language at home, if they spend more time interacting with English-speaking interlocutors and engaging in language and literacy practices using English than their heritage languages in school settings, they often fail to gain native-like proficiency in their heritage language and consequently experience heritage language attrition and loss (Carreira & Kagan, 2011; Murphy, 2014; Polinsky, 2011, 2018; Polinsky & Kagan, 2007; Seals & Peyton, 2017; Shin & Krashen, 1996; Valdés, 2001, 2005).

Kim & Chao, 2009; Lee & Wright, 2014; Li & Wen, 2015; Murphy, 2014; Shin & Lee, 2013). Researchers specifically indicated that the Korean ethnic group was less likely to use their heritage language at home than other Asian ethnic groups (Lee & Wright, 2014; Murphy, 2014; Shin & Lee, 2013). Lee and Shin (2008) correspondingly reported that second-generation Korean Americans showed the highest rate of heritage language attrition among Asian ethnic groups in the US. According to the Pew Research Center (2023), Korean Americans are more likely to hide their heritage identity (25%) than other Asian origin groups (i.e. Chinese (19%), Vietnamese (18%), Filipino (16%) and Japanese (14%)). The same report also revealed that Asian Americans who predominantly speak English are more likely to have hidden part of their heritage (29%) than those who are bilingual (14%) and who primarily speak their Asian origin language (9%).

Factors Affecting Immigrant Children's Heritage Language Attrition

Immigrant children often experience language attrition and loss in their heritage language due to array of factors, such as limited exposure to their heritage language, social pressures to assimilate to the dominant language, negative attitudes toward using their heritage language, the parents' language proficiency and attitudes toward maintaining their heritage language, home language use or policy and a lack of school programs that provide instruction in the target heritage language, among others (Caldas, 2012; Cho, 2015; Fogle, 2013; Hinton, 2008; Kim & Pyun, 2014; Lee, 2013, 2021a; Li, 2006; Lü & Koda, 2011; McCabe, 2016; Nesteruk, 2010; Oh & Fuligni, 2010; Ro & Cheatham, 2009; Shin, 2005, 2014).

One of the contributing factors to immigrant children's heritage language attrition is the scarcity of school programs that provide instruction in their heritage languages. Although there has been an increase in bilingual education programs in the US (Bialystok, 2018), where instruction is provided both with language minority students' heritage language and the dominant language (i.e. English), there is a lack of support for bilingual schools for Asian American students in the US. Specifically, more than 3000 Spanish dual language schools were available in 2021. In contrast, only 385 dual language schools (comprising all Asian languages, such as Chinese, Japanese, Korean, Hmong and Vietnamese) existed for children of Asian immigrants (American Council for International Education, 2021). Asian language bilingual programs are scarce, even in large school districts that serve significant Asian American student populations. Accordingly, Asian or Asian American students in the US are less likely to have opportunities to learn their heritage language in school settings.

It is essential to recognize that language shift and loss are closely tied to the power dynamics between two languages. When people immigrate to a new country, the language used in that country is often regarded as the dominant language, which holds privilege and supremacy, while the immigrants' heritage languages are often viewed as minority or less privileged languages (Schmid, 2010; Veltman, 1983). For this reason, some immigrants want to assimilate into the mainstream culture. They actively participate in the dominant language group by using the majority language, thereby reducing or ceasing their active participation in their communities of origin (Shin, 2005).

Studies have found that second-generation immigrant children often encounter the vicious cycle that explains the close relationship between social interaction or networks and language use or proficiency. In the vicious cycle, immigrant children's language anxiety leads them to avoid using the language and have less practice and social interaction in that language, which causes limited proficiency and, in turn, results in language anxiety and avoidance. Avoiding speaking the heritage language then negatively affects the quality of communication or causes pressure and tension within the family, which further leads them to feel alienated in their ethnic community or home country (Cavicchiolo *et al.*, 2020; Foner & Kasinitz, 2007; Köpke & Schmid, 2019; Park, 2006; Schmid, 2016).

The Significance of Heritage Language Learning and Education

Language instruction is considered a crucial component in preserving and transmitting cultural connections to younger generations, as language serves as a vehicle for conveying cultural values, traditions and history within a community (Fishman, 2001; McCarty, 2002; Valdes, 2001). Maintaining the heritage language has the political strength to keep the language alive for future generations, allowing it to connect deeply with the cultural heritage and social practices associated with that language (Abourehab & Azaz, 2023; Abraham *et al.*, 2021; Cun, 2024; Wu & Leung, 2022). Researchers have reported that when emergent bilingual students maintain their heritage languages, numerous cognitive, metalinguistic, social and cultural advantages occur. Although many immigrant children in the US tend to experience the challenge of preserving their heritage language as they acquire and develop the majority/societal language (i.e. English), scholars have emphasized the significance and value of heritage language learning (Budiyana, 2017; Cho, 2000; Guardado & Becker, 2013; Keh & Stoessel, 2017; King & Fogle, 2006; Lee, 2021a; Lynch, 2014; Nesteruk, 2010; Polinsky, 2011, 2018). Maintaining a heritage language while acquiring English has been indicated to support students' development in many areas.

Speaking a heritage language bolsters family relationships and creates a bond with extended family members by enhancing communication with older generations. Heritage language learning can strengthen children's connection to their family traditions, cultural roots and ancestral history, ultimately fostering a stronger sense of belonging within their community. It was found that children who developed skills in their heritage language experienced stronger connections and more positive relationships with their parents and extended family members compared to those who did not have the opportunity to develop their heritage language (Oh & Fuligni, 2010; Tseng & Fuligni, 2000). In other words, heritage language learning facilitates cultural understanding, practices and values within the family unit. Research also showed that developing a heritage language facilitated children's academic achievement and cognitive development, encompassing executive function skills such as sustained attention, problem-solving, cognitive flexibility and self-regulation, which are important for learning in and out of school contexts (Barac et al., 2014; Esposito, 2021; Merculief et al., 2023). As demonstrated in past studies, becoming bilingual in English and one's heritage language provides significant educational advantages.

Heritage language education is important for children from immigrant families, not only for their cultural connection and academic/cognitive development but also for their identity construction. Research revealed a close relationship between children's heritage language learning and their positive identity conformation (Arredondo et al., 2016; Mu, 2015; Umaña-Taylor, 2023; Wu et al., 2014). The studies found that sustaining heritage language helped children develop higher self-esteem, a greater sense of belonging and a stronger ethnic–racial identity. Learning a heritage language can instill pride and confidence in children's cultural identity, helping them mitigate the harmful effects of racial or ethnic discrimination by combating marginalization and building resilience (Yip et al., 2019). Research correspondingly showed that individuals who did not actively maintain but lost their heritage language often confused their sense of identity, as they were not fully accepted by either culture (Shin, 2010). Thus, learning a heritage language helps individuals reconcile their dual identities, such as being part of both the dominant and heritage cultures in their environment. It also enables them to feel more comfortable and confident navigating multicultural environments by bridging their personal and societal identities.

Since language is one of the most important factors in building a strong ethnic and cultural identity, particularly for marginalized children, language-minority children who are proficient in their heritage language tend to have a more positive sense of their ethnic identity and higher self-esteem compared to those who do not achieve proficiency in their heritage language. Thus, fluency in their heritage language contributes to a stronger connection to their cultural background, leading to a more positive self-image. Studies showed that heritage language learners (re)construct and negotiate their ethnic identity through the process of learning and engaging with their heritage language (Gyogi, 2020; Jing-Schmidt *et al.*, 2016; Kang, 2013; Lee, 2021a; Leeman, 2015; Park, 2021; Tseng, 2020; Yang, 2023; Yu, 2015; Zhou & Liu, 2022). Specifically, speakers with greater proficiency in their heritage language showed a stronger feeling of belonging to and affiliation with their ethnic group (Bankston & Zhou, 1995; Cho, 2000; Lee, 2021a). As language shapes an individual's identity, research consistently demonstrates a strong correlation between heritage language maintenance, ethnic identity and self-esteem.

The Need and Role of Heritage Language Schools for Asian Languages in the US

As the student demographics in the US become much more racially, culturally and linguistically diverse (RCLD), educators must understand the significance of heritage language learning and cultural inclusiveness to embrace students' linguistic variation and cultural diversity (Gutiérrez *et al.*, 2014; Rogoff *et al.*, 2016). Since RCLD students or children of immigrant families encounter two different cultures, values and views, they often reshape and negotiate their identities based on unique lived experiences and social participations that comprise distinctive cultural practices and linguistic knowledge (Giroux, 2005; Sánchez & Kasun, 2012). Researchers and educators have pursued ways to integrate immigrant students' dynamic life journeys into school curricula by transitioning from traditional school-based education to learning from real-world experiences (Compton-Lilly *et al.*, 2017; Sánchez & Kasun, 2012; Skerrett & Bomer, 2013; Souto-Manning, 2013) so that they can support students' everyday practices in horizontal forms rather than pursuing vertical knowledge only (Gutiérrez *et al.*, 2017; Rogoff *et al.*, 2016). Although there have been increased efforts to make school environments more inclusive and relevant for underrepresented minority groups by moving away from conventional teaching methods and practices (e.g. Souto-Manning & Lanza, 2019), many schools in the US still lack the necessary resources and knowledge to assist RCLD students effectively.

Due to the absence of resources to recognize and appreciate immigrant students' cultural heritage in public schools, as well as the lack of bilingual programs for specific Asian languages (e.g. Korean) in the US, there is a significant gap in educational options for students who learn those heritage languages at home or local communities. Thus, community-based heritage language schools – where children who have ancestral ties to the same national language and culture attend on the weekend to develop their language and literacy skills in their heritage language and develop their cultural knowledge (Compton, 2001; Fishman, 2001; Valdés, 2005) – play a pivotal role for Asian American students in not only supporting their bilingualism and biliteracy but also fostering the dynamics of their ethnic and cultural identity construction. Due to the strong emphasis on English-only instruction in US K-12 schools, the role of community-based heritage language schools has become even more vital in maintaining cultural identity and linguistic diversity across generations (Kondo-Brown, 2011; Lee, 2021b). In other words, heritage language schools provide 'an environment for cultural adjustment, identity confirmation, and social acceptance, which is essential to their [immigrant children's] psychological well-being and quality of life' (Lu, 2001: 217) in mainstream society.

Heritage language schools are privately organized by community members from the same heritage language group (Fishman, 2001) and are motivated by the community's needs and desire to pass on their linguistic and cultural heritage to future generations (Webb & Miller, 2000). Hence, the primary goal of heritage language schools is not only to teach the heritage language but also to build cultural connections. Since curricula in mainstream school settings do not provide instruction or opportunities for Asian immigrant students to learn their heritage languages and cultures, heritage language schools become the places where students learn and develop the language and culture of their heritage community (Lee, 2024b). Heritage language schools play important linguistic and non-linguistic roles by helping children of immigrants develop a sense of belonging, community connections, cultural knowledge and competence, a positive national identity and strong ethnic and cultural pride. By creating a more inclusive and culturally and linguistically diverse environment, heritage language schools validate speakers of minoritized languages and communities, thereby eradicating language disparities (García & Leiva, 2014; Peace-Hughes, 2022) and offering equal educational opportunities and equity (Lee, 2024b).

Navigating a Third Space: What Is Third Space Theory?

By acknowledging that immigrant students' everyday practices, including their cultural values, heritage and tradition, are not appreciated nor expanded in mainstream classrooms (Lagman, 2018; Lee, 2024b), scholars have called attention to Third Spaces (Bhabha, 1994) that allow students to bring their everyday funds of knowledge (Moll *et al.*, 1992) (see Chapter 5 for funds of knowledge) into the academic space by embracing their varied experiences, cultures and literacies. The term 'Third Space' was coined by the postcolonial sociolinguist Homi Bhabha (1994) to describe the construction of new cultural identities in settings where power imbalances and social inequities exist between colonizers and colonized populations, leading to the emergence of hybrid cultural forms that blend elements from both sides.

Bhabha offered insights into the emancipatory potential to disrupt antagonism against colonialism and revamped the idea of the Third Space in areas of language and cultural studies and scholarship. For Bhabha (1994: 1), the Third Space provides 'innovative sites of collaboration and contestation'; thus, the Third Space underscores the spatial politics of inclusion, negotiation and transformation, promoting dynamic transformation rather than exclusion, separation or marginalization. Pane (2007) extended the notion of Third Space by defining it as a zone of transformation where everyday and academic discourses merge, creating new potentials for learning and interaction. The concept of the Third Space contributes to an approach that contests the perpetuation of divisive and binary ways of thinking, while fostering inclusive and richly diverse patterns of cultural exchange and maturation.

Since the colonizer presents a normalizing and hegemonic culture, the Third Space further opens up for the re-articulation of negotiation and mediation by maintaining counterhegemonic agency, stance and practice (Bhabha, 1994; Soja, 1996). Third Spaces mediate the intersection of cultures and identities as they interrogate dominant notions of 'primordial unity and fixity' (Bhabha, 1994: 37). Bhabha, thus, considered Third Spaces as hybrid, liminal, ambivalent and in-between conceptual spaces since cultural meaning and representation are dynamic and evolving, not static or fixed. Gutiérrez and her associates (1999a: 287) described Third Spaces as centers of 'hybridity and diversity', which are fundamental in fostering innovative learning practices. Hybrid literacy practices within Third Spaces facilitate collaboration, which catalyzes learners' social and cognitive development, breaking traditional educational norms and conventional teaching methods to inspire more inclusive and engaging learning environments (Gutiérrez, 2014; Gutiérrez *et al.*, 1999b).

Building on Bhabha's (1994) concept of the Third Space, Flores and García (2014) proposed a pedagogical approach to creating a linguistic Third Space where learners' full linguistic and semiotic repertoires are valued and honored. Since bi/multi/plurilingual students' dynamic translanguaging practices allow them to draw on their entire linguistic knowledge and semiotic resources without limiting their language capabilities (see Chapter 3 for comprehensive discussion regarding translanguaging), providing a third space in the classroom can assist bi/multi/plurilingual students to extend their communicative competence in a creative and meaningful way (García *et al.*, 2017; Lee, 2024b; Mendoza *et al.*, 2023; Palmer *et al.*, 2019; Solorza, 2019). Encouraging students to use their entire range of languages can also preserve and sustain students' heritage languages, which are often marginalized in a dominant language environment (García *et al.*, 2017; Lee, 2021b, 2023).

Studies (e.g. Flores & García, 2014; Kakos, 2022; Tai & Li, 2021) discovered that teachers in bi/multilingual classrooms constructed pedagogical third spaces by valuing students' diverse linguistic and semiotic resources. This approach helped students develop their dynamic linguistic and cultural identities, challenging the dominant power relations that stigmatized and marginalized minority groups. In turn, the Third Space contributed to dismantling language hierarchies and power structures. Since a key goal of translanguaging is to support and protect minoritized languages, speakers and communities (Lee, 2021a; Otheguy *et al.*, 2015), providing a Third Space through translanguaging can interrogate linguistic inequality and the power imbalance among languages in different learning contexts (Cenoz & Gorter, 2017; García *et al.*, 2017).

Korean Heritage Language School Generating the Third Space

I proposed that heritage language schools offer a new lens into Third Spaces, allowing students to utilize their fluid languaging practices, value dynamic discursive practices and embrace the diverse aspects of their identities (Lee, 2024b). Since children of immigrant families in local heritage language schools constantly adapt and develop their cultural understanding and knowledge to make sense of themselves as Asian Americans (Cuero, 2010; Cun, 2024; Lee, 2024a; Wu & Leung, 2022), heritage language schools can be communal learning sites for these students to (re)construct and negotiate their multifaceted identities (Lee, 2024b). I sought to examine whether a Third Space can be created and developed in a heritage language classroom, and how this space becomes conducive to navigating students' diverse cultural and linguistic backgrounds and bridging home and school discourses.

In one of my studies (Lee, 2024b), I identified that the Korean heritage language school where I worked as a fifth-grade classroom teacher could generate a Third Space for Korean American students to bring their out-of-school knowledge into the classroom to construct their 'hybrid identit[ies] ... from many different everyday funds of knowledge and Discourse' (Moje *et al.*, 2004: 61). As I understood that my students' everyday worlds could significantly influence how they learn, understand and engage with classroom materials and resources, I decided to create my classroom as an inclusive learning space by embracing the students' linguistic hybridity and cultural diversity from their lived experiences. By acknowledging that the students needed to see themselves and their family members through literature, I designed my curricula, including transnationally inclusive literature (Skerrett, 2012, 2015) that portray a variety of cultural practices and experiences by illustrating the lives of immigrant families and their border-crossing stories (Dutro & Haberl, 2018; Skerrett & Bomer, 2013) so that the students could freely use overall sets of their lived experiences, cultural understanding and diverse perspectives. Close analysis of the literacy events in my fifth-grade class-room provided opportunities to build and co-construct a Third Space by incorporating three key features: hybridity, transformation and democracy, which are discussed in the next section.

Heritage language classroom as a hybrid Third Space

The fifth-grade heritage language classroom was developed as a hybrid learning space where students' entire linguistic repertoires, their collective knowledge from everyday practices and multifaceted identities are accepted and valued. Specifically, I created an interactive hybrid Third Space by including and valuing the students' linguistic funds of knowledge they acquired from out-of-school contexts. For instance, I often led the class discussion using both Korean and English, moving between the languages so that students were allowed to use all the languages and linguistic abilities they possessed when sharing their responses. Utilizing my entire linguistic resources indeed encouraged the students to leverage their full range of language skills for richer engagement and more profound comprehension of learning. The students acknowledged that using both languages was a normal and natural practice as they were bilinguals who effortlessly and fluidly employed their entire language repertoires. The students recognized their heritage language classroom as a hybrid learning space where the fluid employment of their language resources is accepted and valued.

The heritage language classroom was established as a hybrid learning space where each student's unique and distinctive identity is embraced in an identity-safe learning environment. The class discussion in Excerpt 2.1 demonstrates how the students constructed their multifaceted identities as bilingual, multilingual or multicultural individuals after reading the poem titled 'A Bridge' from the literature *Somewhere Among* (Donwerth-Chikamatsu, 2016).

Excerpt 2.1 Constructing multi-layered identities

(1) Ms Lee: Can you all understand what it says here? 'I am one foot here, one foot there between two worlds, Japan and America. Binational, bicultural, bilingual and biracial.'
(2) Emma: Yes, I think it describes me. I stand between Korea and America. I live in America but visit Korea often. I travel a lot.

(3) Ben: That's me. I am bilingual and bicultural because I use two lan-
     guages and celebrate two cultures, Korean and American.
(4) Kenny: I am bilingual in English and Koran, but I know three cul-
     tures – Korean, Vietnamese and American cultures. I forgot how to
     call the person who knows three cultures.
(5) Ms Lee: We can call you 'tricultural' if you want to be specific. The
     prefix 'tri' means three.
(6) Sunny: Then, I am 'tricultural' and 'trilingual.' I know how to speak
     Vietnamese a little bit.
(7) Ben: Are you fluent in Vietnamese?
(8) Sunny: No, my English and Korean are much better.
(9) Ben: Then can you be trilingual? I think I am bicultural but not bilin-
     gual because I know both American and Korean cultures well, but
     my Korean is bad, so I am not bilingual.
(10) Sunny: No, your Korean is good. You are bilingual. You don't have
     to be perfectly fluent in two languages to be bilingual.

Note. Although the students used both Korean and English during class discussions, their
language use was translated into English because the analyses in this chapter did not focus
on translanguaging. As Chapters 3 and 4 specifically examine students' translanguaging
practices, the excerpts in those chapters include their use of both Korean and English.

As shown, my question in line 1 led the students to think about and
see themselves through the protagonist who moves across Japan and
America. Emma and Ben stated that 'it describes me' and 'that's me' by
identifying the characteristics of being bicultural and bilingual (lines 2
and 3). Kenny and Sunny, whose parents were of Korean and Vietnamese
descent, developed their trilingual and tricultural identities by reflecting
on the languages and cultures they were familiar with (lines 4 and 6).
The students actively participated in their discussions to (re)construct
and negotiate their identities using the terminologies from the literature.
The students not only understood that they shared an identity as Asian
Americans and transnational individuals (see Chapter 6 for a discussion
regarding transnationalism) but also recognized that an individual's
collective identities could be different depending on their cultural and
linguistic practices, even when people share the same racial or national
identity. As I created an interactive hybrid Third Space in the classroom
using relevant literature, the dialogic engagement and interaction helped
students move forward toward constructing their multifaceted yet indi-
vidually distinctive identities.

Heritage language classroom as a transformative Third Space

The heritage language classroom was developed as a space for
transformation, as the class advocated for social justice by examining
and challenging inequality and injustice. The storylines in the selected

literature featuring Asian children as protagonists commonly portray negative biases and prejudices toward Asian people. I, as a teacher, often tried to confront the issues Asian Americans face in society and asked the class to think about ways to reduce discrimination and prejudiced attitudes. When reading the literature *Inside Out and Back Again* (Lai, 2013), I initiated the discussion by pointing out the issue the Vietnamese protagonist faced in the story (being called a 'pancake' due to the absence of concavity and convexity in her face). The students began to share their honest feelings and accumulated knowledge regarding stereotyped referents (i.e. banana, Twinkie, Chink) that describe Asian people living in the US. Specifically, the students addressed the unequal behaviors and unjust treatment toward Asians, demonstrating their understanding of the widespread injustice in society. Excerpt 2.2 displays the students' responses when I asked the class to think about ways they could fight inequality and address injustice issues.

Excerpt 2.2 Finding ways to contribute to social change and equality

(1) Ms Lee: What can we and should we do to prevent racial inequality and injustice?
(2) Rosa: Teach children about kindness, fairness and how to respect others.
(3) Julie: Schools teach how to be kind and nice, but maybe they are not always teaching how to be nice and fair to people who are different from us.
(4) Emma: Our schools should teach Asian American history, people and cultures so that Americans know and understand who we are, where we are coming from, why we are living here and what we do and celebrate.
(5) Ben: We need to be confident in who we are and our culture.
(6) Kris: Asians need to gather to stop Asian hate crimes.
(7) Sunny: We can create stop Asian hate campaign signs.

As shown, the students shared the ways they would do in preventing unfair discrimination and injustice issues. When engaging in literature that portrays negative biases and prejudices toward Asian people, the students considered and shared ideas to combat pervasive inequities and racism. As shown, the students addressed several ways that they could combat inequality and prevent unfair discrimination against Asians (i.e. teaching Asian culture and values to people, being confident as Asians, making their voices heard and actions seen) (lines 4–7). The students' responses indicate that examining pervasive race-related social problems after reading relevant literature provided them with opportunities to contemplate ideas for advocating equality and social justice. This classroom discourse shows how the heritage language classroom can bring transformative forms of learning. Hence, the heritage language classroom served as a transformative space where the students discussed how to contribute to social changes for justice and equity.

Heritage language classroom as a democratic Third Space

The heritage language classroom was developed as a democratic learning space where students have linguistic freedom and rights, as they are permitted to bring in their entire language and linguistic resources to liberate their voices and expressions. The students identified that their heritage language classroom was an autonomous learning space where they had autonomy in their language use in the classroom. By comparing the language policy in their previous heritage language classrooms, where they were required to use Korean only, the students recognized that their current classroom had become a space where they had freedom of language choice and linguistic rights.

The heritage language classroom was also established as a democratic Third Space, as it disrupts traditional social roles and power structures while building horizontal relationships between the teacher and students. For instance, I disrupted the traditional role of the teacher by positioning the two students (children of Vietnamese and Korean descent) as experts in Vietnamese culture on a classroom culture day. The interviews with the two students (Sunny and Kenny) demonstrate how they valued reciprocal processes of teaching and the horizontal dimension of learning in their current heritage language classroom. Excerpt 2.3 displays what Sunny and Kenny shared during the interview.

Excerpt 2.3 Disrupting traditional social roles and power structures in the classroom

(1) Sunny: I felt valued when you [her teacher; Ms Lee] asked me to teach you and the class about the Vietnamese language and culture. It was the first time I felt that what I knew was valuable and useful in class. I was nervous but felt good to be a teacher.
(2) Kenny: It was a different experience for me because I taught the teacher and the other kids in class. I felt I had become a teacher on that day. It was different from the former classroom experiences because in my previous classrooms, teachers were always talking, and we [the students] were always supposed to follow him or her.

Sunny and Kenny commonly addressed that they had experienced a power imbalance that situated the teacher and students in a hierarchical relationship in their previous classrooms. Yet, they recognized that the current heritage language classroom disrupted the traditional classroom setting and became a democratic learning space where the balance of power can be shifted depending on the content of learning and topics of conversation. The two students' responses indicate that they appreciated the classroom environment where there were equal rights between teacher and students so that both were actively engaged in and contributing to the learning process. In this democratic Third Space, the students' testimonies suggest that I, as the classroom teacher, intentionally disrupted traditional teacher–student hierarchies by prioritizing students' voices and perspectives to create a more collaborative learning environment where everyone participates equally.

Implications for Educational Practice of Creating a Transformative Third Space

In the US, languages other than English are often referred to as 'foreign' languages. However, these languages are not foreign to people who learn and speak them because the speakers have personal and cultural connections and strong familial ties to those languages as their heritage language. Even if they may not be fully fluent in their heritage language, it remains an integral part of their cultural heritage and shared identity. Thus, educators need to recognize and appreciate RCLD students' heritage language learning and cultural heritage development by creating a more inclusive and enriching learning environment. This chapter emphasizes the significant role of creating a Third Space (i.e. a conceptual space that serves as a bridge between students' home experiences and school discourses).

As the empirical study in this chapter demonstrates that a Korean heritage language classroom can create a hybrid, transformative and democratic Third Space for Korean American students, educators are encouraged to understand that they can offer a learning space that has transformative potential so that the learning zone becomes an arena for constructing new knowledge and fostering individual and collective agency through engagement and empowerment. Educators can work toward transformative change by moving away from traditional teaching methods and practices and making school environments more inclusive, relevant and meaningful for their students. As the findings in this chapter illustrate, educators are required to understand that providing literature that includes a variety of cultures, experiences and perspectives can serve as a valuable medium and a powerful pedagogical tool for students in positively (re)constructing their fluid and multifaceted identities.

Educators are expected to recognize that their classroom can be a vital democratic space that challenges traditional social roles and power structures, fostering horizontal relationships between the teacher and students. Teachers can create a horizontal learning zone in their classrooms from a democratic perspective by fostering a collaborative learning environment where everyone is actively involved and contributing to the interaction. To create and develop their classroom as a Third Space where diverse perspectives, practices and ideologies coexist and reinforce one another, educators need to value inclusion and diversity (hybridity), dismantle social injustice (transformation) and provide opportunities for autonomy and equality (democracy) (Lee, 2024b). Overall, the chapter offers educators and researchers powerful insights into creating conducive Third Spaces in various learning contexts, thereby providing hybrid, transformational and democratic educational experiences.

References

Abourehab, Y. and Azaz, M. (2023) Pedagogical translanguaging in community/heritage Arabic language learning. *Journal of Multilingual and Multicultural Development* 44, 398–411.

Abraham, S., Kedley, K., Fall, M., Krishnamurthy, S. and Tulino, D. (2021) Creating a translanguaging space in a bilingual community-based writing program. *International Multilingual Research Journal* 15 (3), 211–234.

American Council for International Education (2021) https://www.americancouncils.org/news/announcements-featured-content/arc-completes-national-canvass-dual-language-immersion-programs.

Arredondo, M.M., Rosado, M. and Satterfield, T. (2016) Understanding the impact of heritage language on ethnic identity formation and literacy for U.S. Latino children. *Journal of Cognition and Culture* 16 (3/4), 245–266. https://doi.org/10.1163/15685373-12342179.

Bankston, C. and Zhou, M. (1995) Effects of minority-language literacy on the academic achievement of Vietnamese youths in New Orleans. *Sociology of Education* 68 (1), 1–17.

Barac, R., Bialystok, E., Castro, D.C. and Sanchez, M. (2014) The cognitive development of young dual language learners: A critical review. *Early Childhood Research Quarterly* 29 (4), 699–714.

Bhabha, H.K. (1994) *The Location of Culture*. Routledge.

Bialystok, E. (2018) Bilingual education for young children: Review of the effects and consequences. *International Journal of Bilingual Education and Bilingualism* 21 (6), 666–679. https://doi.org/10.1080/13670050.2016.1203859.

Budiyana, Y.E. (2017) Students' parents' attitude toward Chinese heritage language maintenance. *Theory and Practice in Language Studies* 7 (3), 195–200.

Caldas, S. (2012) Language policy in the family. In B. Spolsky (ed.) *The Cambridge Handbook of Language Policy* (pp. 351–373). Cambridge University Press.

Carreira, M. and Kagan, O. (2011) The results of the national heritage language survey: Implications for teaching, curriculum design, and professional development. *Foreign Language Annals* 44 (1), 40–64.

Cavicchiolo, E., Manganelli, S., Girelli, L., Chirico, A., Lucidi, F. and Alivernini, F. (2020) Immigrant children's proficiency in the host country language is more important than individual, family and peer characteristics in predicting their psychological well-being. *Journal of Immigrant and Minority Health* 22 (6), 1225–1231. https://www.jstor.org/stable/48709775.

Cenoz, J. and Gorter, D. (2017) Minority languages and sustainable translanguaging: Threat or opportunity? *Journal of Multilingual and Multicultural Development* 38, 901–912.

Cho, G. (2000) The role of heritage language in social interactions and relationships: Reflections from a language minority group. *Bilingual Research Journal* 24, 369–384.

Cho, G. (2015) Perspectives vs. reality of heritage language development: Voices from second-generation Korean-American high school students. *Multicultural Education* 22 (2), 30–38.

Compton, C. (2001) Heritage language communities and schools: Challenges and recommendations. In J.K. Peyton, D.A. Ranard and Scott McGinnis (eds) *Heritage Languages in America: Preserving a National Resource* (pp. 145–166). Center for Applied Linguistics & Delta Systems.

Compton-Lilly, C., Papoi, K., Venegas, P., Hamman, L. and Schwabenbauer, B. (2017) Intersectional identity negotiation: The case of young immigrant children. *Journal of Literacy Research* 49 (1), 115–140.

Cuero, K.K. (2010) Artisan with words: Transnational funds of knowledge in a bilingual Latina's stories. *Language Arts* 87 (6), 427–436.

Cun, A. (2024) Translanguaging practices in a community-based Chinese heritage early childhood classroom. *International Journal of Bilingualism* 29 (3), 667–683. https://doi.org/10.1177/13670069241243204.

Donwerth-Chikamatsu, A. (2016) *Somewhere Among*. Atheneum Caitlyn Dlouhy Books Publisher.

Dutro, E. and Haberl, E. (2018) Blurring material and rhetorical walls: Children writing the border/lands in a second-grade classroom. *Journal of Literacy Research* 50 (2), 167–189.

Eng, D. and Han, S. (2019) *Racial Melancholia, Racial Dissociation: On the Social and Psychic Lives of Asian Americans*. Duke.

Esposito, A.G. (2021) Executive functions in two-way dual-language education: A mechanism for academic performance. *Bilingual Research Journal* 43 (4), 417–432. https://doi.org/10.1080/15235882.2021.1874570.

Fishman, J.A. (2001) 300-plus years of heritage language education in the United States. In J.K. Peyton, D.A. Ranard and S. McGinnis (eds) *Heritage Languages in America: Preserving a National Resource* (pp. 81–98). Center for Applied Linguistics & Delta Systems.

Flores, N. and García, O. (2014) Linguistic third spaces in education: Teachers' translanguaging across the bilingual continuum. In D. Little, C. Leung and P. Van Avermaet (eds) *Managing Diversity in Education: Languages, Policies, Pedagogies* (pp. 243–256). Multilingual Matters.

Fogle, L.W. (2013) Parental ethnotheories and family language policy in transnational adoptive families. *Language Policy* 12, 83–102.

Foner, N. and Kasinitz, P. (2007) The second generation. In M. Waters, R. Ueda and H. Marrow (eds) *The New Americans: A Guide to Immigration Since 1965* (pp. 270–282). Harvard University Press.

García, O. and Leiva, L. (2014). Theorizing and enacting translanguaging for social justice. In A. Blackledge and A. Creese (eds) *Heteroglossia as Practice and Pedagogy* 20 (pp. 199–216). Springer.

García, O., Johnson, S. and Seltzer, K. (2017) *The Translanguaging Classroom. Leveraging Student Bilingualism for Learning*. Caslon.

Giroux, H. (2005) *Border Crossings: Cultural Workers and the Politics of Education*. Routledge.

Guardado, M. (2017) Spanish as a minority/heritage language in Canada and the UK. In K. Potowski (ed.) *The Routledge Handbook of Spanish as a Heritage/Minority Language*. Routledge.

Guardado, M. and Becker, A. (2013) Fostering heritage languages and diasporic identities: The role of grassroots initiatives in Alberta and British Columbia. In K. Arnett and C. Mady (eds) *Minority Populations in Canadian Second Language Education* (pp. 55–70). Multilingual Matters.

Guijarro-Fuentes, P. and Schmitz, K. (2015) The nature and nurture of heritage language acquisition. *Lingua* 164 (3), 239–250.

Gutiérrez, K. (2014) Integrative research review: Syncretic approaches to literacy learning. In P. Dunston, L. Gambrell, K. Headley, S. Fullerton and P. Stecker (eds) *Leveraging Horizontal Knowledge and Expertise: 63rd Literacy Research Association Yearbook* (pp. 48–61). Literacy Research Association.

Gutiérrez, K., Baquedano-Lopez, P. and Tejeda, C. (1999a) Rethinking diversity: Hybridity and hybrid language practices in the third space. *Mind, Culture, & Activity* 6, 286–303.

Gutiérrez, K., Baquedano-Lopez, P., Alvarez, H. and Chiu, M. (1999b) A cultural-historical approach to collaboration: Building a culture of collaboration through hybrid language practices. *Theory Into Practice* 38 (2), 87–93.

Gyogi, E. (2020) Fixity and fluidity in two heritage language learners' identity narratives. *Language and Education* 34 (4), 328–344. https://doi.org/10.1080/09500782.2020.1720228.

Hinton, L. (2008) Trading tongues: Loss of heritage languages in the United States. In A. Reyes and A. Lo (eds) *Beyond Yellow English: Toward a Linguistic Anthropology of Asian Pacific America* (pp. 331–346). Oxford University Press.

Jing-Schmidt, Z., Chen, J.Y. and Zhang, Z. (2016) Identity development in the ancestral homeland: A Chinese heritage perspective. *The Modern Language Journal* 100 (4), 797–812. https://doi.org/10.1111/modl.12348.

Kakos, M. (2022) A third space for inclusion: Multilingual teaching assistants reporting on the use of their marginal position, translation and translanguaging to construct inclusive environments. *International Journal of Inclusive Education* 1–16. https://doi.org/10.1080/13603116.2022.2073060.

Kang, H.S. (2013) Korean American college students' language practices and identity positioning: "Not Korean, but not American." *Journal of Language, Identity & Education* 12 (4), 248–261. https://doi.org/10.1080/15348458.2013.818473.

Keh, M.L. and Stoessel, S. (2017) How first is first? Revisiting language maintenance and shift and the meaning of L1/L2 in three case studies. *International Multilingual Research Journal* 11, 101–114.

Kim, S.Y. and Chao, R.K. (2009) Heritage language fluency, ethnic identity, and school effort of immigrant Chinese and Mexican adolescents. *Cultural Diversity & Ethnic Minority Psychology* 15 (1), 27–37. https://doi.org/10.1037/a0013052.

Kim, C. and Pyun, D. (2014) Heritage language literacy maintenance: A study of Korean-American heritage learners. *Language, Culture, and Curriculum* 27 (3), 294–315.

King, K.A. and Fogle, L.W. (2006) Bilingual parenting as good parenting: Parents' perspectives on family language policy for additive bilingualism. *International Journal of Bilingual Education and Bilingualism* 9 (6), 695–712.

Kondo-Brown, K. (2011) Maintaining heritage language perspectives of Korean parents. *Multicultural Education* 19 (1), 31–37.

Köpke, B. and Schmid, M.S. (2019) *The Oxford Handbook of Language Attrition*. Oxford University Press.

Lagman, E. (2018) Literacy remains: Loss and affects in transnational literacies. *College English* 81 (1), 27–49.

Lai, T. (2013) *Inside Out and Back Again*. HarperCollins Publisher.

Lee, B.Y. (2013) Heritage language maintenance and cultural identity formation: The case of Korean immigrant parents and their children in the USA. *Early Child Development and Care* 183 (11), 1576–1588.

Lee, C. (2021a) Role of immigrant parents' attitudes and practices in emergent bilingual students' language use and translanguaging performance. In G. Onchwari and S. Keengwe (eds) *Research Anthology on Bilingual and Multilingual Education*. IGI Global.

Lee, C. (2021b) *Understanding the Oral and Written Translanguaging Practices of Emergent Bilinguals: Insights from a Korean Heritage Language Classroom in the U.S.* Routledge.

Lee, C. (2023) How do children go through a heteroglossic path to becoming bilingual? Comparison of Korean children's translanguaging performance in first and third grades. *International Journal of Bilingual Education and Bilingualism* 27 (4), 612–630. https://doi.org/10.1080/13670050.2023.2232088.

Lee, C. (2024a) Sanctioning a space for literacy practices to promote transnational students' identity development in a HL classroom. *International Multilingual Research Journal* 19 (1), 1–22. https://doi.org/10.1080/19313152.2024.2309695.

Lee, C. (2024b) (Co)constructing hybrid, transformative, and democratic third spaces in a heritage classroom for Asian American transnational students. *Language & Education* 39 (3), 699–716.

Lee, J.S. and Shin, S. (2008) Korean heritage language education in the United States: The current state, opportunities, and possibilities. *Heritage Language Journal* 6 (2), 1–20.

Lee, J.S. and Wright, W.E. (2014) The rediscovery of heritage and community language education in the United States. *Review of Research in Education* 38 (1), 137–165.

Leeman, J. (2015) Heritage language education and identity in the United States. *Annual Review of Applied Linguistics* 35, 100–119.

Li, G. (2006) Biliteracy and trilingual practices in the home context: Case studies of Chinese-Canadian children. *Journal of Early Childhood Literacy* 6 (3), 355–381.

Li, G. and Wen, K. (2015) East Asian heritage language education for a plurilingual reality in the United States: Practices, potholes, and possibilities. *International Multilingual Research Journal* 9 (4), 274–290.

Lu, X. (2001) Bicultural identity development and Chinese community formation: An ethnographic study of Chinese schools in Chicago. *The Howard Journal of Communications* 12, 203–220.

Lü, C. and Koda, K. (2011) The impact of home language and literacy support on English-Chinese biliteracy acquisition among Chinese heritage language learners. *Heritage Language Journal* 8, 119–231.

Lynch, A. (2014) The first decade of the heritage language journal: A retrospective view of research on heritage languages. *Heritage Language Journal* 11 (3), 224–242.

McCabe, M. (2016) Transnationalism and language maintenance: Czech and Slovak as heritage languages in the Southeastern United States. *International Journal of the Sociology of Language* 238, 169–191.

McCarty, T.L. (2002) *A Place to be Navajo: Rough Rock and the Struggle for Self-Determination in Indigenous Schooling*. Lawrence Erlbaum.

Mendoza, A., Hamman-Ortiz, L., Tian, Z., Rajendram, S., Tai, K.W.H., Ho, W.Y.J. and Sah, P.K. (2023) Sustaining critical approaches to translanguaging in education: A contextual framework. *TESOL Quarterly* 58 (2), 664–692. https://doi.org/10.1002/tesq.3240.

Merculief, A., Lipscomb, S.T., McClelland, M.M., Geldhof, J. and Tsethlikai, M.T. (2023) Nurturing resilience in AI/ AN preschool children: The role of cultural socialization, executive function, and neighborhood risk. *Frontiers in Psychology* 14. https://doi.org/10.3389/fpsyg.2023.1279336.

Moje, E.B., Ciechanoswi, K., Kramer, K., Ellis, L., Carrillo, R. and Collazo, T. (2004) Working toward third space in content area literacy: An examination of everyday funds of knowledge and Discourse. *Reading Research Quarterly* 39 (1), 38–70.

Moll, L., Amanti, C., Neff, D. and González, N. (1992) Funds of knowledge for teaching: Using a qualitative approach to connect homes and classrooms. *Theory into Practice* 31 (2), 132–141.

Montrul, S. (2008) *Incomplete Acquisition in Bilingualism: Re-examining the Age Factor*. John Benjamins.

Montrul, S. (2010) Current issues in heritage language acquisition. *Annual Review of Applied Linguistics* 30, 3–23.

Montrul, S.A. (2012) Is the heritage language like a second language? *EUROSLA Yearbook* 12, 1–29. https://doi.org/10.1075/eurosla.12.03mon.

Montrul, S.A. (2018) Heritage language development: Connecting the dots. *International Journal of Bilingualism* 22 (5), 530–546.

Montrul, S. (2023) Heritage languages: Language acquired, language lost, language regained. *Annual Review of Linguistics* 9, 399–418. https://doi.org/10.1146/annurev-linguistics-030521-050236.

Montrul, S. and Bowles, M. (2009) Back to basics: Incomplete knowledge of differential object marking in Spanish heritage speakers. *Bilingualism: Language and Cognition* 12 (3), 363–383. https://doi.org/10.1017/S1366728909990071.

Mu, M. (2015) A meta-analysis of the correlation between heritage language and ethnic identity. *Journal of Multilingual and Multicultural Development* 36 (3), 239–254.

Murphy, V. (2014) *Second Language Learning in the Early School Years: Trends and Contexts*. Oxford University Press.

Nesteruk, O. (2010) Heritage language maintenance and loss among the children of Eastern European immigrants in the USA. *Journal of Multilingual and Multicultural Development* 31 (3), 271–286.

Oh, J.S. and Fuligni, A.J. (2010) The role of heritage language development in the ethnic identity and family relationships of adolescents from immigrant backgrounds. *Social Development* 19, 202–220.

Otheguy, R., García, O. and Reid, W. (2015) Clarifying translanguaging and deconstructing named languages: A perspective from linguistics. *Applied Linguistics Review* 6, 281–307. https://doi.org/10.1515/applirev-2015-0014.

Palmer, D.K., Cervantes-Soon, C., Dorner, L. and Heiman, D. (2019) Bilingualism, biliteracy, biculturalism, and critical consciousness for all: Proposing a fourth fundamental goal for two-way dual language education. *Theory Into Practice* 58 (2), 121–133. https://doi.org/10.1080/00405841.2019.1569376.

Pane, D.M. (2007) Third space theory: Reconceptualizing content literacy learning. *Reading and Writing* 20 (1), 78–83.

Park, E. (2006) Grandparents, grandchildren, and heritage language. In K. Kondo-Brown (ed.) *Heritage Language Development: Focus on East Asian Immigrants* (pp. 57–86). John Benjamins.

Park, M.Y. (2021) Language ideologies, heritage language use, and identity construction among 1.5-generation Korean immigrants in New Zealand. *International Journal of Bilingual Education and Bilingualism* 25 (7), 2469–2481. https://doi.org/10.1080/1367 0050.2021.1913988.

Peace-Hughes, T., Cohen, B.J., Jamieson, L. and Tisdall, E.K.M. (2022) Children, childhoods and bilingualism: Exploring experiences, perspectives and policies. *Children & Society* 36, 301–304. https://doi.org/10.1111/chso.12556.

Pew Research Center (2023, September 11) Among Asian Americans, U.S. born children of immigrants are most likely to have hidden part of their heritage. Retrieved from:

Pires, A. and Rothman, J. (2009). Disentangling sources of incomplete acquisition: An explanation for competence divergence across heritage grammars. *International Journal of Bilingualism* 13 (2), 211–238..

Pires, A. and Rothman, J. (2009) Disentangling sources of incomplete acquisition: An explanation for competence divergence across heritage grammars. *International Journal of Bilingualism* 13 (2), 211–238.

Polinsky, M. (2011) Reanalysis in adult heritage language. *Studies in Second Language Acquisition* 33 (2), 305–328.

Polinsky, M. (2018) Bilingual children and adult heritage speakers: The range of comparison. *International Journal of Bilingualism* 22 (5), 547–563.

Polinsky, M. and Kagan, O. (2007) Heritage languages: In the "wild" and in the classroom. *Language and Linguistics Compass* 1 (5), 368–395.

Ro, Y.E. and Cheatham, G.A. (2009) Biliteracy and bilingual development in a second-generation Korean child: A case study. *Journal of Research in Childhood Education* 23, 290–308.

Rogoff, B., Callanan, M., Gutiérrez, K.D. and Erickson, F. (2016) The organization of informal learning. *Review of Research in Education* 40, 356–401.

Sánchez, P. and Kasun, G.S. (2012) Connecting transnationalism to the classroom and to theories of immigrant student adaptation. *Berkeley Review of Education* 3, 71–93.

Schmid, M.S. (2008) Defining language attrition. *Babylonia* 2, 9–12.

Schmid, M.S. (2010) Languages at play: The relevance of L1 attrition to the study of bilingualism. *Bilingualism: Language and Cognition* 13 (1), 1–7. https://doi.org/10.1017/S1366728909990368.

Seals, C. and Peyton, J.K. (2017) Heritage language education: Valuing the languages, literacies and cultural competencies of immigrant youth. *Current Issues of Language Planning* 18 (1), 87–101.

Shin, S.J. (2005) *Developing in Two Languages: Korean Children in America*. Multilingual Matters.

Shin, S.J. (2010) "What about me? I'm not like Chinese but I'm not like American": Heritage-language learning and identity of mixed-heritage adults. *Journal of Language, Identity & Education* 9 (3), 203–219.

Shin, S.J. (2014) Language learning as culture keeping: Family language policies of transnational adoptive parents. *International Multilingual Research Journal* 8 (3), 189–207.

Shin, F.H. and Krashen, S. (1996) Teacher attitudes toward the principles of bilingual education and toward students' participation in bilingual programs: Same or different? *Bilingual Research Journal* 20, 45–53.

Shin, S.J. and Lee, J.S. (2013) Expanding capacity, opportunity, and desire to learn Korean as a heritage language. *Heritage Language Journal* 10 (3), 64–73.

Skerrett, A. (2012) Language and literacies in translocation: Experiences and perspectives of a transnational youth. *Journal of Literacy Research* 44, 364–395.

Skerrett, A. (2015) *Teaching Transnational Youth: Literacy and Education in a Changing World*. Teachers College Press.

Skerrett, A. and Bomer, R. (2013) Recruiting languages and lifeworlds for border-crossing compositions. *Research in the Teaching of English* 47, 313–337.

Soja, E.W. (1996) *Third Space: Journeys to Los Angeles and Other Real-and-Imagined Places*. Blackwell.

Solorza, C.R. (2019) Trans + Languaging: Beyond dual language bilingual education. *Journal of Multilingual Education Research* 9 (15), 99–112.

Souto-Manning, M. (2013) Teaching young children from immigrant and diverse families. *YC Young Children* 68 (4), 72–80.

Souto-Manning, M. and Lanza, A. (2019) Pedagogical third spaces: Inclusion and representation of LGBTQ Communities in and through teaching as a matter of justice. *Theory Into Practice* 58 (1), 39–50.

Tai, K. and Li, W. (2021) Constructing playful talk through translanguaging in English medium instruction mathematics classrooms. *Applied Linguistics* 42 (4), 607–640.

Tse, L. (1998). Affecting affect: The impact of heritage language programs on student attitudes. In S. Krashen, L. Tse and J. McQuillan (eds) *Heritage Language Development* (pp. 51–72). Language Education Associates.

Tse, L. (2001) *Why Don't They Learn English? Separating Fact from Fallacy in the U.S. Language Debate*. Teachers College Press.

Tseng, A. (2020) Identity in home-language maintenance. In A.C. Schalley and S.A. Eisenchlas (eds) *Handbook of Home Language Maintenance and Development* (pp. 109–129). De Gruyter Mouton.

Tseng, V. and Fuligni, A.J. (2000) Parent-adolescent language use and relationships among immigrant families with East Asian, Filipino, and Latin American backgrounds. *Journal of Marriage and Family* 62, 465–476.

Umaña-Taylor, A.J. (2023) Promoting adolescent adjustment by intervening in ethnic-racial identity development: Opportunities for developmental prevention science and considerations for a global theory of change. *International Journal of Behavioral Development* 47 (4), 352–365. https://doi:10.1177/01650254231162614.

Valdés, G. (2000) Teaching heritage languages: An introduction for Slavic-language-teaching professionals. In O. Kagan and B. Rifkin (eds) *Learning and Teaching of Slavic Languages and Cultures: Toward the 21st Century* (pp. 37–403). Slavica.

Valdés, G. (2001) Heritage language students: Profiles and possibilities. In J. Peyton, J. Ranard and S. McGinnis (eds) *Heritage Languages in America: Preserving a National Resource* (pp. 37–80). The Center for Applied Linguistics and Delta Systems.

Valdés, G. (2005) Bilingualism, heritage language learners, and SLA research: Opportunities lost or seized? *Modern Language Journal* 89 (3), 410–426.

Veltman, C. (1983) *Language Shift in the United States*. Mouton.

Webb, J.B. and Miller, B.L. (2000) *Teaching Heritage Language Learners: Voices from the Classroom*. American Council on the Teaching of Foreign Languages.

Wu, M.H., Lee, K. and Leung, G. (2014) Heritage language education and investment among Asian American middle schoolers: Insights from a charter school. *Language and Education* 28 (1), 19–33.

Wu, M.H. and Leung, G. (2022) 'It's not my Chinese': A teacher and her students disrupting and dismantling conventional notions of 'Chinese' through translanguaging in a heritage language classroom. *International Journal of Bilingual Education and Bilingualism* 25 (5), 1811–1824.

Yang, Y. (2023) The role of heritage language in multiple dimensions of ethnic identity: A case study of Chinese-Australian adolescents. *International Journal of Multilingualism* 21 (4), 1775–1798. https://doi:10.1080/14790718.2023.2210284.

Yip, T., Wang, Y., Mootoo, C. and Mirpuri, S. (2019) Moderating the association between discrimination and adjustment: A meta-analysis of ethnic/racial identity. *Developmental Psychology* 55 (6), 1274–1298. https://doi:10.1037/dev0000708.

Yu, S. (2015). The relationships among heritage language proficiency, ethnic identity, and self-esteem. *Forum for International Research in Education* 2 (2), 57–71.

Zhou, Y. and Liu, Y. (2022) Theorising the dynamics of heritage language identity development: A narrative inquiry of the life histories of three Chinese heritage speakers. *Language and Education* 37 (3), 383–400. https://doi.org/10.1080/09500782.2022.206 8351.

3 Enacting Translanguaging Pedagogy in Creating an Inclusive and Rich Learning Environment

As I invite the third graders in Mrs Park's class to participate in my translanguaging research, I have a conversation with Mrs Park about emergent bilingual learners' translanguaging practices and performance. Mrs Park admits that she is not familiar with the term 'translanguaging', but she understands the concept of code-switching as the practice of alternating between different languages during a verbal interaction. Mrs Park, however, has a negative view of students' use of code-switching in the classroom, as she believes it hinders her bilingual students' language learning and communication skills. I explain the notion of translanguaging by differentiating it from code-switching so that she can understand that translanguaging describes how bi/multilingual speakers access and utilize all their linguistic resources as one interconnected system rather than separate languages for communication. Although Mrs Park understands that translanguaging is a natural practice for bi/multilingual students, she is doubtful about providing time and space for translanguaging in her heritage language classroom because she is concerned about her students' overuse of English rather than focusing on the target language (Korean) if she allows her students to translanguage. Mrs Park shows her hesitancy in implementing translanguaging in her heritage language classroom.

***

This vignette highlights that classroom teachers may hold uncertain, ambivalent or negative perceptions of translanguaging, as they may not fully understand what translanguaging is or how it can benefit their bilingual or multilingual students. Like Mrs Park, many classroom teachers may fear that incorporating translanguaging would negatively impact their students' progress in the language of instruction. Classroom teachers like Mrs Park, who serve linguistically and culturally diverse students, are expected to understand that translanguaging pedagogy is a teaching approach that empowers bi/multilingual students to leverage their entire linguistic repertoire to enhance learning. Mrs Park later understood that translanguaging extends beyond traditional language instruction by recognizing that students do not learn in isolation within a single language but rather utilize all their linguistic resources to make sense of their meaning and the world around them.

Introduction to the Chapter

By moving away from the traditional or fractional view of bilingualism, this chapter introduces a holistic view and a heteroglossic perspective on bi/multi/plurilingualism, which describes a bi/multi/plurilingual individual as an integrated whole, with their language processes and linguistic knowledge not stored in separate compartments. From this holistic and heteroglossic perspective, a translanguaging (García, 2009) paradigm has emerged. The purpose of this chapter is to review the core concept and idea behind translanguaging theory within bi/multi/plurilingual education settings. The chapter thoroughly discusses translanguaging in the post-multilingualism era and explores how translanguaging promotes inclusiveness of language use, fairness, equality and justice for bi/multi/plurilingual learners by resisting colonial logic and decolonizing language and education. The chapter then presents translanguaging pedagogy along with various teaching methods and strategies to validate students' bi/multi/plurilingual abilities and humanize their learning processes. The implications of translanguaging pedagogy to foster a more inclusive learning environment for bi/multi/plurilingual students are discussed at the end of the chapter.

From a Fractional View of Bilingualism to a Holistic View of Bilingualism

Bilingual educators in the past believed that bilingual students' languages should be kept separate in the classroom to provide sufficient instruction in each target language and to prevent confusion or language interference (August & Hakuta, 1998; Fillmore, 1991). Traditional models of bilingual education have traditionally indicated a strict separation of the languages and a clear boundary between the two (Baker, 2011; Lindholm-Leary, 2001). The language policy in many dual language immersion programs in the past aimed to provide one language at a time by discouraging the mixing of the two languages, as the goal was to ensure students developed strong proficiency in each language separately before fully integrating them (Crawford, 2004). Thus, the approach to bilingual education used to be described as 'parallel monolingualism' (Heller, 2001), 'separate bilingualism' (Creese & Blackledge, 2010), 'two solitudes' (Cummins, 2005), 'code-segregation' (Guerra, 2012) and 'bilingualism with diglossia' (Baker, 2011).

Based on this notion of bilingualism, educators formerly believed that bilingual speakers' two languages were used under different conditions and for distinct social functions. This traditional view of bilingualism, also known as the monolingual or fractional view of bilingualism, considered that bilinguals have two separate language systems in their brains (Gravelle, 1996; Grosjean, 1989, 2024). By outlining several negative consequences associated with this fractional view of bilingualism, Grosjean (1989) proposed a 'holistic' view of bilingualism, which describes a bilingual individual as an integrated whole, and their language processing and linguistic knowledge cannot be separated into two compartments. From a holistic bilingual perspective, bilinguals have a unique and fluid linguistic configuration, and the coexistence and constant interaction of their languages construct a distinctive but complete language system (Grosjean, 1989, 2024; Soltero-González *et al.*, 2016).

Rethinking and Reimagining Bi/Multi/Plurilingualism from a Heteroglossic Perspective

To move away from the concept of bilingualism as parallel monolingualism or the notion that bilinguals are two monolinguals in one person, Mikhail Bakhtin (1981) coined the term 'heteroglossia' to describe the phenomenon where speakers utilize a variety of registers, voices, languages or codes within communication in their daily lives, emphasizing the coexistent of varied perspectives and multi-layered social meanings within a single utterance. The Bakhtinian notion of heteroglossia has rejected and replaced monolingual ideology in language learning, advancing multi/plurilingual pedagogy and practices by accepting and appreciating all kinds of multimodal languaging practices (Canagarajah, 2011; Creese & Blackledge, 2010; García, 2011; Li, 2011, 2018).

Influenced by Bakhtin's theory, scholars made a clear distinction between monoglossic and heteroglossic ideologies by arguing that heteroglossia does not explain the existence of different varieties, dialects and styles of speech as a unitary system; instead, it refers to the coexistence of distinct linguistic varieties, multiple voices, different styles of discourse or multiple points of view within a single language (Bailey, 2007; Busch, 2012; Canagarajah, 2011). That is, heteroglossia creates a dynamic and diverse linguistic landscape rather than identifying a unified or singular form of speech and highlights the plurality of language (Creese & Blackledge, 2010; Li, 2011). The heteroglossia perspective allows speakers to draw upon their diverse and collective linguistic repertoires to effectively communicate and achieve their communicative aims depending on their desired meaning in a given situation or under different circumstances.

Heteroglossia opened the spaces to acknowledge the existence of diverse language varieties and voices, to embrace the integration of different modes of communication and to accept all kinds of multimodal translanguaging practices as an inclusive approach rather than solely focusing on a single, dominant language or holding the monolingual perspective (Busch, 2012; Canagarajah, 2011). A translanguaging paradigm has emerged and developed from this heteroglossic viewpoint. That is, the heteroglossic viewpoint directly aligns with the concept of translanguaging (García, 2009) as both approaches recognize the value of diverse linguistic varieties and challenge the traditional view of language learning (Creese & Blackledge, 2010; García *et al.*, 2017; Lee, 2021; Lewis *et al.*, 2012; Li, 2011, 2018; Li & García, 2022).

Translanguaging as Heteroglossic Pedagogy

Translanguaging was initially coined by a Welsh educator, Cen Williams (1994), to refer to pedagogical practice where bi/multi/plurilingual students can 'alternate languages for the purposes of receptive or productive use' (as cited in García *et al.*, 2017: 2). Colin Baker (2011) later translated the Welsh term 'trawsieithu' to the English word 'translanguaging'. Ofelia García (2009, 2011, 2014) and her colleagues (e.g. García *et al.*, 2017; García & Li, 2014; Velasco & García, 2014) broadened the concept of translanguaging to describe the practice where bi/multi/plurilingual individuals utilize their entire linguistic repertoire to communicate flexibly and effectively both in oral and written forms (Lee, 2021). A translanguaging paradigm has been established and utilized in research on bi/multi/plurilingualism, bi/multi/pluriliteracies and bi/multi/plurilingual education over the past 15 years.

Translanguaging refers to speakers' normal and natural practices that diverge from the 'diglossic functional separation' (Creese & Blackledge, 2010: 106). As bi/multi/plurilingual individuals have access to their integrated linguistic system and use their languages from their 'internal perspectives' (García, Johnson & Seltzer, 2017: 20), translanguaging enables them to 'turn off their language switching function' (García & Li, 2014: 23) and supports the flexible use of the speaker's entire language repertoires. The notion of codeswitching 'put[s] to the service of the majority language and encourag[es] switching towards the dominant language only and used progressively to take space and time away from the minority language until it disappears completely' (García, 2009: 297). Yet, in translanguaging practice, there are 'no clear-cut boundaries between the languages of bilinguals ... what we have is a languaging continuum that is accessed' (García, 2009: 47). Unlike code-switching that views language from an external perspective (i.e. national or standard languages) as if speakers' language process and linguistic knowledge are stored in separate compartments, translanguaging focuses on the ways that speakers use their languages from their internal perspectives by actively fluidly drawing on their multiple languages (García *et al.*, 2017; García & Lin, 2017).

Although translanguaging is a linguistic practice that involves the use of multiple languages and semiotic resources (García, 2009, 2014; García & Lin, 2017; García *et al.*, 2017; García & Li, 2014), it is not a shift from one language or code to another. Rather, translanguaging is 'rooted in the principle that bilingual speakers select language features from a repertoire and "soft assemble" their language practices in ways that fit their communicative situations' (García & Kano, 2014: 260). Thus, the concept of translanguaging not only indicates the flexible use of languages by bi/multi/plurilingual speakers (Lewis *et al.*, 2012) but also theorizes their language practices as a unified linguistic repertoire (García & Li, 2014). As translanguaging rejects the monolingual ideologies in language use, Sembiante and Tian (2023) described translanguaging as a pedagogy of hope. They claimed that translanguaging could counteract monoglossic bias by promoting unbiased, equitable and humanizing instructional practices in multilingual classrooms.

Although the term 'translanguaging' was primarily used to refer to the teacher's pedagogical practices to scaffold bilingual students' learning (Canagarajah, 2011; Cenoz & Gorter, 2021, 2022), scholars also consider translanguaging as complex language practices of bi/multi/plurilingual individuals using their full linguistic repertoires (García, 2009; Lee, 2021; Otheguy *et al.*, 2015). Specifically, Flores and Schissel (2014) defined translanguaging on two different levels, namely from the sociolinguistic and pedagogical perspectives. According to them, translanguaging refers to the fluid language practices of bi/multi/plurilingual learners from a sociolinguistic perspective. From a pedagogical perspective, translanguaging also indicates teachers' instructional approach to leverage the language practices of their bi/multi/plurilingual students.

Similarly, Cenoz (2017) distinguished between pedagogical translanguaging and spontaneous translanguaging. According to her, spontaneous translanguaging indicates 'fluid discursive practices that can take place inside or outside the classroom' (2017: 194), which describes the natural and instinctive use of bi/multi/plurilingual learners' full linguistic repertoire. In comparison, pedagogical translanguaging denotes a teaching approach where a teacher intentionally plans to use students' whole linguistic repertoire within the classroom by valuing their multiple language abilities, which explains the intentional practice of alternating between languages for pedagogical purposes (Hamman, 2018). In other words, translanguaging represents both a natural act of bi/multi/plurilingual performance and a pedagogical approach to teaching (García & Kleifgen, 2019; García & Leiva, 2014).

Translanguaging in the Post-Multilingualism Era

Scholars have noted that the world is currently in an era of superdiversity (Vertovec, 2007, 2023), and individuals are entering the post-multilingualism era (Li, 2016, 2018) where both linguistic and cultural diversity is unavoidable, and various linguistic, social, cultural, multimodal and multisemiotic resources are viewed as valuable assets. Language education has been going through multiple shifts in relatively recent years, including a 'multilingual turn' (Conteh & Meier, 2014; Huckle, 2021; May, 2014; Meier, 2017; Sembiante, 2016) and the 'translanguaging turn' (García & Li, 2014), which are based on the idea that learners bring various but integrated linguistic knowledge to the classroom.

In the past, language dialects (both regional and social dialects, which are not identified as Standard English) and varieties (languages other than English) were criticized as inappropriate, incongruous and less privileged or unintelligent in the US (Harris, 1989). Yet, this notion has been reevaluated in this increasingly interconnected globalized world. As society respects the internal variations of languages and the numerous external influences on them, linguistic purism (i.e. the notion that one variety of a language is superior to others) and linguistic protectionism (i.e. the idea that a language should be protected from external influences) have been criticized. The dominance of English as the most powerful language has raised several challenges, as it promotes language imperialism and linguistic inequality. Since creative expressions and critical approaches to language use and learning are highly encouraged and considered a valuable aspect of learning in translanguaging spaces (Li, 2018), we should understand that individual speakers integrate and orchestrate all semiotic systems to make meaning in a creative and critical way (García, 2018; Lee, 2021, 2023a; Lee & García, 2020).

According to Li (2016: 20), post-multilingualism goes beyond simply having multiple languages, rather, '[i]t is about the dilemma of protecting the identity and integrity of individual languages whilst promoting translanguaging practices'. Post-multilingualism navigates the complex dynamic systems of employing multiple languages while appreciating and valuing the distinctive features of each language through translanguaging (Li, 2016). As people are actively constructing and negotiating their social identities, belief systems and fluid ideologies in response to evolving societal dynamics or transformations and adapting to ever-changing cultural contexts and trends, Li highlighted that 'new identities, new subjectivities, and new ideologies are being constituted and reconstituted' (2016: 20) in this post-multilingualism era.

Translanguaging That Deconstruct and Transcend Named Languages

Now, it has become clear that translanguaging refers to fluid language practices, describing bi/multi/plurilingual speakers' dynamic and integrated ways of communication, rather than strictly alternating between separate languages (Allard, 2017). Although translanguaging opened spaces to recognize the 'dynamic bilingualism' (García & Li, 2014) and 'dynamic multilingualism' (Li & García, 2022) of learners in classrooms, translanguaging is still often seen as simply enabling bi/multi/plurilingual students to use their home or heritage language.

Teachers often understand translanguaging as an instructional approach that allows students to move across two or multiple languages when communicating and making meaning. However, the prefix 'trans' in translanguaging implies 'the transcendence of named languages, the going beyond named languages as have been socially constructed' (Li & García, 2022: 314). In this post-multilingual era, where linguistic boundaries across and between languages have been blurred, recognizing the complex interweaving of language variations and valuing the creative and critical expression of multiple languages, codes and meanings has become essential and inevitable.

Although acknowledging named languages (e.g. English, Spanish, Korean) is important for social purposes such as identity embodiment or (re)construction and belongingness, it is essential to understand that reifying languages as separate entities can easily overlook or exclude students who live in the intersections of languages and cultures that are neither one nor the other. It is also worth noting that the language performances of bi/multi/plurilingual learners are much more fluid, dynamic and complex, and their languages cannot be decomposed into separate parts because the boundaries between them are not clear. Hence, we should understand that bi/multi/plurilingual learners have a unique and specific linguistic configuration (García, 2009, 2014; Lee, 2021; Lee & García, 2021). As bi/multi/plurilingual speakers' language practices fall along the languaging continuum, we need to recognize and appreciate that bi/multi/plurilingual learners construct and produce the coexistence and constant interaction of languages as their unitary and complete linguistic entity (Li, 2022; Otheguy *et al.*, 2015).

Translanguaging to Promote Inclusiveness in Language and Advocate Equity and Justice

Translanguaging not only promotes inclusiveness of language use and linguistic diversity by valuing learners' bi/multi/plurilingual resources but also pursues educational equity and justice by countering linguistic discrimination and empowering learners' racial, linguistic and cultural identities (García & Leiva, 2014; Li & García, 2022). Translanguaging fosters an inclusive pedagogy that considers issues of diversity, valuing and respecting learners' diverse backgrounds, experiences and learning styles. In other words, translanguaging aims not only to include bi/multi/plurilingual individuals' all-inclusive language practices but also to endorse minority languages by balancing the power relations among languages in the classroom (Allard, 2017; Bartlett & García, 2011; Cenoz, 2017), thereby ensuring equitable access to education.

The translanguaging approach further challenges raciolinguistic ideologies (see Chapter 8 for a discussion of raciolinguistics) by rejecting the notion that certain languages or linguistic features are inherently associated with specific racial or ethnic groups deemed inferior and subordinate. Since translanguaging recognizes the entire linguistic repertoire of bi/multi/plurilingual individuals as valuable and empowering, it dismantles the deficit view that is often associated with racialized languages and linguistic racism (Rosa & Flores, 2017). Thus, translanguaging promotes the development of social justice and facilitates educational equity (García, 2009; García *et al.*, 2017; Li, 2024; Wang, 2024). The translanguaging lens not only recognizes learners' full repertoire to facilitate learning but also promotes learning as a decolonizing project (Li & García, 2022); thus, learners can develop an understanding of social justice and educational equity through translanguaging.

Translanguaging as a Decolonizing Language Education

As translanguaging-informed scholarship advocates for linguistic equity and justice for bi/multi/plurilingual learners, translanguaging further advances the decolonization of language education (García & Li, 2014; Li & García, 2022; Wang, 2024). By shifting the monolingual bias that is deeply rooted in language education, translanguaging adopts a decolonizing approach to promote bi/multi/plurilingualism, endorsing pluriversal thinking and stance in understanding bi/multi/plurilingual students' translanguaging performance (Wang, 2024). According to Li and García (2022: 314), translanguaging is a decolonizing project because it can 'undo the process through which the knowledge base and linguistic/cultural practices of colonized people was obliterated'.

Researchers have recently employed translanguaging as a decolonial approach to challenge the predominant Eurocentric way of thinking and to critique the Western centrality assumption in language education (Canagarajah, 2022; Kramsch, 2019; Phipps, 2019; Reagan & Osborn, 2019; Wang, 2024). To invigorate and revitalize minority languages (i.e. heritage languages, Indigenous languages), it is vital to support the equal status of cultures and the knowledge of minority languages and their speakers. By highlighting the intersection of translanguaging and decoloniality, Wang (2024) suggests that teachers should incorporate decolonial activities to foster diverse worldviews and promote the harmonious coexistence of languages, cultures and bodies of knowledge within their learning environment, all with mutual respect. Educators should strive to explore transformative approaches to incorporate pluriversal worldviews and knowledge within their curriculum and classroom practices.

Decolonization in education or pedagogy toward decoloniality can make 'visible the invisible [and] unmuting the muted' (Wang, 2024: 1388), which endeavors to combat Western imperialism and colonialism (Mignolo & Walsh, 2018). As translanguaging acknowledges the diversity and coexistence of all linguistic and semiotic repertoires, translanguaging criticizes the hegemonic ideological regimes of monolingualism and rejects the normative colonial-era ideologies that often consider the purist monolingual view as a universal standard (García & Li, 2014). According to Li and García (2022), transforming the classroom environment by embracing bi/multi/plurilingual students' translanguaging practices and capacities is 'a top priority in decolonizing education in the 21st century' (2022: 322). Scholars and researchers in language education have used a decolonial approach to challenge the predominant Eurocentric educational system and to contest the imperial/colonial view of language teaching through translanguaging (Wang, 2024). In this respect, translanguaging disrupts monolingual perspectives and racial hierarchies, pursuing decolonizing language education to promote a more equitable and inclusive learning environment.

Translanguaging as Teachers' Instructional Approach and Pedagogical Practices

Since the term 'translanguaging' was primarily used to refer to the teacher's pedagogical practices to scaffold bi/multi/plurilingual students' learning (Canagarajah, 2011), a large number of studies focused on teachers' use of translanguaging as an instructional strategy when working with bi/multi/plurilingual students (Cenoz & Gorter, 2021, 2022). Studies have been conducted in bilingual education settings (i.e. Dual Language Bilingual Education (DLBE) schools), particularly in Two-Way Bilingual Education (TWBE) programs where speakers of a common minority language (e.g. Spanish) and native-English speakers are taught together in the same classroom and receive instruction in two languages (e.g. Baca, 2024; Duarte, 2020; Esquinca et al., 2014; Gort & Sembiante, 2015; Hamman-Ortiz & Prasad, 2025; Martínez et al., 2015; Palmer et al., 2014; Sembiante et al., 2023; Tian & Lau, 2022; Worthy et al., 2013). Since TWBE programs have three primary objectives – academic achievement, bilingualism/biliteracy and sociocultural competence (Howard et al., 2018), translanguaging not only pursues students' language and linguistic proficiency in both languages equally but also promotes students' cultural heritage, values and positive identity construction. Specifically, the sociocultural competence tenet aims to provide inclusive pedagogy that facilitates the ethnic, racial, linguistic and cultural identity formation of bi/multi/plurilingual students in a non-stereotypical manner.

Although TWBE programs are considered one of the most promising options to boost learners' bilingualism, biliteracy and biculturalism (Li, 2016), instructions are delivered in a particular language due to the school's 'language of the day' policy. Teachers are less likely to employ their dual language resources during instruction to endorse students' understanding nor guide students to utilize their entire language repertoires when engaging in learning. Accordingly, students' languages often remain separate in class discussions unless teachers position translanguaging as a natural practice for their students in the classrooms.

Scholars argue that these strict language allocation policies prevent emergent bilingual students from activating their creativity and critical thinking because the ideas of language separation disrespect and reprimand the discursive practices of bi/multi/plurilingual individuals (Li, 2011; Sánchez et al., 2018). Although the language performances of bi/multi/plurilingual students are now more fluid, the language allocation policy still disregards the actual performance of those students' languaging practices (Sánchez et al., 2018). Li and García (2022) indeed criticized the fact that bi/multilingual education classrooms still operate under the same logic as English monolingual classrooms. In addition, language minority students in TWBE are less likely to obtain the same benefits compared to their English-speaking counterparts due to linguistic inequality and the existing power structures in the classrooms (Cervantes-Soon, 2014; Hamman-Ortiz & Palmer, 2023; Heiman, 2017; Howard & Simpson, 2023; Palmer et al., 2019; Valdés et al., 2016).

Scholars pointed out complex historical, sociocultural and political tensions and inequities in TWBE programs (e.g. Rubinstein-Aliva, 2002), such as normalizing White racial and linguistic identity or prioritizing the needs and interests of the English dominant group (Dorner, 2010; Hamman, 2018; Palmer, 2009; Valdés et al., 2016). Since the hegemony of English and White privilege are pervasive in TWBE classrooms, those inequitable practices and outcomes shape and drive classroom dynamics. Specifically, studies have discovered that White, native English-speaking students tend to dominate classroom conversations in TWBE programs (e.g. Hamman, 2018; Palmer, 2009), but language minority speakers are less likely to see their cultures and values at school as they are relatively less represented in the school curriculum (Lee, 2023b).

To address the controversial issues in the TWBE programs that create disparities in educational opportunities between two language groups, such as unequal distribution of resources and prioritizing English language acquisition over the partner language, scholars suggested a shift in teaching practices by rethinking language allocation in TWBE programs and challenging the dichotomy of languages in the classroom (e.g. Cervantes-Soon et al., 2017; Dorner et al., 2023; Flores & García, 2014; García & Leiva, 2014; Palmer et al., 2019; Palmer & Martinez, 2013; Sánchez et al., 2018). Scholars explicitly argued for a transformative practice that goes beyond conventional or named language separation by creating a translanguaging space (García & Kleyn, 2016; Li, 2018).

Since translanguaging fulfills its promise to open up spaces for equity and social justice by challenging traditional views of bilingualism (Allard, 2017; García & Li, 2014), TWBE programs should provide flexibility to the use of language that includes more translanguaging practices. That is, teachers are asked to actively use their students' multiple languages to support learning rather than strictly adhering to a set language division between English and the partner language throughout lessons. To effectively utilize multiple languages in the classroom and foster deeper student learning, educators must not only change their teaching methods (i.e. acting with translanguaging pedagogical shift) but also gain a thorough understanding of how students can leverage their diverse linguistic abilities to access and critically analyze information across different languages. By doing so, educators can essentially empower their bi/multi/plurilingual students to develop their critical consciousness (Cervantes-Soon et al., 2017; Dorner et al., 2023; García et al., 2017; Palmer et al., 2019).

Teachers' Strategic Use of Translanguaging to Protect Heritage Languages

Translanguaging additionally suggests a move away from hierarchical notions of language (e.g. English as a majority language versus languages other than English as minority languages) and linguistic distinctions between societal or school language (i.e. English) versus heritage or home language (e.g. Spanish, Korean) (Lee, 2021; Mendoza et al., 2023; Palmer et al., 2019). From a translanguaging perspective, speakers of more than one language do not separate their languages; instead, they strategically move across their language (i.e. translanguage) for different reasons or to attain specific purposes (García, 2011; García & Kleifgen, 2019). Because translanguaging provides 'a smoother conceptual path than previous approaches to the goal of protecting minoritized communities, their languages, and their learners and schools' (Otheguy et al., 2015: 283), it prioritizes the preservation and continued use of heritage languages (Bartlett & García, 2011; Cummins & Persad, 2014; Duarte, 2020; García & Kano, 2014; García et al., 2021; Lee, 2023b). One of the goals of translanguaging is to endorse and protect minoritized languages, speakers and communities by recognizing and valuing the sustainability of heritage languages (Otheguy et al., 2015). Accordingly, translanguaging disrupts the power dynamics among languages and pursues linguistic equality (Allard, 2017; Arreguín-Anderson et al., 2018; Axelrod & Cole, 2018; Bartlett & García, 2011; Cenoz, 2017; Cenoz & Gorter, 2017, 2019; Cummins & Persad, 2014; García et al., 2021; Hamman-Ortiz & Palmer, 2023; Howard & Simpson, 2023; Kirsch & Mortini, 2023; Palmer et al., 2019).

There have been numerous empirical studies that explored how teachers adopted translanguaging pedagogy as part of their instruction and interaction (e.g. Caldas, 2019; Dikilitas et al., 2023; Dikilitas & Bahrami, 2023; Hamman, 2018; Herrera, 2023; Holdway & Hitchcock, 2018; McClain et al., 2021; Phyak et al., 2022; Sohn et al., 2022). These studies have highlighted the influential role of translanguaging pedagogy by showing how teachers create translanguaging spaces to ensure that all students, regardless of their language background or proficiency level, have equal opportunities and equitable access to participate in meaning-ful interactions. The teachers in these studies allowed and encouraged their students to utilize all available linguistic resources by constructing dialogic classrooms to enhance student interaction and learning.

A set of empirical studies that were conducted in English–Spanish bilingual schools reported that teachers in these programs favored and privileged Spanish to confront English hegemony ideologies (e.g. Alamillo *et al.*, 2017; Escamilla *et al.*, 2023; Gort & Sembiante, 2015; Martínez *et al.*, 2015; Sembiante *et al.*, 2023; Worthy *et al.*, 2013). One of the common findings from the above studies is that teachers prevalently and intentionally incorporated more Spanish by resisting the greater focus on English over Spanish to protect the position and value of the students' heritage language (i.e. Spanish) in the classroom where English was regarded as a more powerful language than Spanish. The teachers provided a space for students to use Spanish when they were designated to teach English, supporting the students' bilingualism and their identity development as bilinguals. In other words, the teachers cultivated their students' heritage language proficiency to sustain Spanish since they believed that there was a power imbalance between the two languages. The teachers' intentional and purposeful use of Spanish challenged the hegemony of English and raciolinguistic ideologies (Rosa & Flores, 2017) (see Chapter 8 for discussion regarding raciolinguistics) that deprecate minority students' cultural and linguistic assets.

Cenoz and Gorter (2017) similarly demonstrated how teachers' translanguaging practices contribute to the protection and promotion of heritage languages. They discovered that translanguaging pedagogy empowered language minority students by allowing them to integrate their entire linguistic repertoire to express themselves authentically, which in turn fostered a sense of pride in their cultural background and identity. Meanwhile, Cenoz and Gorter asserted that translanguaging needs to be carefully managed in the context of teaching regional minor-ity languages (e.g. Basque, Māori) because regional minority languages are vastly vulnerable in the US. Sanctioning translanguaging in a pre-dominantly English-speaking setting might easily lead students, who speak regional minority languages as their heritage languages, to use more of the majority language (English). In a similar vein, Dikilitaş and Öztüfekçi (2024) stated that teachers tend to unconsciously prioritize the majority language (i.e. English) because they often believe it is more significant than students' heritage languages. The teachers in their study incorporated translanguaging pedagogies into their teaching practices to mitigate the risk of social, linguistic and cultural disparities within the classroom, thereby fostering an inclusive environment where all students feel included and respected for their unique linguistic abilities and cul-tural backgrounds.

Other scholars have also argued that bilingual schools need to incorporate a substantial amount of instruction in Indigenous languages to the fullest extent to dismantle the colonial power dynamics embedded within a solely English-based education system (May, 2023; Nicholas & McCarty, 2022). Translanguaging, thus, should be restricted in contexts where one language is more dominant than another because allowing students to translanguage in these classroom settings can be a threat to minority languages. If translanguaging is not implemented carefully, it can lead to a dominance of the majority language and potentially weaken the usage and development of the minority language.

Educators are responsible for being conscious and intentional about how they implement translanguaging in their classrooms. Teachers specifically need to monitor their translanguaging practices to ensure they are avoiding the unconscious favoring of the dominant language and neglecting the languages spoken by minority groups (Arreguín-Anderson et al., 2018; Axelrod & Cole, 2018; Kirsch & Mortini, 2023). Concurrently, educators also must thoroughly understand the specific characteristics of the sociolinguistic context so that translanguaging can be a sustainable practice for regional or minority languages, acting as a tool to support and revitalize heritage languages (Faltis, 2022; Ramirez & Faltis, 2019). By doing so, teachers can challenge societal beliefs and combat language ideologies that might devalue students' heritage languages.

Translanguaging in Heritage Language School Contexts

Although there has been an increasing number of translanguaging studies, translanguaging is less likely to be seen as a normal and natural means of communication in classroom settings where the monolingual norm prevails and students' languages remain separate, such as heritage language schools (Abourehab & Azaz, 2023; Abraham et al., 2021; Lee, 2021; Leeman & King, 2014; Wu & Leung, 2020). Research has discovered that teachers in heritage language schools hold an appreciative view of translanguaging, considering it a useful tool for empowering students (Abourehab & Azaz, 2023; Beaudrie et al., 2020; Lee, 2023b; Leeman, 2018). Heritage language teachers understand that bilingual students engage in everyday translanguaging practices by incorporating their whole body of linguistic resources flexibly rather than seeing them as separate entities. However, given the monolingual ideological stance in the US schools, where developing the societal language (i.e. English) is regarded as much more important than heritage language learning (Beaudrie, 2015; Valdés & Parra, 2018), heritage language teachers often feel compelled to use the target language (i.e. heritage language) only in their classrooms, knowing that their classroom may be the only place where students can actively practice and develop their heritage language (Lee, 2023b).

Teachers in local heritage language schools often believe or are informed that maintaining the target language throughout the school day is an ideal pedagogy approach. Accordingly, heritage language teachers may hold paradoxical and ambivalent attitudes toward translanguaging; they may theoretically support the idea of translanguaging but struggle to fully implement it in practice due to the pressures of maintaining a traditional educational system that values language separation. Heritage language educators may encounter contradictions between the ideal classroom language ideologies (i.e. implementing translanguaging) and their actual language use (i.e. language separation according to the mono-lingual norm) (Lee, 2023b). For this reason, a translanguaging approach needs to be carefully planned and implemented in the context of teaching minority languages (Cenoz & Gorter, 2017; Faltis, 2022; Martínez *et al.*, 2017; May, 2023; Nicholas & McCarty, 2022; Ramirez & Faltis, 2019).

Heritage Language Teachers' Instructional Methods to Validate Students' Bilingualism

Since many heritage languages are vulnerable and susceptible to loss in mainstream society (Cenoz & Gorter, 2017; Montrul, 2018), I, as a Korean heritage language teacher, acknowledged that allowing Korean American emergent bilingual students to freely translanguage could lead them to use the majority language (English) (Lee, 2023b; Sánchez *et al.*, 2018). I understood that classroom translanguaging needs to be supported by a thoughtfully designed curriculum and strategically imple-mented instruction. As my ideological orientation guided me to provide pedagogies that harness the full range of bilingual students' linguistic resources, I consciously planned and implemented translanguaging pedagogies to create a language-rich environment considering the Korean American bilingual students' dynamic bilingualism. Several applicable translanguaging pedagogies I implemented in my heritage language class-rooms are shared and discussed in the following sections.

Using Bilingual Books to Create a Translanguaging Space. When selecting books for class materials, I understood that bilingual books (also known as dual language texts) could be informative classroom resources as they allow students to integrate their entire linguistic reper-toire for richer engagement and deeper comprehension of reading. Bilin-gual books deliver information in two different languages, which help students develop their bilingual identities while reading, comprehending and discussing the stories. There are at least three different types of bilin-gual texts: They are (1) books published in different versions for each language, (2) books that include parallel use of two languages and (3) books that alternate between languages (Ernst-Slavit & Mulhern, 2003). I selected and included three different types of bilingual books. When considering content for book selection, I believed that the students could engage in more profound reflections and discussions if they are given literature portraying contemporary Korea with a vibrant mixture of traditions and culture or depicting Korean Americans' experiences, such as immigration to the US. I consciously chose books that delve into a wide range of Korean culture and their lived experiences so that I could incorporate the students' heritage cultures, bilingual identities and bicultural life experiences into my curriculum. Table 3.1 displays the selection of children's literature I used when working with second graders that depict Korean ethnic groups along with their contemporary or traditional life (hi)stories and experiences.

During the literature discussions after reading the selected bilingual texts, I purposefully and strategically employed both languages through translanguaging to make sure that the class understood the dialogues and engaged in the discussions. For instance, I often asked the class questions in Korean and then translanguaged to restate the same questions in English or vice versa by moving across the two languages. I also intentionally chose a page or paragraph by selecting the English version of the book and then provided a summary of a particular scene in Korean, or asked the class to share what happened in the scene in Korean verbally. By demonstrating how I flexibly translated, I enabled students to engage in the flexible use of their languages, allowing them to fully understand and actively participate in the book discussions.

Table 3.1 Bilingual books with diverse genres and types

Title of the books	Authors (Year)	Genre of the books	Type of the books
My Name is Yoon	Recorvits (2003)	Contemporary realistic fiction	Books published in different versions for each language
The Name Jar	Choi (2003)	Contemporary realistic fiction	Books published in different versions for each language
Goodbye, 382 Shin Dang Dong	Park (2002)	Contemporary realistic fiction	Books published in different versions for each language
Behind the Mask	Choi (2006)	Fiction about Korean traditional story	Books published in different versions for each language
This Next New Year	Wong (2000)	Fiction about Korean traditional story	Books that include parallel use of two languages
The Mysterious Stream	Smit (2015)	Folktale	Books that include parallel use of two languages
Where's Halmoni?	Kim (2017)	Adapted fiction based on a Korean folktale	Books that switch between languages or alternate use of languages

The following examples demonstrate how I incorporated translanguaging pedagogy to encourage the students' meaning-making processes, creating a rich learning space (Li, 2018) and facilitating their bilingual identity construction through dialogic interaction.

Building a Rich Learning Space through Language Exploration Activity. In the adapted fiction *Where's Halmoni?* (Kim, 2017) that was based on a Korean folktale, the literary characters alternate languages between English and Korean. Although the book is primarily written in English, Korean words are interspersed within English phrases and sentences through transliteration, which indicates using sounds from one language to write letters in another language (García *et al.*, 2017). The transliterated words *halmoni* (grandmother in Korean) and *noona* (older sister in Korean) are incorporated into English sentences throughout the book.

During reading, I highlighted these sentences and asked questions to the class to deepen the conversation. Excerpt 3.1 presents the students' responses, which demonstrate how the translanguaging space can be expanded through social practices in the classroom.

Excerpt 3.1 Providing a language exploration activity to support the integrated use of linguistic resources

(1) Ms Lee: (Read aloud) '*Noona* [older sister], I smell *Halmoni*'s [grandmother's] red bean soup.' (To class) 애들아, 여기 보면 너희는 어떤 말이 들리니? 한국말 아님 영어?
[Class, what language is being spoken here? Korean or English?]

(2) Joy: 영어. 오, 아니 한국말도 있어요 like 누나 and 할머니. 그거 내가 맨날 하는건데. I say something like '엄마 [*umma*; mom], I wanna go with my 언니 [*unni*; older sister].'
[I hear English, Oh, no, there are Korean words, too, like sister and grandmother. That's what I always say. I say something like 'Mom, I wanna go with my sister.'].

(3) Juho: Me, too. I use English with my older sister, but I always calling her 누나 [*noona*; older sister]. I never call her by her first name.

(4) Ms Lee: Why do you think you always call her *noona* [older sister]?

(5) Juho: Hmm … I don't know. I think I just do. My parents tell me noona when they are referring to her. And I got used to call her *noona*. And my mom told me that calling her Sofia [his sister's English name] is quite rude.

(6) Joy: I like to call *umma* [mom] rather than mom because she is Korean. So she is *umma* to me [laughs]. I feel like I am closer to her when I call her *umma*.

(7) Ms Lee: What language do the rabbit and other animals use here?

(8) Ian: Korean. It is interesting that they speak Korean.

(9) Juho: The children are speaking in English, but the animals speak Korean.

(10) Eva: This is what we do at home with my parents. My brothers and I use English, and my parents use Korean. But we understand each other.

(11) Joy: We do the same at home. My sister and I use English with each other. My parents use Korean each other. My sister and I understand Korean, and they understand English. So, it was okay, but we are different from other families.

Responding to my question in line 1 about the literary characters' language use that switched between English and Korean, Joy and Juho identified that both English and Korean are embedded in the sentence and then shared that they engaged in similar translanguaging practices when referring to their family members (lines 2–3). The students indicated that they purposefully used transliterated words in Korean when indicating their family to show respect or intimacy (lines 5–6). Another question I raised in line 7 further led the class to analyze the protagonists' language use and to engage in language exploration activity (Flores, 2020) by comparing language variations. This language exploration practice – analyzing how other bilingual speakers use language – guided the class to reflect on their language use and practices at home (see lines 10–11). Using the bilingual text that demonstrates translanguaging by bilingual individuals, I created a social space to build a rich bilingual learning community (Li, 2018) that supported the use of integrated linguistic knowledge and valued recursive translanguaging practices (Lee, 2021, 2023b).

Translanguaging to Promote Students' Criticality on Cultural Hegemony. One of the bilingual books *This Next New Year* (Wong, 2000) illustrates how Koreans celebrate the Lunar New Year. Excerpt 3.2 presents a segment of the literature discussion after the class read the book. In this excerpt, I generated transformative power through translanguaging to promote students' criticality on cultural hegemony.

Excerpt 3.2 Generating transformative power through translanguaging to promote

(1) Ms Lee: 여기 보면 멕시코에서 온 친구도 Korean New Year 를 좋아 한대. 아까 프랑스, 독일에서 온 친구도 한국 새해를 celebrate 한다고 했어. 다른 나라 친구들도 우리 holiday 를 아네. It is interesting that the children from other countries know our holiday. 저 친구들이 어떻게 알까요?
[In the story, the Mexican child says that Korean New Year is her favorite holiday. The child who is French and German also mentions that he celebrates Korean New Year. Children from other countries know our holiday. It is interesting that the children from other countries know our holiday. How can they know it?]

(2) Juho: 진짜요? [Really?] I don't think they know about Korean New Year.

(3) Ms Lee: Why do you think so?

(4) Juho: Because I have some friends from Mexico, and they didn't seem to know.

(5) Ms Lee: They might have learned in school...? What holidays or celebrations did you learn about in your school?

(6) Juho: We learned about Halloween and Christmas. We did some activities for Halloween and Christmas. We did Halloween rock painting and made a classroom Christmas tree.

(7) Eva: I did it, too. We made pumpkins for Halloween. Mine was a scary pumpkin.

(8) Ms Lee: So, you were learning about American holidays in school. You didn't learn anything about the Korean holidays?

(9) Juho: No, we don't do anything about Korea. My friends don't know about Korean holidays.

(10) Sky: I wish we celebrate the Korean New Year in my American school. It would be great if we do both Korean and American holidays. Then no school on those days! [laughs].

(11) Runa: Me, too. My mom told me that there is a children's day in Korea. Korean children get presents from their parents on that day. I wish we could have that day here.

As shown, I highlighted the part of the story where the protagonist's friends from other countries celebrate the Korean New Year (line 1). When I asked the class to think about how children in other countries would know about Korean New Year, Juho raised his doubt about the scene and provided his reason (lines 2 and 4). Based on Juho's responses, I asked the class about holidays or celebrations they had learned about in their American schools (line 5). Juho and Eva listed a few prominent American holidays, but their answers imply that their American schools lack a diverse cultural curriculum (lines 6–7). Juho further indicated that his heritage culture was excluded from his mainstream curricula (line 9). The following statements by Sky and Runa showed their desire to learn about and celebrate Korean holidays in their American schools (lines 10–11). The literature discussion, using the storyline from the book, allowed the class to identify and critique dominant cultural norms and practices embedded in their American schools, further promoting the students' criticality of cultural hegemony.

It is shown that including bilingual books in the curriculum suggests the possible translanguaging transformation space (Sánchez *et al.*, 2017). The act of translanguaging in the example excerpts enabled bilingual students to create a shared social space (Li, 2011) by integrating different aspects of their linguistic identity, cultural experiences and social perspectives into a unified performance (Lee, 2023b). As displayed, the carefully chosen bilingual texts not only encompassed the hybridity of the students' linguistic and cultural resources but also assisted them in criticizing the cultural hegemony living in the US. The students' responses reveal that the translanguaging space generated transformative power (Sánchez et al., 2017) where they can voice their opinions and perspectives critically by challenging dominant narratives and power structures within a given context. In implementing a pedagogy that counters language or cultural hegemony and dominant ideologies, teachers can act as agents of educational change and transformation (Brown et al., 2021; Gort & Sembiante, 2015).

Using wordless picture books in promoting bilinguals' translanguaging practices

The Characteristics and Merits of Wordless Picture Books. Unlike picture books with texts, wordless picture books carry the meaning of the narrative exclusively through the use of pictorial images (Arizpe, 2013). Readers of wordless picture books must actively interpret the illustrations by entirely relying on the visual details presented in the images to understand the storyline (Bosch, 2014; Chaparro-Moreno et al., 2018). Since readers can develop plots based on the provided visual images and make references to the pictorial characteristics, engaging in wordless picture books is regarded as an open-ended process (Serafini, 2014a). In other words, each reader could create a different story based on their experiences, backgrounds and prior knowledge of the reading events (Louie & Sierschynski, 2015; Lubis, 2018; Jalongo et al., 2002). The reader's interpretation can vary depending on how each reader comprehends the visual images, leading to a range of possible narratives from the same book.

A significant number of studies have discovered that young readers benefit from exposure to wordless picture books (e.g. Arizpe, 2013; Jalongo et al., 2002; Serafini, 2014b). Studies report that engaging in wordless picture books accelerates young readers' engagement by actively requiring them to use their creativity, imagination, critical thinking and storytelling abilities (Arizpe, 2014; Lee, 2023c, 2023d; Lysaker & Miller, 2012; Ramos & Ramos, 2011; Salisbury & Styles, 2012; Serafini, 2014b). Given the context in which readers encounter books that contain printed texts and illustrations versus illustrations only without texts, it is assumed that visual cues are more profound in the construction of meaning when reading wordless picture books than in books accompanied by both texts and pictures. Studies have demonstrated that children who read wordless picture books engage in more discussions about the pictures and have longer conversations focusing on the visual aspects of the story compared to when they read books with text only (e.g. Arif & Hashim, 2008; Chaparro-Moreno et al., 2017; Hammett-Price et al.,

2009). In other words, research indicates that wordless picture books encourage young readers to engage in active participation using higher levels of story verbalization rather than passively following written texts.

Wordless picture books can work as powerful instructional materials for students who use more than two languages. Even when bi/multi/plurilingual readers are given a text written in one language, they often naturally activate their linguistic knowledge from both or multiple languages, drawing on their entire linguistic repertoire to fully understand and interpret the text. Thus, when encountering wordless picture books, bi/multi/plurilingual students incorporate the whole linguistic knowledge they possess to make sense of their thinking, learning and the world around them (García & Sylvan, 2011; Lee, 2023c). Furthermore, since visual narratives are rendered through non-verbal pictorial features in wordless picture books (Arizpe, 2013; Lubis, 2018), bi/multi/plurilingual students can use their language skills and understanding to interpret the visuals and create their unique narratives by drawing on all the linguistic features and tools they possess (Li, 2018; Otheguy *et al.*, 2015; Vogel & García, 2017). Studies have shown that incorporating wordless picture books into the curriculum for bi/multi/plurilingual students had positive effects, for instance, by allowing them to draw on the strengths of each language to construct a plot and enrich their narrative (e.g. Hu *et al.*, 2016; Lee, 2023c, 2023d; Louie & Sierschynski, 2015).

Enhancing Students' Meaning-Making Process through Translanguaging. In an attempt to document the translanguaging performance of Korean bilingual students when reading wordless picture books, I conducted a study using classroom discourse methodology in my first-grade Korean heritage language classroom. I created a translanguaging space (Li, 2018) by using wordless picture books as class materials (see Table 3.2 for suggested wordless picture books for early elementary-grade students) and investigated how emergent bilingual students utilized their integrated linguistic resources during their meaning-making process when analyzing visual literacy and building their own storylines.

Table 3.2 Wordless picture books selection

Title of the book	Name of the author
Journey (2020)	Aaron Becker
Here I Am (2015)	Petti Kim
The Red Book (2011)	Barbara Lehman
Chalk (2011)	Bill Thomson
Fossil (2013)	Bill Thomson
Mr Wuffles! (2013)	David Wiesner
I Got It! (2018)	David Wiesner

Enhancing Students' Meaning-Making Process through Translanguaging. In an attempt to document the translanguaging performance of Korean bilingual students when reading wordless picture books, I conducted a study using classroom discourse methodology in my first-grade Korean heritage language classroom. I created a translanguaging space (Li, 2018) by using wordless picture books as class materials (see Table 3.2 for suggested wordless picture books for early elementary-grade students) and investigated how emergent bilingual students utilized their integrated linguistic resources during their meaning-making process when analyzing visual literacy and building their own storylines.

As a teacher, I allowed and encouraged students to construct the meaning of stories and develop plots by employing both Korean and English when encountering wordless picture books. Because wordless picture books convey meanings of the narratives exclusively through illustrations, visualizing was the primary strategy the students employed. Yet, I demonstrated how I could use and incorporate other reading strategies beyond visualizing (i.e. making text-to-self or text-to-text connections, using prior knowledge, asking questions, making predictions or inferences and revising predictions) to build and develop a plot by flexibly drawing on the entire linguistic and semiotic resources. Based on my demonstration, the students were able to integrate their linguistic repertoires flexibly; thus, their translanguaging naturally occurred when elaborating on the stories and building their plots from visual literacy. Chapter 4 presents and discusses how bilingual students employed translanguaging to construct the meaning of the stories when encountering wordless picture books and creating their own storylines.

Implications for Educational Practice of Implementing Translanguaging Pedagogy

The findings in this chapter reinforce the argument that translanguaging can be beneficial and transformative if teachers are thoughtful in creating an inclusive classroom environment by valuing and respecting all students' linguistic resources and integrating them into their lessons (Dutton & Rushton, 2021; Kirsch & Mortini, 2023; Li & García, 2022). Since students' languages do not remain separate in class discussions even in monoglossic learning contexts (i.e. heritage language classrooms), teachers should recognize the value of creating translanguaging spaces. Such spaces allow bi/multi/plurilingual students to draw on their full linguistic repertoires in meaning- and sense-making processes. It is essential for educators to recognize, value and validate each learner's flexible use of whole language repertoires by fostering positive attitudes toward translanguaging and strategically design and create an inclusive learning community.

As the empirical studies in this chapter indicated that the teacher's instructional pedagogy leveraged the emergent bilingual students' language use and learning experiences through culturally relevant reading materials and biliteracy activities, the chapter insinuates the promises of including literacy instruction to sanction a safe translanguaging space to embrace and sustain students' bi/multi/plurilingualism. In diverse classroom settings, teachers are encouraged to utilize multilingual resources by valuing the diverse linguistic resources students bring to dynamic interactions, rather than adhering solely to the target language only, which has been a longstanding ideology.

Although the popularity of and concerns about translanguaging pedagogy have increased, it is essential to note that translanguaging highlights the preservation and sustainability of heritage languages by addressing linguistic inequality. Hence, educators are encouraged to understand that translanguaging can disrupt power dynamics among languages by actively valuing and sanctioning speakers of multiple languages. Whenever it is possible, educators are expected to incorporate a substantial amount of instruction in students' heritage languages to dismantle colonial power structures embedded within a solely English-based education system. It is important to remember that classroom teachers are key agents of educational change in schools. Although this chapter focused on translanguaging pedagogy, not everything we need to know about translanguaging was covered in this chapter. How bi/multi/plurilingual learners engage in translanguaging as their learning practice or meaning-making process is covered in more detail in Chapter 4.

Children's Literature Bibliography

Becker, A. (2020) *Journey*. Walker Books Publishing.
Choi, Y. (2003) *The Name Jar*. Dragonfly Books.
Choi, Y. (2006) *Behind the Mask*. Farrar, Straus and Giroux.
Kim, J. (2017) *Where's Halmoni?* Little Bigfoot.
Kim, P. (2015) *Here I Am*. Picture Window Books.
Lehman, B. (2011) *The Red Book*. Houghton Mifflin.
Park, F. (2002) *Goodbye, 382 Shin Dang Dong*. National Geographic Kids.
Recorvits, H. (2003) *My Name is Yoon*. Square Fish.
Smit, F.B. (2015) *The Mysterious Stream: A Korean folktale*. Eeyagi Tales.
Thomson, B. (2011) *Chalk*. Amazon Children's Publishing.
Thomson, B. (2013) *Fossil*. Amazon Children's Publishing.
Wiesner, D. (2013) *Mr Wuffles!* Clarion Books.
Wiesner, D. (2018) *I Got It!* Clarion Books.
Wong, J.S. (2000) *This Next New Year*. Pomelo Books.

References

Abourehab, Y. and Azaz, M. (2023) Pedagogical translanguaging in community/heritage Arabic language learning. *Journal of Multilingual and Multicultural Development* 44, 398–411.

Abraham, S., Kedley, K., Fall, M., Krishnamurthy, S. and Tulino, D. (2021) Creating a translanguaging space in a bilingual community-based writing program. *International Multilingual Research Journal* 15 (3), 211–234.

Alamillo, L., Yun, C. and Bennett, L.H. (2017) Translanguaging in a Reggio-Inspired Spanish dual-language immersion programme. *Early Child Development and Care* 187 (3/4), 469486. https://doi.org/10.1080/03004430.2016.1236091.

Allard, E. (2017) Re-examining teacher translanguaging: An ecological perspective. *Bilingual Research Journal* 40 (2), 116–130.

Arif, M.M. and Hashim, F. (2008) Reading from the wordless: A case study on the use of wordless picture books. *English Language Teaching* 1 (1), 121–126. https://doi.org/10.5539/ELT.V1N1P121-.

Arizpe, E. (2013) Meaning-making from wordless (or nearly wordless) picture books: What educational research expects and what readers have to say. *Cambridge Journal of Education* 43 (2), 1–14. https://doi.org/10.1080/ 0305764X.2013.767879.

Arizpe, E. (2014) Wordless picturebooks: Critical and educational perspectives on meaning-making. In B. Kümmerling Meibauer (ed.) *Picturebooks: Representation and Narration* (pp. 91–106). Routledge.

Arreguín-Anderson, M.G., Salinas-Gonzalez, I. and Alanis, I. (2018) Translingual play that promotes cultural connections, invention, and regulation: A LatCrit perspective. *International Multilingual Research Journal* 12 (4), 273–287. https://doi.org/10.1080/ 19313152.2018.1470434.

August, D. and Hakuta, K. (eds) (1998) *Educating Language-Minority Children*. National Academy Press.

Axelrod, Y. and Cole, M.W. (2018) "The pumpkins are coming . . . vienen las calabazas . . . that sounds funny": Translanguaging practices of young emergent bilinguals. *Journal of Early Childhood Literacy* 18, 129–153.

Baca, E.C. (2024) Teaching in two-way dual-language-bilingual education: An analysis of teacher language ideologies and linguistic practices. *Journal of Language, Identity & Education*, 1–16. https://doi.org/10.1080/15348458.2024.2392647.

Bailey, B. (2007) Heteroglossia and boundaries. In M. Heller (ed.) *Bilingualism: A Social Approach* (pp. 257–276). Palgrave.

Baker, C. (2011) *Foundations of Bilingual Education and Bilingualism* (5th edn). Multilingual Matters.

Bakhtin, M.M. (1981) *The Dialogic Imagination: Four Essays*. University of Texas Press.

Bartlett, L. and García, O. (2011) *Additive Schooling in Subtractive Times: Bilingual Education and Dominican Immigrant Youth in the Heights*. Vanderbilt University Press. https://doi.org/10.2307/j.ctv16b78cp.

Beaudrie, S. (2015) Approaches to language variation: Goals and objectives of the Spanish heritage language syllabus. *Heritage Language Journal* 12 (1), 1–21.

Beaudrie, S., Angelica, A. and Sergio, L. (2020) Critical language awareness in the heritage language classroom: Design, implementation, and evaluation of a curricular intervention. *International Multilingual Research Journal* 15 (1), 1–21.

Bosch, E. (2014) Texts and peritexts in wordless and almost wordless picturebooks. In B. Kümmerling-Meibauer (eds) *Picturebooks: Representation and Narration* (pp. 71–90). Routledge.

Brown, C., White, R. and Kelly, A. (2021) Teachers as educational change agents: What do we currently know? Findings from a systematic review. *Emerald Open Research* 3 (26). https://doi.org/10.35241/emeraldopenres.14385.1.

Busch, B. (2012) The linguistic repertoire revisited. *Applied Linguistics* 33 (5), 503–523.

Caldas, S. (2019) To switch or not to switch: Bilingual preservice teachers and translanguaging in teaching and learning. *TESOL Journal* 10 (4). https://doi.org/10.1002/tesj.485.

Canagarajah, S. (2011) Codemeshing in academic writing: Identifying teachable strategies of translanguaging. *Modern Language Journal* 95 (3), 401–417.

Canagarajah, S. (2022) Language diversity in academic writing: Toward decolonizing scholarly publishing. *Journal of Multicultural Discourses* 17 (2), 107–128. https://doi.org/10.1080/17447143.2022.2063873.

Cenoz, J. (2017) Translanguaging in school contexts: International perspectives. *Journal of Language, Identity & Education* 16 (4), 193–198.

Cenoz, J. and Gorter, D. (2017) Minority languages and sustainable translanguaging: Threat or opportunity? *Journal of Multilingual and Multicultural Development* 38 (10), 901–912.

Cenoz, J. and Gorter, D. (2019) Multilingualism, translanguaging, and minority languages in SLA. *The Modern Language Journal* 103 (1), 130–135.

Cenoz, J. and Gorter, D. (2021) *Pedagogical Translanguaging*. Cambridge University Press.

Cenoz, J. and Gorter, D. (2022) Pedagogical translanguaging and its application to language classes. *RELC Journal* 53 (2), 342–354.

Cervantes-Soon, C.G. (2014) A critical look at dual language immersion in the new Latin@ diaspora. *Bilingual Research Journal* 37 (1), 64–82. https://doi.org/10.1080/15235882.2014.893267.

Cervantes-Soon, C.G., Dorner, L., Palmer, D., Heiman, D., Schwerdtfeger, R. and Choi, J. (2017) Combating inequalities in two-way language immersion programs: Toward critical consciousness in bilingual education spaces. *Review of Research in Education* 41 (1), 403–427.

Chaparro-Moreno, L., Reali, F. and Maldonado-Carreno, C. (2017) Wordless picture books boost preschoolers' language production during shared reading. *Early Childhood Research Quarterly* 40 (2), 52–62.

Conteh, J. and Meier, G. (eds) (2014) *The Multilingual Turn in Languages Education: Opportunities and Challenges*. Multilingual Matters.

Crawford, J. (2004) *Educating English Learners. Language Diversity in the Classroom* (5th edn). Bilingual Educational Services, Inc.

Creese, A. and Blackledge, A. (2010) Translanguaging in the bilingual classroom: A pedagogy for teaching and learning. *The Modern Language Journal* 94, 103–115.

Cummins, J. (2005) A proposal for action: Strategies for recognizing heritage language competence as a learning resource with the mainstream classroom. *The Modern Language Journal* 89 (4), 585–592.

Cummins, J. and Persad, R. (2014) Teaching through a multilingual lens: The evolution of EAL policy and practice in Canada. *Education Matters* 2, 3–40.

Dikilitaş, K. and Bahrami, V. (2023) Teacher identity (re)construction in collaborative bilingual education: The emergence of dyadic identity. *TESOL Quarterly* 1–26.

Dikilitaş, K. and Öztüfekçi, A. (2024) English language teachers' implementation of collaborative translanguaging. *System* 126. https://doi.org/10.1016/j.system.2024.103488.

Dikilitaş, K., Bahrami, V. and Erbakan, N.T. (2023) Bilingual education teachers and learners in a preschool context: Instructional and interactional translanguaging spaces. *Learning and instruction* 86, 101754. https://doi.org/10.1016/j.learninstruc.2023.101754.

Dorner, L.M. (2010) English and Spanish "para un futuro" – or just English? Immigrant family perspectives on two-way immersion. *International Journal of Bilingual Education and Bilingualism* 13 (3), 303–323.

Dorner, L., Palmer, D., Cervantes-Soon, C., Heiman, D. and Crawford, E. (2023) *Critical Consciousness in Dual Language Bilingual Education: Case Studies on Policy and Practice*. Routledge.

Duarte, J. (2020) Translanguaging in the context of mainstream multilingual education. *International Journal of Multilingualism* 17 (2), 232–247.

Dutton, J. and Rushton, K. (2021) Using the translanguaging space to facilitate poetic representation of language and identity. *Language Teaching Research* 25 (1), 105–133. https://doi.org/10.1177/1362168820951215.

Ernst-Slavit, G. and Mulhern, M. (2003) Bilingual books: Promoting literacy and biliteracy in the second-language and mainstream classroom. *Reading Online* 7 (2), 1–5.

Escamilla, I.M., Alanís, I. and Meier, D.R. (2023) Translanguaging in preschool: Supporting language rights and social justice for Latino/a children, families, and educators. *Contemporary Issues in Early Childhood* 25 (2), 162–185.

Esquinca, A., Araujo, B. and de la Piedra, M.T. (2014) Meaning making and translanguaging in a two-way dual-language program on the U.S.- Mexico border. *Bilingual Research Journal* 37 (2), 164–181.

Faltis, C. (2022) Understanding and resisting perfect language and eugenics-based language ideologies in bilingual teacher education. In J. MacSwan (ed.) *Multilingual Perspectives on Translanguaging* (pp. 321–342). Multilingual Matters.

Fillmore, L. (1991) When learning a second language means losing the first. *Early Childhood Research Quarterly* 6 (3), 323–346.

Flores N. L. (2020) From academic language to language architecture: Challenging raciolinguistic ideologies in research and practice. *Theory Into Practice* 59 (1), 22–31.

Flores, N. and García, O. (2014) Linguistic third spaces in education: Teachers' translanguaging across the bilingual continuum. In D. Little, C. Leung and P. Van Avermaet (eds) *Managing Diversity in Education: Languages, Policies, Pedagogies* (pp. 243–256). Multilingual Matters.

Flores, N. and Rosa, J. (2015) Undoing appropriateness: Raciolinguistic ideologies and language diversity in education. *Harvard Educational Review* 85, 149–171.

Flores, N. and Schissel, J.L. (2014) Dynamic bilingualism as the norm: Envisioning a heteroglossic approach to standards-based reform. *TESOL Quarterly* 48 (3), 454–479. https://doi.org/10.1002/tesq.182.

García, O. (2009) *Bilingual Education in the 21st Century: A Global Perspective.* Wiley-Blackwell.

García, O. (2011) Educating New York's bilingual children: Constructing a future from the past. *International Journal of Bilingual Education and Bilingualism* 14, 133–153.

García, O. (2014) What is translanguaging? Expanded questions and answers for U.S. educators. In S. Hesson, K. Seltzer and H.H. Woodley (eds) *Translanguaging in Curriculum and Instruction: A CUNY-NYSIEB Guide for Educators* (pp. 1–13). CUNY- NYSIEB.

García, O. (2018) The multiplicities of multilingual interaction. *International Journal of Bilingual Education and Bilingualism* 21 (7), 881–891.

García, O. and Kano, N. (2014) Translanguaging as process and pedagogy: Developing the English writing of Japanese students in the US. In J. Conteh and G. Meier (eds) *The Multilingual Turn in Languages Education: Opportunities and Challenges* (pp. 258–277). Multilingual Matters.

García, O. and Kleifgen, J. (2019) Translanguaging and literacies. *Reading Research Quarterly* 55 (4), 553–571. https://doi.org/10.1002/rrq.286.

García, O. and Kleyn, T. (eds) (2016) *Translanguaging with Multilingual Students: Learning from Classroom Moments.* Routledge.

García, O. and Leiva, C. (2014) Theorizing and enacting translanguaging for social justice. In A. Blackledge and A. Creese (eds) *Heteroglossia as Practice and Pedagogy* (pp. 199–216). Springer.

García, O. and Li, W. (2014) *Translanguaging: Language, Bilingualism and Education.* Palgrave Macmillan Pivot.

García, O. and Lin, A. (2017) Translanguaging and bilingual education. In O. García, A. Lin and S. May (eds) *Bilingual and Multilingual Education* (pp. 117–130). Springer.

García, O. and Sylvan, C. (2011) Pedagogies and practices in multilingual classrooms: Singularities in pluralities. *Modern Language Journal* 95 (3), 385–400. https://doi.org/10.1111/j.1540-4781.2011.01208.x.

García, O., Flores, N., Seltzer, K., Li, W. Otheguy, R. and Rosa, J. (2021) Rejecting abyssal thinking in the language and education of racialized bilinguals: A manifesto.

Critical Inquiry in Language Studies 18 (3), 203–228. https://doi.org/10.1080/154275 87.2021.1935957.

García, O., Johnson, I. and Seltzer, K. (2017) *The Translanguaging Classroom: Leveraging Student Bilingualism for Learning.* Caslon Publishing.

Gort, M. and Sembiante, S. (2015) Navigating hybridized language learning spaces through translanguaging pedagogy: Dual language preschool teachers' languaging practices in support of emergent bilingual children's performance of academic discourse. *International Multilingual Research Journal* 9, 7–25.

Gravelle, M. (1996). *Supporting Bilingual Learners in Schools.* Trentham.

Grosjean, F. (1989) Neurolinguists, beware! The bilingual is not two monolinguals in one person. *Brain and Language* 36 (1), 3–15. https://doi.org/10.1016/0093-934X(89)90048-5.

Grosjean, F. (2024) *On Bilinguals and Bilingualism.* Cambridge University Press.

Guerra, J. (2012). From code-segregation to code-switching to code-meshing: Finding deliverance from deficit thinking through language awareness and performance. *Literacy Research Association Yearbook* 61, 29–39.

Hamman, L. (2018) Translanguaging and positioning in two-way dual language classrooms: A case for criticality. *Language and Education* 32 (1), 21–42. https://doi.org/10.1080/09500782.2017.1384006.

Hamman-Ortiz, L. and Palmer, D. (2023) Identity and two-way bilingual education: Considering student perspectives: Introduction to the special issue. *International Journal of Bilingual Education and Bilingualism* 26, 1. https://doi.org/10.1080/13670050.2020.1819096.

Hamman-Ortiz, L., and Prasad, G. (2025) Reimagining bilingual education: A linguistically expansive orientation. *Journal of Language, Identity & Education* 24 (2), 413–432. https://doi.org/10.1080/15348458.2022.2147526.

Hammett-Price, L., van Kleeck, A. and Huberty, C.J. (2009) Talk during book sharing between parents and preschool children: A comparison between storybook and expository book conditions. *Reading Research Quarterly* 44 (2), 171–194. https://doi.org/10.1598/RRQ.44.2.4.

Harris, P.L. (1989) *Children and Emotion: The Development of Psychological Understanding.* Basil Blackwell.

Heiman, D. (2017) "So, is gentrification good or bad?": One teacher's implementation of the fourth goal in her TWBE Classroom. *Anthropology & Education* 52 (1), 63–81.

Heller, M. (2001) Undoing the macro/micro dichotomy: Ideology and categorization in a linguistic minority school. In N. Coupland, S. Sarangi and C.N. Candlin (eds) *Sociolinguistics and Social Theory* (pp. 212–234). Routledge.

Herrera, L.Y. (2023) Translanguaging in teacher education: Engaging preservice teachers in culturally and linguistically sustaining pedagogies. *Language and Education* 37 (5), 610–623. https://doi.org/10.1080/09500782.2023.2203677.

Holdway, J. and Hitchcock, C.H. (2018) Exploring ideological becoming in professional development for teachers of multilingual learners: Perspectives on translanguaging in the classroom. *Teaching and Teacher Education* 75, 60–70. https://doi.org/10.1016/j.tate.2018.05.015.

Howard, E.R., Lindholm-Leary, K.J., Rogers, D., Olague, N., Medina, J., Kennedy, B., Sugarman, J. and Christian, D. (2018) *Guiding Principles for Dual Language Education* (3rd edn). Center for Applied Linguistics, Dual Language Education of New Mexico, and Santilla.

Howard, E.R. and Simpson, S. (2023) Navigating the tensions between translanguaging and separation of languages in dual language programs. *Dual Language Education of New Mexico Monograph Series-Promising Practices from the Field* 7, 1–28.

Huckle, J. (2021) Multilingualism and the international baccalaureate diploma programme (IBDP): An analysis of language learning in the IBDP in light of the 'Multilingual Turn.' *Journal of Research in International Education* 20 (3), 263–280.

Hu, R., Liu, X. and Zheng, X. (2016) Examining meaning making from reading wordless picture books in Chinese and English by three bilingual children. *Journal of Early Childhood Literacy* 18 (2), 214–238.

Jalongo, M.R., Dragich, D., Conrad, N.K. and Zhang, A. (2002) Using wordless picture books to support emergent literacy. *Early Childhood Education Journal* 29 (3), 167–177. https://doi.org/10.1023/A:1014584509011.

Jiang, Y.B., García, G.E. and Willis, I.W. (2014) Code-mixing as a bilingual instructional strategy. *Bilingual Research Journal* 37 (3), 311–326. https://doi.org/10.1080/1523588 2.2014.963738.

Kirsch, C. and Mortini, S. (2023) Engaging in and creatively reproducing translanguaging practices with peers: A longitudinal study with three-year-olds in Luxembourg. *International Journal of Bilingual Education and Bilingualism* 26 (8), 943–959.

Kramsch, C. (2019) Between globalization and decolonization: Foreign languages in the crossfire. In D. Macedo (ed.) *Decolonizing Foreign Language Education: The Misteaching English and Other Colonial Languages* (pp. 50–72). Routledge.

Lee, C. (2021) *Understanding the Oral and Written Translanguaging Practices of Emergent Bilinguals: Insights from a Korean Heritage Language Classroom in the U.S.* Routledge.

Lee, C. (2023a) How do children go through a heteroglossic path to becoming bilingual? Comparison of Korean children's translanguaging performance in first and third grades. *International Journal of Bilingual Education and Bilingualism* 27 (4), 612–630. https://doi.org/10.1080/13670050.2023.2232088.

Lee, C. (2023b) Translanguaging in action: Incorporating translanguaging pedagogy in a Korean heritage language classroom. In H. Cho and K. Song (eds) *Korean as a Heritage Language from Transnational and Translanguaging Perspectives*. Routledge.

Lee, C. (2023c) Using wordless picturebooks to promote bilingual students' translanguaging. *Journal of Research in Childhood Education* 38 (1), 123–144. https://doi.org/10.1080/02568543.2023.2193258.

Lee, C. (2023d) Bilingual students' meaning-making strategies when exploring wordless picturebooks in interactive shared reading. *Early Childhood Education Journal* 52, 1375–1392. https://doi.org/10.1007/s10643-023-01501-y.

Lee, C. and García, G. (2020) Unpacking the oral translanguaging practices of Korean-American first graders. *Bilingual Research Journal* 43 (1), 32–49.

Lee, C. and García, G. (2021) Understanding Korean American first graders' written translanguaging practices. *Linguistic and Education* 66. https://doi.org/10.1016/j.linged.2021.100998.

Leeman, J. (2018) Critical language awareness and Spanish as a heritage language: Challenging the linguistic subordination of US Latinxs. In K. Potowski (ed.) *The Routledge Handbook of Spanish as a Heritage Language* (pp. 345–358). Routledge.

Leeman, J. and King, K. (2014) *Heritage Language Education: Minority Language Speakers, Second Language Instruction, and Monolingual Schooling*. Routledge.

Lewis, G., Jones, B. and Baker, C. (2012) Translanguaging: Developing its conceptualization and contextualization. *Educational Research and Evaluation* 18, 655–670.

Li, W. (2011) Moment analysis and translanguaging space: Discursive construction of identities by multilingual Chinese youth in Britain. *Journal of Pragmatics* 43 (5), 1222–1235.

Li, W. (2016) New Chinglish and the Post-Multilingualism challenge: Translanguaging ELF in China. *Journal of English as a Lingua Franca* 5 (1), 1–25. https://doi.org/10.1515/jelf-2016-0001.

Li, W. (2018) Translanguaging as a practical theory of language. *Applied Linguistics* 39 (1), 9–30.

Li, W. (2022) Translanguaging as a political stance: Implications for English language education. *ELT Journal* 76 (2), 172–182.

Li, W. (2024) Transformative pedagogy for inclusion and social justice through translanguaging, co-learning, and transpositioning. *Language Teaching* 57 (2), 203–214. https://doi.org/10.1017/S0261444823000186.

Li, W. and García, O. (2022) Not a first language but one repertoire: Translanguaging as a decolonizing project. *RELC Journal* 53 (2), 313–324.

Lindholm-Leary, K.J. (2001) *Dual Language Education*. Multilingual Matters.

Louie, B. and Sierschynski, J. (2015) Enhancing English learners' language development using wordless picture books. *The Reading Teacher* 69 (1), 103–111. https://doi.org/10.1002/trtr.1376.

Lubis, R. (2018) The progress of students reading comprehension through wordless picture books. *Advances in Language and Literacy Studies* 9 (1), 48–52. https://doi.org/10.7575/aiac.alls.v.9n.1p.48.

Lysaker, J.T. and Miller, A. (2012) Engaging social imagination: The developmental work of wordless book. *Journal of Early Childhood Literacy* 13 (2), 147–174. https://doi.org/10.1177/1468798411430425.

Martin-Beltran, M. (2010) The two-way language bridge: Co-constructing bilingual language learning opportunities. *The Modern Language Journal* 94 (2), 254–277.

Martínez, R., Durán, A.L., and Hikida, M. (2017) Becoming "Spanish learners": Identity and interaction among multilingual children in a Spanish-English dual language classroom. *International Multilingual Research Journal* 11 (3), 167–183.

Martínez, R., Hikida, M. and Durán, L. (2015) Unpacking ideologies of linguistic purism: How dual language teachers make sense of everyday translanguaging. *International Multilingual Research Journal* 9, 26–42. https://doi.org/10.1080/19313152.2014.977712.

May, S. (ed.) (2014) *The Multilingual Turn: Implications for SLA, TESOL, and Bilingual Education*. Routledge.

May, S. (2023) Linguistic racism: Origins and implications. *Ethnicities* 23 (5), 651–661.

McClain, J.B., Mancilla-Martinez, J., Flores, I. and Buckley, L. (2021) Translanguaging to support emergent bilingual students in English dominant preschools: An explanatory sequential mixed-method study. *Bilingual Research Journal* 44 (2), 158–173. https://doi.org/10.1080/15235882.2021.1963014.

Meier, G.S. (2017) The multilingual turn as a critical movement in education: Assumptions, challenges and a need for reflection. *Applied Linguistics Review* 8 (1), 131–161.

Mendoza, N., Yan, Z. and King, R. (2023) Supporting students' intrinsic motivation for online learning tasks: The effect of need-supportive task instructions on motivation, self-assessment, and task performance. *Computers & Education* 193, 104663. https://doi.org/10.1016/j.compedu.2022.104663.

Mignolo, W.D. and Walsh, C.E. (2018) *On Decoloniality: Concepts, Analytics, Praxis*. Duke University Press. https://doi.org/10.2307/j.ctv11g9616.

Montrul, S.A. (2018) Heritage language development: Connecting the dots. *International Journal of Bilingualism* 22 (5), 530–546.

Nicholas, S.E. and McCarty, T.L. (2022) To 'think in a different way' – A relational paradigm for Indigenous language rights. In J. MacSwan (ed.) *Multilingual Perspectives on Translanguaging* (pp. 227–247). Multilingual Matters.

Otheguy, R., García, O. and Reid, W. (2015) Clarifying translanguaging and deconstructing named languages: A perspective from linguistics. *Applied Linguistics Review* 6 (3), 281–307.

Palmer, D.K. (2009) Middle-class English speakers in a two-way immersion bilingual classroom: "Everybody should be listening to Jonathan right now." *TESOL Quarterly* 43 (2), 177–202. https://doi.org/10.1002/j.1545-7249.2009.tb00164.x.

Palmer, D. and Martinez, R. (2013) Teacher agency in bilingual spaces: A fresh look at preparing teachers to educate Latina/o bilingual children. *Review of Research in Education* 37, 269–297. https://doi.org/10.3102/0091732X12463556.

Palmer, D.K., Martinez, R.A., Mateus, S.G. and Henderson, K. (2014) Reframing the debate on language separation: Toward a vision for translanguaging pedagogies in the dual language classroom. *The Modern Language Journal* 98 (3), 757–772.

Palmer, D.K., Cervantes-Soon, C., Dorner, L. and Heiman, D. (2019) Bilingualism, biliteracy, biculturalism, and critical consciousness for all: Proposing a fourth fundamental goal for two-way dual language education. *Theory Into Practice* 58 (2), 121–133. https://doi.org/10.1080/00405841.2019.1569376.

Phipps, A. (2019) *Decolonising Multilingualism: Struggles to Decreate.* Multilingual Matters.

Phyak, P., Sah, P.K., Ghimire, N.B. and Lama, A. (2022) Teacher agency in creating a translingual space in Nepal's multilingual English-medium schools. *RELC Journal* 53 (2), 431–451. https://doi.org/10.1177/00336882221113950.

Ramirez, P. and Faltis, C. (2019) Re-imagining dual language education in the US. *Theory Into Practice.* https://doi.org/10.1080/00405841.2019.1569401.

Ramos, A.M. and Ramos, R. (2011) Ecoliteracy through imagery: A close reading of two wordless picture books. *Children's Literature in Education* 42 (4), 325–339.

Reagan, T. and Terry, O. (2019) Between globalization and decolonization: Foreign languages in the crossfire. In D. Macedo (ed.) *Decolonizing Foreign Language Education: The Misteaching English and Other Colonial Languages* (pp. 73–110). Routledge.

Rosa, J. and Flores, N. (2017) Unsettling language and race: Toward a raciolinguistic perspective. *Language in Society* 46, 621–647.

Rubinstein-Avila, E. (2002) Problematizing the "dual" in a dual-immersion program: A portrait. *Linguistics and Education* 13 (1), 65–87.

Salisbury, M. and Styles, M. (2012) *Children's Picturebooks: The Art of Visual Storytelling.* Laurence King Publishing.

Sánchez, M.T., García, O. and Solorza, C. (2018) Reframing language allocation policy in dual language bilingual education. *Bilingual Research Journal* 41 (1), 37–51. https://doi.org/10.1080/15235882.2017.1405098.

Seltzer, K. (2022) Enacting a critical translingual approach in teacher preparation: Disrupting oppressive language ideologies and fostering the personal, political, and pedagogical stances of preservice teachers. *TESOL Journal* 13 (2). https://doi.org/10.1002/tesj.649.

Sembiante, S.F. (2016) Translanguaging and the multilingual turn: Epistemological reconceptualization in the fields of language and implications for reframing language in curriculum studies. *Curriculum Inquiry* 46 (1), 45–61.

Sembiante, S.F. and Tian, Z. (2023) Translanguaging: A pedagogy of heteroglossic hope. *International Journal of Bilingual Education and Bilingualism* 26. https://doi.org/10.1080/13670050.2023.2212835.

Sembiante, S.F., Restrepo-Widney, C., Bengochea, A. and Gort, M. (2023) Sustainable translanguaging pedagogy in support of the vulnerable language: Honoring children's ways of 'showing' and 'telling' in an early childhood dual language bilingual education program. *International Journal of Bilingual Education and Bilingualism* 26 (8), 928–942. https://doi.org/10.1080/13670050.2022.2161814.

Serafini, S.F. (2014a) Exploring wordless picture books. *The Reading Teacher* 68 (1), 24–26. https://doi.org/10.1002/trtr.1294.

Serafini, S.F. (2014b) *Reading the Visual: An Introduction to Teaching Multimodal Literacy.* Teachers College Press.

Sohn, B., dos Santos, P. and Lin, A. (2022) Translanguaging as a theory of language for a critical integration of content and language in multilingual educational settings. *RELC Journal* 53 (2), 355–370.

Soltero-González, L., Sparrow, W., Butvilofsky, S., Escamilla, K., and Hopewell, S. (2016) Effects of a paired literacy program on emerging bilingual children's biliteracy outcomes in third grade. *Journal of Literacy Research* 48 (1), 80–104.

Soltero-Gonzalez, L. and Butvilofsky, S. (2016) The early Spanish and English writing development of simultaneous bilingual preschoolers. *Journal of Early Childhood Literacy* 16 (4), 473–497.

Tian, Z. and Lau, S.M.C. (2022) Translanguaging pedagogies in a Mandarin-English dual language bilingual education classroom: Contextualised learning from teacher-researcher collaboration. *International Journal of Bilingual Education and Bilingualism* 26 (8), 960–974. https://doi.org/10.1080/13670050.2022.2161815.

Valdés, V.E., Freire, J.A. and Delavan, M.G. (2016) The gentrification of dual language education. *Urban Review* 48, 601–627. https://doi.org/10.1007/s11256-016-0370-0.

Valdés, G. and Parra, M. (2018) Towards the development of an analytical framework for examining goals and pedagogical approaches in teaching language to heritage speakers. In K. Potowski (ed.) *The Routledge Handbook of Spanish as a Heritage Language* (pp. 301–330). Routledge.

Velasco, P. and García, O. (2014) Translanguaging and the writing of bilingual learners. *Bilingual Research Journal* 37 (1), 6–23.

Vertovec, S. (2007) Super-diversity and its implications. *Ethnic and Racial Studies* 30 (6), 1024–1054. https://doi.org/10.1080/01419870701599465.

Vertovec, S. (2023) *Superdiversity: Migration and Social Complexity*. Routledge.

Vogel, S. and García, O. (2017) *Translanguaging*. Oxford Research Encyclopedia of Education.

Wang, D. (2024) Translanguaging as a decolonising approach: Students' perspectives towards integrating Indigenous epistemology in language teaching. *Applied Linguistics Review* 15 (4), 1385–1406.

Williams, C. (1994) An evaluation of teaching and learning methods in the context of secondary education. Unpublished Doctoral Dissertation, University of Bangor.

Worthy, J., Durán, L., Hikida, M., Pruitt, A. and Peterson, K. (2013) Spaces for dynamic bilingualism in read-aloud discussions: Developing and strengthening bilingual and academic skills. *Bilingual Research Journal* 36, 311–328.

Wu, M.H. and Leung, G. (2020) 'It's not my Chinese': A teacher and her students disrupting and dismantling conventional notions of 'Chinese' through translanguaging in a heritage language classroom. *International Journal of Bilingual Education and Bilingualism* 25 (5), 1811–1824. https://doi.org/10.1080/13670050.2020.1804524.

4 Understanding Bi/Multi/ Plurilingual Learners' Dynamic and Fluid Translanguaging Practices

It is a first-grade classroom at a Korean heritage language school where students who are emergent in both Korean and English enroll. As a first-grade teacher, I observe that students exclusively use English when communicating with one another during recess, but they switch to Korean when participating in a whole-group discussion after reading a storybook written in Korean. During and after reading, I often ask the class questions that range from basic recall to critical thinking. One day, a student named Yuri responded to my basic recall questions in Korean by retrieving information directly from the text. But when she was asked to answer a higher-order thinking and more analytical question, she asked me if she could respond in English. As I approved, Yuri provided her responses in English, and her responses were in great detail and thoughtful. It appears that the use of her translanguaging assisted her in elaborating her ideas and thoughts. Meanwhile, when the class was asked to provide their answers in Korean on a worksheet, Bomi and Jina whispered to each other in English as they were unsure of one of the questions listed on the worksheet. Although they quietly discussed the specific question mainly using English, they successfully provided their answer in Korean. The use of translanguaging during such conversations helps students clarify and confirm uncertain questions, which in turn enables them to process information and complete their writing tasks through translanguaging.

***

This vignette illustrates how bilingual students can naturally and unconsciously move across their languages in their communication, which is considered a natural aspect of bilingual language use. Yet, at the same time, it also shows that they are consciously aware of when, where, why and/or with whom they should use a particular language, which is understood as a unique asset of bilingual learners. Translanguaging as a teacher's pedagogical approach was discussed in the previous chapter. Another dimension of translanguaging revolves around bi/multi/

plurilingual students' translanguaging practices. Today, bi/multi/plurilingual individuals are exposed to a wide range of linguistic and semiotic features due to global mobility and modern technology, providing them with numerous opportunities to interact with speakers from diverse communities, cultures and countries worldwide. Due to this increasing flexibility of people to move around the world, bi/multi/plurilingual learners are more likely to utilize their entire language repertoires to engage in learning and employ their dual or multiple language resources for their meaning-making or sense-making processes.

Introduction to the Chapter

This chapter introduces the dynamic nature of students' bi/multi/plurilingualism by presenting their translanguaging practices when engaging in communication and interactions to construct meaning, as demonstrated by Yuri, Bomi and Jina in the vignette. Acknowledging the less-documented translanguaging practices in the writing of bi/multi/plurilingual learners compared to their oral translanguaging, the chapter illuminates students' written translanguaging practices in addition to their oral translanguaging performance and displays how they draw on their entire linguistic resources during the writing process. The chapter then introduces trans-semiotizing as a new theoretical concept that encompasses both linguistic modality (i.e. spoken or written language) and social/cultural semiotic resources (e.g. visuals, gestures and body language) to maximize meaning-making, engagement and learning potential. By recognizing the importance of incorporating diverse forms of communication, the chapter seeks to view bi/multi/plurilingual learners' linguistic performance holistically and challenge the conventional understanding of language that solely includes spoken or written languages. Then, the heart of the chapter, Korean American bilingual learners' translanguaging, transmodal and trans-semiotizing practices, are displayed and discussed.

Understanding Dynamic Translanguaging Progressions

The flexible and fluid nature of students' bi/multi/plurilingualism is referred to as dynamic translanguaging progressions by García, Johnson and Seltzer (2017). According to García and her colleagues, there are two types of linguistic performance: general linguistic performance and language-specific performance. General linguistic performance indicates the ability of bi/multi/plurilingual learners to flexibly utilize features from multiple languages within their linguistic repertoire to accomplish language- and content-related tasks. In comparison, language-specific performance refers to what bi/multi/plurilingual speakers can strategically select and utilize only the linguistic features from their repertoire that correspond to the specific language being used in a given task (García *et al.*, 2017: 39).

Educators who accept and value translanguaging practices encourage students to develop their proficiency in the specific languages necessary for academic achievement and success. Yet, at the same time, they understand that bi/multi/plurilingual students need to have opportunities to draw on the entire features of their language repertoires. Those teachers believe that bi/multi/plurilingual learners who engage in meaning- and sense-making using their complete language resources can also develop the specific language features required in school. It is essential to value and focus on general linguistic performance if we want to liberate bi/multi/plurilingual students from constraining or suppressing certain features of their language repertoires. Adopting and utilizing translanguaging for students' dynamic language progressions are necessary to challenge monoglossic ideology and recognize the holistic learning outcomes of bi/multi/plurilingual learners (García *et al.*, 2017).

Using the concept of dynamic translanguaging progression (García *et al.*, 2017), it is important to understand that the dynamic nature of students' bi/multi/plurilingualism – that is, students' capability to utilize their entire linguistic skillset, drawing from both or multiple languages they understand – is not static but constantly shifts and adapts depending on the context, social situation and their individual language development. Thus, students' dynamic translanguaging progressions enable them to utilize their complete set of language varieties, dialects, registers and styles, allowing us to observe their capabilities through both language-specific and general linguistic performances. Translanguaging is 'the impetus for the sophisticated general linguistic performance' (García *et al.*, 2017: 43), which leverages bi/multi/plurilingual students' linguistic assets to foster a deeper understanding of academic content and develop their learning, creativity and criticality. By utilizing multiple languages fluidly, bi/multi/plurilingual individuals can achieve a higher level of overall linguistic ability, drawing on the strengths of each language to enhance communication and understanding across contexts.

Studies on Bi/Multi/Plurilingual Learners' Translanguaging Practices

An increasing number of translanguaging research have examined how bilingual students naturally utilize their multiple languages within the school environment, looking at how this practice impacts their learning and participation in the classroom. Most research on bilingual learners' translanguaging practices has been conducted in bilingual education settings, such as Dual Language Bilingual Education (DLBE) or Dual Language Immersion (DLI) programs, where speakers of a common minority language and native-English speakers are taught together in the same classroom, utilizing both languages for instruction. Another common program type for translanguaging research is the Transitional Bilingual Education (TBE) program where students' first language (L1) is utilized as a bridge to acquiring English, to transition to fully English instruction after a certain period (typically three years for early-exit and five to six years for late-exit programs) of using students' L1 for academic content delivery (Baker, 2011; Crawford, 2004; Durán & Palmer, 2014; Howard *et al.*, 2018).

Most research on translanguaging in these classroom settings has examined how bi/multi/plurilingual students actively used all the languages they know during their oral communication (e.g. Alamillo *et al.*, 2017; Axelrod, 2014; Durán & Palmer, 2014; Gort & Pontier, 2012; Gort & Sembiante, 2015; Kirsch, 2017, 2020; Martínez *et al.*, 2017). These studies discovered that bi/multi/plurilingual students strategically and flexibly employed translanguaging to understand information, construct meaning and express their ideas when engaging in communication and learning. When bi/multi/plurilingual students draw on their entire linguistic and semiotic repertoires, including different modes of communication (i.e. verbal and non-verbal, such as gestures or visuals), their translanguaging practices enable them to communicate effectively in diverse ways. Thus, bi/multi/plurilingual learners' translanguaging practices enhance their ability to participate fully in social interactions across different contexts (Kirsch & Mortini, 2023; Song *et al.*, 2022). Since language boundaries across and between languages have been blurred and indistinct for bi/multi/plurilingual speakers, the translanguaging approach acknowledges and embraces the complex interplay between language varieties, valuing the speakers' creativity and criticality in their language practices.

Research on bi/multi/plurilingual learners' translanguaging practices revealed that they made deliberate language choices by purposefully selecting which language to use and consciously including or excluding their interlocutors to engage in meaningful conversations (García *et al.*, 2011; Kirsch, 2018; Lee & García, 2020). Bi/multi/plurilingual learners effectively access their full range of linguistic abilities and actively select specific lexical items, phrases and/or grammatical structures from their multiple languages to acutely comprehend information and fully grasp complex ideas in their meaning-making processes. That is, translanguaging helps learners practice language-based agency (García & Kleifgen, 2010; Kirsch & Mortini, 2023; Martínez *et al.*, 2017; Parra & Proctor, 2021; Schwartz *et al.*, 2020; Toth & Paulsrud, 2017) by giving them the power to support their understanding and further advance their learning as they take ownership of their educational journey across multiple languages.

Translanguaging Practices in Speech

Empirical research on translanguaging has shown that bi/multi/plurilingual learners participate in translanguaging in appropriate ways to engage in classroom interactions, but their translanguaging performance serves various purposes or goals. For instance, students flexibly utilize their full language repertoires to create and redefine who they are by positioning themselves as bi/multi/plurilingual speakers through translanguaging (e.g. Alamillo *et al.*, 2017; García-Mateus & Palmer, 2017; Gort & Sembiante, 2015; Martínez *et al.*, 2017; Tian, 2022). Bi/multi/plurilingual learners engage in translanguaging practices to express, construct and negotiate their dynamic identities by embracing the richness of their unique and diverse ethnic, linguistic and/or cultural backgrounds, which leads them to authentically represent themselves and reshape their individualities in different contexts or situations.

Numerous studies that explored purposes of translanguaging practices showed that bi/multi/plurilingual students engaged in translanguaging, in particular, to fully engage in conversations, interactions and activities (Alamillo *et al.*, 2017; Gort & Sembiante, 2015; Kirsch, 2017, 2020; Lee, 2023a), to effectively convey their ideas and fully express their thoughts (Axelrod, 2014; García, 2011; Gort & Pontier, 2012; Gort & Sembiante, 2015), to accelerate their language learning (Alamillo *et al.*, 2017; Kirsch, 2017; Sanders-Smith & Dávila, 2019), to check comprehension and ensure their understanding (García & Kleifgen, 2019; Jiménez *et al.*, 2015; Lee, 2023b), to conform to a principle of code alignment (Lee & García, 2020; Sayer, 2013), to engage in problem solving and knowledge building (Martin-Beltrán, 2010), to regulate their own behaviors (Arreguín-Anderson *et al.*, 2018), to express emotions (Lee & García, 2021; McCarthey *et al.*, 2020), to socialize with others (García, 2011; Kirsch & Mortini, 2023; Sanders-Smith & Dávila, 2019), to deliver a sense of humor (Creese & Blackledge, 2010; Jönsson, 2013; Lee & García, 2021), to show respect, endearment and excitement (Hopewell & Abril-Gonzalez, 2019; Lee & García, 2021), and to signal camaraderie and express solidarity (Martínez *et al.*, 2017).

For instance, the students in the Hopewell and Abril-Gonzalez (2019) study consistently used Spanish when referring to their family members in their English utterances, even though they knew how to refer to them in English. The students' use of Spanish when indicating their family led them to express endearment; thus, their translanguaging reflected the 'intimacy ... and closeness of [the family] relationship' (2019: 114) that would have been lessened or lost if they had used the referents in English. Hopewell and Abril-Gonzalez pointed out that the students' strategic integration of languages enhanced and augmented the meanings of their communication. Translanguaging studies broadly have demonstrated that bi/multi/plurilingual learners' translanguaging performance helped them develop their metalinguistic awareness (i.e. understanding how language works) (Martin-Beltrán, 2010), metacognitive knowledge (i.e. awareness of one's thinking processes) (Martínez-Roldán, 2015) and pragmatic competence (i.e. ability to use language appropriately in different social contexts) (Almér, 2017; Bergroth & Palviainen, 2017; Schwartz *et al.*, 2020).

Functions of Translanguaging Practices
Performed by Korean Bilingual Students

The majority of translanguaging research conducted over the past 10 years (following the publication of Ofelia García's groundbreaking book in 2009) has been with Spanish–English bilingual students, primarily within bilingual education settings (see Chapter 3). There has been a gradually increasing number of studies that investigated translanguaging practices of emergent bilingual learners from diverse language backgrounds and in various classroom settings beyond traditional bilingual programs in the US (e.g. Lee & García, 2020, 2021; Lee, 2023b; Sanders-Smith & Dávila, 2019; Tian, 2022), but there remains a significant lack of scholarly focus on the translanguaging practices of Asian American students (Lee, 2021). Thus, we have a limited understanding of how children of Asian descent utilize translanguaging practices, particularly within the context of heritage language schools (see Chapter 2 for an overview of the roles and aims of heritage language schools in the US). To narrow the gaps in the literature, I (Lee, 2020, 2021, 2023a, 2023b; Lee & García, 2020, 2021) investigated translanguaging practices by Korean–English emergent bilingual students in Korean heritage language classrooms.

In one study (Lee, 2020), I examined the functions of translanguaging used by first-grade Korean bilingual students in a heritage language classroom through classroom discourse analysis. Jakobson's (1960) six functions of language (i.e. directive, expressive, referential, phatic, metalinguistic and poetic) were adopted to identify the students' translanguaging functions. Based on his six functions of language, I identified the following five functional categories that emerged from the students' translanguaging data: referential, directive, expressive, metalinguistic and poetic functions. As a total, 14 different subsidiary functions were developed under the 5 functional categories (see Table 4.1). Throughout the students' translanguaging data, translanguaging for the referential function was documented as the highest (616 out of 1012 utterances; 60.86%), followed by directive function (201 out of 1012 utterances; 19.86%), expressive function (107 out of 1012 utterances; 10.57%), metalinguistic function (72 out of 1012 utterances; 7.11%) and poetic function (16 out of 1012 utterances; 1.58%).

For instance, the students' translanguaging were reported as directive in the following four functions: (1) building intimate relationships with others, (2) persuading others, (3) requesting information and (4) attracting others' attention. Excerpts 4.1 and 4.2 illustrate how students engaged in translanguaging to build intimate relationships with a peer and attract peers' attention, respectively.

Table 4.1 Functional categories of translanguaging

Functions of translanguaging	Functional categories
Referential	Maintaining conversation and facilitating communication
	Delivering accurate meanings of words or concepts
	Elaborating ideas and thoughts
	Incorporating habitually used terms or referents
Directive	Building intimate relationships with others
	Persuading others
	Requesting information
	Attracting others' attention
Expressive	Expressing their emotions and feelings
	Creating their bilingual identity
Metalinguistic	Clarifying own's understanding
	Comparing languages
	Using metaphors
Poetic	Adding a sense of humor

Excerpt 4.1 Building an intimate relationship through translanguaging

(1) Ms Lee: 지나랑 나래랑 카드게임 하는 거예요? [Are you two playing the card game?].
(2) Jina: 네, 근데 우리 다른 게임 해요. [Yes, but we are playing a different card game.].
(3) Jina: (to Narae) Okay, Narae. Let's do it. Now you got a seven.

Excerpt 4.1 illustrates Jina's translanguaging as she plays a card game with her classmate, Narae, using English during recess. When I, as the teacher, interjected their play and asked a question in Korean (line 1), Jina responded to me using the same language, Korean (line 2). Yet, Jina used English by translanguaging in her subsequent utterance, as her audience had changed to Narae (line 3). Jina strategically switched her language by positioning herself as an English proficient speaker to resume the card game with Narae, who also identified as a fluent English speaker. Jina's language use in this excerpt indicates that she purposefully engaged in translanguaging by aligning the same language with her peer to build intimate relationships.

Excerpt 4.2 Attracting peers' attention

(1) Ms Lee: 여기 지나가 그린 것 좀 봐. 멋지지? [Look at Jina's drawing. Isn't it really great?].
(2) Mino: 와, 진짜 잘했어요. [Wow, it is really great.].
(3) Mino: (loudly, to class) Look at this, guys. This is amazing.

Another directive function of translanguaging is presented in Excerpt 4.2, where the student attempts to attract others' attention. When I complimented Jina's drawing (line 1), Mino praised Jina's drawing using Korean in response to me, but he translanguaged into English to talk to his classmates (line 3). Mino's translanguaging suggests that he fluidly and deliberately switched languages by transcending boundaries between them to draw his classmates' attention.

Purpose of Korean bilingual students' oral translanguaging

My previous study (Lee, 2020) aimed to identify 'how' bilingual students translanguage (i.e. functions of translanguaging). By defining a *function* as a specific action or activity and a *purpose* as the overall reason or goal, I and my colleague (Lee & García, 2020) examined 'why' bilingual students translanguage (i.e. purposes of translanguaging). We scrutinized the translanguaging instances identified by first-grade Korean bilingual students when they interacted in their Korean heritage language classroom. We categorized the students' translanguaging practices according to the following four purposes: sociolinguistic competence (i.e. drawing from integrated linguistic resources to effectively communicate), metalinguistic awareness (i.e. utilizing integrated linguistic resources to create meaning and compare languages), metacognitive insight (i.e. using the entire linguistic repertoires to engage in private speech) and sociocultural understanding (i.e. incorporating linguistic resources for culturally relevant referents).

Translanguaging for Sociolinguistic Competence. The students translanguaged the most for sociolinguistic purposes, accounting for 50% (540 out of 1080 utterances) of their translanguaging. Five different codes that emerged to characterize the students' translanguaging for sociolinguistic purposes are when they (1) respond to the interlocutor's language use, (2) express their bilingual identity, (3) produce dual lexicons, (4) employ borrowed lexical items for non-existing words or terms and (5) achieve quicker lexical access to a specific language.

Excerpt 4.3 illustrates a student's translanguaging as she responds to her interlocutor using the same language.

Excerpt 4.3 Code alignment with interlocutor's bilingual language use

(1) Ms Lee: 아 친구가 영어 책 잘 못 읽어서 그럼 English reading 도와 줘? [Oh, your friend is not good at reading in English, so do you help her with English reading?].

(2) Rena: 응. 나 매일 내 친구 English reading help 해줘. [Yes, I help her with English reading every day.].

(3) Ms Lee: 어떻게 도와줘? [How do you help her?] How do you help her?

(4) Rena: Sometimes she picks up [an] English book, and I help her.

The example illustrates Rena's translanguaging for code alignment. I asked a question in Korean but incorporated the English word 'English reading' in my utterance (line 1). As shown, Rena answered in Korean but included the same words, 'English reading', in her response, demonstrating her translanguaging for code alignment. Responding to my follow-up question, which was initially asked in Korean but translated into English immediately (line 3), Rena provided her response in English (line 4). Rena's language use demonstrates that she seamlessly transitioned between her languages as needed to communicate effectively with me (her teacher) by mirroring the language used by me (her interlocutor). It appears that Rena conformed to a principle of code alignment to my language use when responding to my questions, which demonstrates her sociolinguistic knowledge.

Translanguaging for Metalinguistic Awareness. The second most frequent purpose of translanguaging was for metalinguistic awareness, which characterized 31% (338 out of 1080 utterances). Three codes were characterized by their use of translanguaging for metalinguistic purposes when they (1) apply their language knowledge to create new meanings or jokes, (2) regulate or control their language use and (3) demonstrate their linguistic knowledge of Korean and English. Excerpt 4.4 illustrates how the student regulated his language use and controlled his language choice for a different purpose.

Excerpt 4.4 Controlling language choice to make a joke

(1) Joon: 먼저 jewelry 많이 가지는 거랑 pretty 하게 하는 거. [First, she wanted to have a lot of jewelry and to be pretty.].

(2) Ms Lee: 그렇지. 또 하나가 뭐였지? [Yes, you are right. Do you remember the last one?].

(3) Joon: Um … she wanted to have one hundred dollars. No, one million dollars. I am kidding (laughs).

After the class read the storybook, I asked the class about the three wishes that the protagonist had made in the story. Joon provided his answers for the first two wishes; he used Korean when responding to the question, although he incorporated a few English words ('jewelry' and 'pretty') in his Korean utterance (line 1). Yet, Joon translanguaged when providing his answer for the protagonist's third wish (line 3). His verbal statement ('I am kidding') and his non-verbal communication (i.e. laughing) imply that he exaggerated the story as a joke. This example shows that Joon translanguaged to signal that his answer was untruthful as he inserted a joke. Joon was aware of how he self-regulated and controlled his language use, which demonstrated his metalinguistic awareness.

Translanguaging for Sociocultural Understanding. The students' translanguaging demonstrated their sociocultural understanding by approximately 9% (95 out of 1080 utterances) when they employed Korean words or phrases related to family members, the Korean language, or cultural practices. For instance, the students employed translanguaging to refer to their family, as shown in the following example: 'I am going to go to Chicago next week with my family, 엄마 [mom], 아빠 [dad], 누나 [older sister].' [I am going to go to Chicago next week with my family: my mom, dad and older sister]. During the interview, Joon explained that he always referred to his immediate family members in Korean even when he spoke in English if his interlocutors were Korean bilingual speakers: 'I always say 엄마 [mom], 아빠 [dad], 누나 [older sister] because I have called them that way since I was very young.' Other students also incorporated Korean words, such as 받아쓰기 [Korean dictation practice], 존댓말 [Korean honorifics] and 한복 [traditional Korean dress] in their English utterances as they were accustomed to use those culturally specific words in Korean. These example utterances demonstrate how the students specifically chose and incorporated Korean words, suggesting that they were able to utilize their sociocultural knowledge through translanguaging as socioculturally competent bilingual speakers.

Translanguaging for Metacognitive Insight. The students' translanguaging practices demonstrated their metacognitive insight in approximately 10% (107 out of 1080 utterances) of instances when they reflected on, evaluated and controlled their thinking processes regarding their own language choices and practices through private speech. The examples in Excerpts 4.5, 4.6 and 4.7 exhibit how the students' translanguaging demonstrated their metacognitive insight.

Excerpt 4.5 Private speech for internalization

(1) Yuri: 이거 cartoon 같은 건데. 선생님, 이걸로 search 해서 보여 줄게요. [It is like a cartoon. Ms Lee, I will show you by searching for it on your cell phone.]
(2) Yuri: (To herself) I need to type something here. (Yuri finds the program on the internet by using Ms Lee's cellular phone.)
(3) Yuri: (To Ms Lee) 선생님, 이거가 그 프로그램 이예요. [Ms Lee, this is the program.]

Excerpt 4.6 Bilingual discourse for a private joke

(1) Yuri: 왜냐면 ... lazy 해서. [Because ... he is lazy.]
(2) Joon: (To himself) I know a person who is lazy like the lazy man. He is in Pre-K.

(3) Ms Lee: (To Joon) 뭐라고 했어? [What did you say?].
(4) Joon: 아니예요. 나 그냥 나한테 말했어요. [Nothing. I just said something to me.]

Excerpt 4.7 Respectful bilingual private speech

(1) Nari: 선생님, 저 너무 더워요. [Ms Lee, I am very hot.]
(2) Nari: (To herself) I am hot. I need a fan.

As shown in Excerpts 4.5, 4.6 and 4.7, the students drew on integrated linguistic resources through translanguaging during private speech to express their thoughts out loud, craft a personal joke and avoid the act of showing disrespect, respectively. Specifically, Yuri's self-directed speech (line 2 in Excerpt 4.5) indicates the process of internalization as she transitions from interpersonal dialogue to intrapersonal speech, moving from a conversation with me to a personal internal monologue. Similarly, Joon engaged in self-talk (line 2 in Excerpt 4.6) as he confirmed that he considered his comment to be private speech, a form of thinking out loud to himself (line 4) outside of the Korean classroom discussion. Nari spoke in Korean to express her physical discomfort when talking to me (line 1 in Excerpt 4.7), but she used English by translanguaging when creating negative self-talk to freely voice her complaint (line 2). Her private speech through translanguaging suggests that she attempted to avoid disrespecting me (her teacher) by not presenting her complaint in Korean. The students' classroom discourses show that the Korean bilingual students used Korean when talking to me (i.e. their Korean language teacher), but they chose to use English in their private speech for various purposes; thus, their translanguaging demonstrated their metacognitive awareness and understanding.

Translanguaging when encountering wordless picture books

Chapter 3 discusses the merits of including wordless picture books for classroom teachers who work with bi/multi/plurilingual learners because wordless picture books help students incorporate the whole linguistic knowledge and semiotic resources they possess (Lee, 2021; Li, 2018; Otheguy et al., 2015; Vogel & García, 2017) to make sense of their thinking and understanding when comprehending visual literacy and creating their storylines (Arizpe, 2013; Lubis, 2018). In one of my studies (Lee, 2023a), I used wordless picture books to create a translanguaging space (Li, 2018) in my Korean heritage language classroom. I introduced wordless picture books to first-grade Korean–English bilingual students to investigate whether and how they utilized their language repertoires to construct their plots. Below, I display excerpts from classroom literacy events where the class was reading and analyzing illustrations from the chosen wordless picture books, which demonstrate the students' translanguaging performance, employing their integrated linguistic resources (see Lee, 2023a, for the entire study).

Excerpt 4.8 Making connections from personal experiences using both languages [Translanguaged words, phrases, and sentences are underlined in the English translation.]

Oral storytelling of classroom discourse	Translation	Translanguaging function
1. Tim: 근데 쟤는 몰라. 나도 쟤처럼 그랬어. I felt bad and sad because what my teacher said was blah, blah, blah to me.	But he is not getting it. I was like him. I felt bad and sad because what my teacher said was blah, blah, blah to me.	Expression of emotions
2. Rose: 나도 똑같이 그랬어. 나 선생님이 하는 말 못 알아 들었어 처음에. But not anymore! I am good at English now!	The same thing happened to me. I did not understand what my teacher said on my first day of school. But not anymore! I am good at English now!	Identity construction
3. Ellie: 근데 나도 옛날엔 학교 가기 싫었어 영어 못해서. 근데 지금은 한국말 할 때 worried 하고 nervous 많이 해 왜냐면 어려우니까.	However, I didn't want to go to the school either before because I was not good at English. But now, I am worried a lot and feel nervous when speaking Korean because it is difficult for me.	Expression of emotions
4. Sarah: 영어 keep working on 해야 해. 그러면 잘 할 수 있어. 나도 처음엔 못 알아 들었는데 keep working on English 했어.	He needs to keep working on English. Then, he can be good at English. I didn't understand in the beginning, but I did keep working on English.	Habitual use

Excerpt 4.8 displays that the students interpreted the illustrations by making personal connections between visual images and their own experiences through translanguaging. The students' text-to-self connections from the visual images helped them construct their own stories by selecting and integrating their entire linguistic resources. In this excerpt, three different translanguaging functions were observed. First, as Tim showed, he moved across his languages through translanguaging when reflecting on his personal experiences and memories to express his emotions ('I felt bad and sad') (line 1). Similarly, Ellie incorporated the English words ('worried' and 'nervous') in her Korean utterances (line 3). Her translanguaging was also to express and highlight her feelings. Both Tim and Ellie mentioned during the interviews that, as English-dominant bilingual speakers, they could accurately convey their true feelings when using English.

Another translanguaging function was observed in line 2. Rose chose to use English to effectively demonstrate a high level of English fluency, highlighting the significant improvement in her English proficiency compared to the past. Rose's translanguaging supported her identity (re)construction as a bilingual speaker who became fluent in English.

The third translanguaging function occurred when Sarah used a certain group of English words. Sarah inserted an English phrasal verb ('keep working on') in her Korean utterances (line 4). During the interview, Sarah explained that she habitually used English for frequently used phrasal verbs. As shown, Sarah's translanguaging appeared to happen routinely as she naturally incorporated English language patterns into her speech.

Excerpt 4.9 Making predictions through translanguaging by searching for pictorial clues

Oral storytelling of classroom discourse	Translation	Translanguaging function
1. Ellie: 그 작은 빨간 거. I don't know what it is. 그거 뭐 같아?	The small red thing. I don't know what it is. What does it look like for you guys?	Private speech
2. Sue: 무슨 작은 장난감 같은 거 집에서 가져온.	It looks like a little toy that he brought from his home.	
3. John: 난 돌멩이 인 거 같아. 음 빨간 돌멩이? But I am not 100% sure.	I think it is a stone. Maybe a red pebble? But I am not 100% sure.	Private speech
4. Sue: Oh, wait! 난 이거 씨앗 같아. 이거 봐, 나무 있어 여기 그 씨앗한테 나온 거야.	Oh, wait! I think it is a seed. Look, there is a tree from that seed.	Spontaneous responses
5. Ms Lee: 좋은 guess네. Why do you think so?	That is a good guess. Why do you guys think so?	
6. Sue: All the leaves and singing birds on the tree make me believe it is a seed.	All the leaves and singing birds on the Code alignment tree make me believe it is a seed.	Code alignment
7. Tim: Oh, you are right! 그리고난 씨앗이 있어야 나무 생기는 거 알아요.	Oh, you are right! And I know that we need a seed to have a tree.	Spontaneous responses
8. Sarah: 여기 같이 씨앗 심어. 우리 맞았어. 이거 진짜 씨앗이였어.	They planted the seed. We were right. It was indeed the seed.	

Excerpt 4.9 particularly shows how the students made predictions when interpreting the visual narratives and developing a storyline by employing translanguaging. This excerpt illustrates that the students combined visual information and their schemata through translanguaging to make their predictions logically. The class showcased three other translanguaging functions in this excerpt. First, the students occasionally employed translanguaging to present their private speech by talking to themselves for self-regulation (i.e. 'I don't know what it is' and 'But I am not 100% sure' in lines 1 and 3, respectively). The two students (Ellie and John) responded during the interviews that they naturally and unconsciously used English as they were thinking aloud and having internal dialogues.

Second, the students translanguaged when providing spontaneous responses. As displayed, Sue and Tim used English to denote their automatic responses (i.e. 'Oh, wait!' 'Oh, you are right!'; lines 4 and 7). The students instinctively used English by engaging in translanguaging when exclaiming or agreeing with others' utterances. Finally, it shows that Sue translanguaged by adjusting her language to match my language use as I asked the question in English (line 5). To correspond with her interlocutor using the same language, Sue transitioned into English (line 6). In other words, Sue's translanguaging was influenced by her interlocutor's language use and choice.

Translanguaging Practices in Writing

Although translanguaging is a strategy that encourages bi/multi/plurilingual learners to utilize their entire linguistic resources to fully participate in the learning process, research on translanguaging has generally focused more on how bi/multi/plurilingual learners utilize their linguistic repertoire in oral communication rather than written communication (Lee & García, 2021). Yet, what Hornberger (2005: 607) asserted – 'bi/multilinguals' learning is maximized when they are allowed and enabled to draw from across all their existing language skills (in two+ languages), rather than being constrained and inhibited from doing so by monolingual instructional assumptions and practices' – is and should be applied to writing. Similarly, researchers argued that bi/multi/plurilingual learners should not be restricted to compose in only one language, dialect, or register; instead, they should be empowered to engage in translanguaging by employing their entire linguistic and semiotic resources during the drafting stage of the writing process (Lee & García, 2021; Otheguy et al., 2015; Velasco & García, 2014).

However, some educators in the past took the stand that translanguaging was not appropriate when writing (Barbour, 2002) because writing was considered a more formal language domain than speaking. Canagarajah (2011) yet challenged this idea; he argued that emergent bi/multi/plurilingual students should be allowed and encouraged to translanguage not only when delivering their thoughts orally but also when expressing themselves in a written form. Canagarajah criticized the earlier assumption that translanguaging while writing was an inappropriate behavior. He pointed out that classroom teachers traditionally instructed students to write solely in the standard form of a language, assuming their audience would understand only one particular language. Thus, the 'target-language-only or one language-at-a-time monolingual ideologies' (Li, 2018: 15) have dominated writing instruction for bi/multi/plurilingual students (Velasco & García, 2014). For this reason, the presence of translanguaging in the writing of bi/multi/plurilingual students in the US has not been well-documented compared to oral translanguaging (Lee & García, 2021).

Although bi/multi/plurilingual learners are restricted to producing their writing in a target language for their final product, they still employ and leverage their understanding and knowledge in other language(s) during the initial brainstorming, planning, pre-writing, organizing, revising and/or editing stages to formulate their ideas better and refine their writing in the target language. Bi/multi/plurilingual writers intuitively express themselves by engaging in translanguaging during different writing processes, for instance, when establishing their thinking and elaborating ideas. Thus, translanguaging can occur as part of their writing processes. By arguing that writing is a highly complex and demanding task, Velasco and García (2014) stated:

> The writer must negotiate the rules and mechanics of writing while maintaining a focus on factors such as organization, form and features, purposes and goals, as well as audience needs and perspectives. Self-regulation of the writing process is critical. The writer must be goal oriented, resourceful, and reflective. Skilled writers are able to use powerful strategies to support them in accomplishing specific writing goals. In emergent bilinguals, translanguaging is one such strategy. (2014: 13)

When we allow and encourage bi/multi/plurilingual students to draw upon their entire linguistic repertoire, we can empower them to be their complete and genuine selves using their most authentic voice. Engaging in translanguaging practices while writing also facilitates students' critical thinking as they are asked to construct knowledge not only by going beyond the named languages (García & Otheguy, 2019) but also by bringing their entire knowledge and expertise to a given writing task. Because 'one cannot push or break boundaries without being critical' (García & Li, 2014: 67), translanguaging facilitates and scaffolds the development of bi/multi/plurilingual learners' criticality.

Bi/Multi/Plurilingual Students' Translanguaging During the Process of Writing

Several researchers (e.g. Bauer & Gort, 2012; Bauer *et al.*, 2017; Gort, 2012; Machado & Hartman, 2019; Soltero-Gonzalez & Butvilofsky, 2016) have provided evidence for García *et al.*'s (2017) contention that bilingual students employ translanguaging during the writing process. For instance, Gort (2012) discovered that Spanish-bilingual first graders in a dual-language classroom strategically employed both languages through oral translanguaging to discuss and revise their writing. Specifically, one student engaged in 'bilingual metacognitive statements'

(2012: 59) by talking to herself, moving across English and Spanish about how to revise her Spanish writing.

Other young bilingual students in Soltero-Gonzalez and Butvilofsky's (2016) and Machado and Hartman's (2019) studies employed transliteration – using the phonology from one language to write characters/letters in another language – in their writing by applying their phonetic knowledge of their heritage languages (Spanish and Urdu/Amharic, respectively) to write words in English to show how those words sound in English. According to García, Johnson and Seltzer (2017), using transliteration is an example of translanguaging, as bi/multilingual individuals employ the phonology and writing systems of their languages. Although bilingual students in these two studies provided their writing in a single language, the students used their dual-language repertoires as they engaged in bilingual interactions to carry out their writing tasks. Hence, translanguaging practices appeared during their writing process (i.e. oral translanguaging during planning and revising, employing transliteration while drafting). Past studies have provided evidence that young bilingual students utilize their knowledge of two languages in the writing process to enrich the quality of their writing. However, their composition or final production does not display the incorporation of dual languages, nor does it show any visible mixing of words or phrases from both languages (Lee & García, 2021).

By exploring the intersections of language, power and identity, Seltzer (2020) examined bilingual students' language practices in their poetry writing after teaching a critical translingual approach (Seltzer, 2019) in a secondary English Language Arts classroom. The students' poems unveiled their ideas and expressions in a way that embraced and acknowledged the fluidity and interconnectedness of their languages, resisting the idea of the hegemony of English 'through the voicing of a translingual sensibility' (2020: 297) to create meaning. In Kiramba's (2017) study, fourth-grade emergent multilinguals shared that they often faced challenges in keeping languages distinct from each other because of the pressure to keep 'the authoritarian single voicedness required by the school and the national curriculum' (2017: 115). Although the students reported the threat of single-language ideologies, which created a sense of tension in their writing process, they utilized multiple semiotic resources to achieve their communication goals through translanguaging when writing. Both Kiramba and Seltzer suggested that translanguaging process in writing can disrupt standard language ideologies and hierarchies by challenging the notion of a single correct language.

Different functions of written translanguaging

As discussed earlier in this chapter that bi/multi/plurilingual learners employ translanguaging when speaking for various purposes and functions, different functions of written translanguaging have also been observed by these students. Research indicated that bi/multi/plurilingual students engaged in written translanguaging for numerous purposes, such as to demonstrate their agency and identities (Axelrod & Cole, 2018; Machado & Hartman, 2019; Seltzer, 2020), to plan and evaluate their writing (Lee & García, 2021; Velasco & García, 2014), to express their feelings and make jokes (Jonsson, 2013), to solve problems independently (Lee & García, 2021; Velasco & García, 2014), to reduce their anxiety caused by a lack of linguistic knowledge (Adamson & Coulson, 2015; Tsai, 2022), to boost confidence and enhance self-esteem (Parmegiani, 2022), to improve organization of their ideas and arguments (Turnbull, 2019), to respect and express their heritage culture and cultural identities (García & Lee, 2022; Song *et al.*, 2022) and to tailor their language choices according to their readers by demonstrating audience awareness (Axelrod & Cole, 2018; Canagarajah, 2011; Durán, 2017; Lee, 2023b; Lee & Handsfield, 2018).

For instance, a second grader in Velasco and García's (2014) study temporarily wrote words in English as he did not know them in Korean when composing his draft in Korean. Velasco and García referred to the writing tactic employed by the student as a 'postponing' strategy (2014: 10). The bilingual writer used his problem-solving strategy through translanguaging, utilizing his entire linguistic repertoire to complete his writing task. As another example, the first-grade Spanish bilingual students in Durán's (2017) study demonstrated their audience awareness by choosing the language in which to write according to their readers' language use and proficiency level. Similarly, the multilingual students in Lee and Handsfield (2018) were also able to tailor and adapt their writing, knowing when to contextualize their use of translanguaging. They consciously identified their intended audiences and intuitively gauged the situation.

Multimodal and Social Semiotic Translanguaging in Writing

Since translanguaging refers to 'the ability of multilingual speakers to shuttle between languages, treating the diverse languages that form their repertoire as an integrated system' (Canagarajah, 2011: 401), the integratedness of communicative repertoires (Rymes, 2014) is fundamental and significant to understand how bi/multi/plurilingual speakers construct their messages. Individuals' linguistic repertoire includes languages, dialects and registers (Busch, 2012), but their communicative repertoires encompass not only the languages they speak or write but also other modes of communication, such as gestures, posture, artifacts, signs, facial expressions, clothing choices and other non-verbal cues, to actively engage and meaningfully contribute in various social groups or multiple communities they participate (Rymes, 2010, 2014). Effective communication is inherently multifaceted and includes a complex interplay of various elements, as people use a combination of multimodal communication methods, not relying solely on spoken words to convey messages and understand meaning.

As speakers' communicative repertoires include both linguistic and other non-verbal semiotic resources, the focus should be on how people use their communicative repertoires in an integrated manner, noting that the linguistic repertoire is only one mode of communication to deliver information and make meaning. Kress (1997, 2003, 2010) indeed called for a transcendence of the pervasiveness of print-only forms of text by including a wide range of semiotic and multimodal resources. Since multiple languages and cultures intersect in today's diverse world, it demands the use of various semiotic resources in multimodal texts. As we identify ideas and meanings from linguistic structure, visual information also guides us in understanding how messages are delivered, which facilitates our comprehension of the visual representation of social dynamics (Kress & van Leeuwen, 2001).

The notion of translanguaging enables us to view an individual's entire set of linguistic and non-linguistic resources as a unified system (Busch, 2012), rather than treating them as separate or distinct entities. Translanguaging also encourages us to recognize that individuals develop knowledge and construct meaning through diverse linguistic and semiotic resources (Tai & Li, 2024). Since translanguaging 'reconceptualizes language as a multilingual, multisemiotic, multisensory and multimodal resource for sense- and meaning-making' (Li, 2018: 22), language users activate, assemble and orchestrate their multilingual, multimodal, multisensory and multi-semiotic repertoires (Hua et al., 2017). Within a translanguaging space (Li, 2011, 2018), which is transformative and offers the possibility to create 'new configurations of language practices' (Hua et al., 2017: 412), speakers actively leverage their diverse linguistic abilities and utilize their dynamic multimodalities and semiotic resources to effectively communicate with different audiences in achieving various goals.

According to a monolingual orientation, people should speak a single, widely understood language with consistent rules that prioritize a dominant language but devalue other linguistic variations (Canagarajah, 2013). However, when viewed through a multimodal social semiotic lens, translanguaging recognizes that language is not just words but rather a part of a broader set of tools people use to communicate and create specific social, cultural, historical and political meanings (Li, 2018). Thus, bi/multi/plurilingual speakers' translanguaging practices should be understood and analyzed from a multimodal social semiotic perspective (Kress, 2010; Kress & van Leeuwen, 2006) in which languages are part of a more expansive repertoire of multimodal resources and a larger toolkit for creating meaning. From this multimodal social semiotic lens, bi/multi/plurilingual speakers are viewed as 'sign makers [who] employ, create, and interpret different kinds of signs to communicate across contexts and participants and perform their subjectivities' (Kress, 2010: 14).

Translanguaging is not seen as a static system; rather, it emphasizes learners' fluid integration of meaning-making resources to communicate (García & Li, 2014; Pierson & Grapin, 2021). Pennycook (2017) denotes explicitly that translanguaging includes the incorporation of 'semiotic assemblages' (2017: 278), which refers to the dynamic and fluid process of using various multimodal resources (such as language, gestures, movement, music and images) to create and construct meaning in communication instead of exclusively solely relying on language as the primary communication source. Thus, the notion of multimodal or semiotic assemblages helps us understand how individuals employ a wide array of communication tools depending on different localities, situations, audiences and/or contexts by bringing their various experiences, knowledge and social/cultural backgrounds to create a unique sense-making event for communication (Curiel & Ponzio, 2021; Pennycook, 2017).

Trans-Semiotizing through a Translanguaging Lens

By emphasizing the connection between linguistic (i.e. spoken and written language) and other semiotic resources (e.g. gestures, bodily movement, visuals images and artifacts), Lin (2015, 2018) coined the term 'trans-semiotizing' as a theoretical framework to analyze how the use of multiple languages and dynamic semiotic resources creates meaning. Lin (2018: 11) argued that trans-semiotizing through a translanguaging lens enables bi/multi/plurilingual learners to sustain the 'uninterrupted flow of meaning-making with their emotional involvement and momentum in extending their understanding of the world'. Trans-semiotizing is considered more encompassing and comprehensive than translanguaging because translanguaging 'indexes the central role of linguistic resources in bi/multilingual communication, [whereas] trans-semiotizing gives primacy to the full range of semiotic resources that make up the semiotic repertoire of meaning-makers' (Valencia, 2022: 181). That is, trans-semiotizing denotes the act of moving fluidly between different semiotic resources, which includes not just linguistic modality (i.e. both spoken and written language) but also other modes of communication, maximizing bi/multi/plurilingual learners' engagement and learning potential in the classroom (Lin, 2015, 2018; Valencia, 2022).

In trans-semiotizing theory, both the verbal and the iconic (Kress & Van Leeuwen, 2001; Mills, 2015) are blended and integrated into the process of making meaning in this complex world (Harman, 2018; Mora, 2019; Mora et al., 2022). Bi/multi/plurilingual learners engage in trans-semiotizing practices that involve combining multiple languages and diverse semiotic funds in complex sense-making situations, which emphasizes the connection between language and other modes of communication (Lin, 2018). This implies the importance of multimodal features for communication in the learning context and further suggests a disruption to traditional notions of languages that often fail to incorporate diverse forms of communication (Blommaert *et al.*, 2019). By recognizing the importance of multimodal features for communication, scholars seek to integrate translanguaging, transmodal and trans-semiotizing practices, challenging the conventional understanding of language that solely includes spoken or written languages but often omits diverse semiotic funds and multimodal resources (Blommaert *et al.*, 2019; Curiel & Ponzio, 2021).

Trans-semiotizing is a new approach to understanding bi/multilingualism in a globalized world, viewing it not just as the ability to speak multiple languages but also as a dynamic process where individuals creatively blend and leverage various semiotic resources to communicate effectively across different contexts. Trans-semiotizing moves away from the assumptions such as 'homogeneity, stability and boundedness' (Blommaert & Rampton, 2011: 3). Instead, the notion of trans-semiotizing refers to the concept of analyzing language not as a standalone system but as interwoven with other semiotic features, essentially viewing communication as a holistic process where multiple modes of meaning-making work together to produce a richer and more comprehensive understanding of a message. Thus, trans-semiotizing conceptualizes how language and other semiotic resources interact and intertwine in human interaction and communication (Harman, 2018; Mora, 2019; Mora *et al.*, 2022).

Korean bilingual students' written translanguaging practices

Canagarajah (2011) recommended that researchers investigate the translanguaging process by analyzing how and why bilingual students employ translanguaging while writing rather than documenting translanguaging as a finished product (i.e. what they produce). Consistent with Canagarajah's call for research on students' translanguaging processes, my colleague and I (Lee & García, 2021) conducted a functional analysis of Korean bilingual first-graders' written translanguaging to investigate how they implement translanguaging for their writing tasks in a heritage language classroom. To categorize the function of the students' written translanguaging practices, we employed a coding framework that we had previously developed when analyzing oral translanguaging practices by the same bilingual student group (see the section 'Purpose of Korean Bilingual Students' Oral Translanguaging' in this chapter). The following four functions were identified in the students' written translanguaging:

sociolinguistic competence, metalinguistic awareness, metacognitive insight and sociocultural understanding.

The subcategories that emerged for sociolinguistic competence were observed when the Korean bilingual students (1) expressed their bilingual identities, (2) considered their perceived audiences, (3) utilized their dual lexicons and (4) showed quicker word retrieval in their dominant language. The subcategories that emerged for metalinguistic awareness were when the students (1) were aware of their language choice and use, (2) understood similarities and differences between the two languages and (3) purposefully regulated and controlled their language use. The only subcategory for metacognitive insight was when students resolved a writing problem through meta-talk (i.e. verbal reflection on their writing) (Swain, 2010). Lastly, the subcategories that emerged for sociocultural understanding were when the students referenced people or cultural activities that were specifically related to Korea(n). The following section displays the students' dynamic translanguaging practices when they engaged in writing.

Written Translanguaging for Sociolinguistic Competence. The students' translanguaging in writing often functioned as sociolinguistic knowledge as they seamlessly drew upon their entire linguistic repertoires to create written content, ensuring clear communication with their readers. Figure 4.1 illustrates how one of the first-grade students (Yuri) utilized her dual lexicon, comprising both Korean and English, to ensure her readers' understanding.

As shown, Yuri composed her diary entry using both languages. It was discovered that Yuri wrote her diary in Korean first and then rewrote all the sentences in English using the spaces between the lines. It is revealed that she translanguaged by translating what she had written in Korean into English because she wanted to ensure her readers'

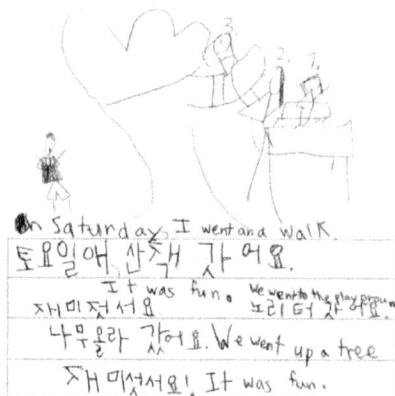

Figure 4.1 Utilizing dual lexicon through translanguaging to ensure reader's understanding

understanding. Yuri explained during the interview that she decided to translate what she had written in Korean to English again by stating, 'I was not sure about my Korean writing, so I rewrote them in English. If I make mistakes in Korean but rewrite them in English, people can know what I write about.' Yuri's statement suggests that she leveraged her linguistic knowledge of English to improve the quality of her Korean writing for her potential readers. Yuri was able to access and use words and sentences from both languages she was proficient in, effectively drawing from her mental storage of vocabulary in each language and identifying different sentence structures to communicate with her audiences.

Written Translanguaging for Metacognitive Insight. The students' translanguaging in writing functioned as a metacognitive insight when they engaged in inner speech during or after writing to evaluate and problem-solve their writing. For instance, Joon (first grader) engaged in oral translanguaging when he evaluated his written work through self-talk. When Joon read aloud his Korean writing, he noticed that he had forgotten to write the object in the following sentence: 'Dragonflies eat --- [three hyphens indicate the forgotten object] and they can fly.' (The original sentence was written in Korean, but it has been translated into English). Joon talked to himself in English, exclaiming, 'Oh, I forgot. Small insects. They eat small insects.' He verbalized the object he had missed (i.e. small insects) in his draft using English, but he added the words in Korean (i.e. 조그만 벌레 [small insects]) using the margin in the text. The type of translanguaging Joon implemented in this example – i.e. his English verbalization to his Korean composition through meta-talk – appeared to involve his 'dual-modal mental translation' (Lee & García, 2021: 11). In other words, by reflecting on his thought process about his writing (i.e. meta-talk), Joon was able to identify a key element that was missing from his written work, demonstrating his metacognitive insight, which ultimately enabled him to complete his writing with precision and accuracy.

Written Translanguaging for Metalinguistic Awareness. The students' translanguaging while writing also demonstrated their metalinguistic awareness as they were able to regulate or control their language use by being aware of their language choice and linguistic knowledge. For instance, Nari's (first grader) written translanguaging was often characterized by transliteration as she employed English phonology to write English words using Korean letter characters. Her transliteration mainly occurred when she wrote English proper nouns (e.g. her American friends' names) and English words that do not have corresponding counterparts in Korean (e.g. playdate). Nari understood that she needed to provide her writing in Korean to the maximum degree. During the interview, Nari said that 'I know that I should be writing in Korean because this is writing for my Korean class.' Her response implies that she identified the language she needed to use, primarily depending on the context and purpose of the communication. Thus, her use of transliteration demonstrated her metalinguistic awareness (i.e. her ability to consciously reflect on and control her language use) beyond her sociolinguistic competence (i.e. her linguistic skills in both languages) when writing.

Utilizing trans-semiotizing for multimodal communication

The Korean bilingual students used the trans-semioticity and translanguaging of their repertoires by drawing upon various linguistic resources and combining different modes of communication from both languages and cultural backgrounds to communicate and create meaning effectively. In one of my studies (Lee, 2023b), where I explored first- and third-grade Korean bilingual students' written translanguaging performance, the findings revealed that both graders created multimodal texts that combined linguistic and visual elements (i.e. writing, drawings and including symbols) to create a more comprehensive and engaging story.

Figure 4.2 displays one of the first graders' (Joon) multimodal text when he wrote about his three wishes, and his writing piece includes trans-semiotizing and translanguaging. As shown, Joon primarily composed his text using Korean but incorporated the English words 'zoo' and 'gold' in his Korean sentences, indicating he utilized his linguistic repertoires from both languages. Similarly, when he drew each of his wishes, he provided the text labels both in English (for the words 'zoo', 'gold' and 'My house') and in Korean (when referring to his family members: '아빠' [dad], '엄마' [mom] and '누나' [older sister]) around his drawing.

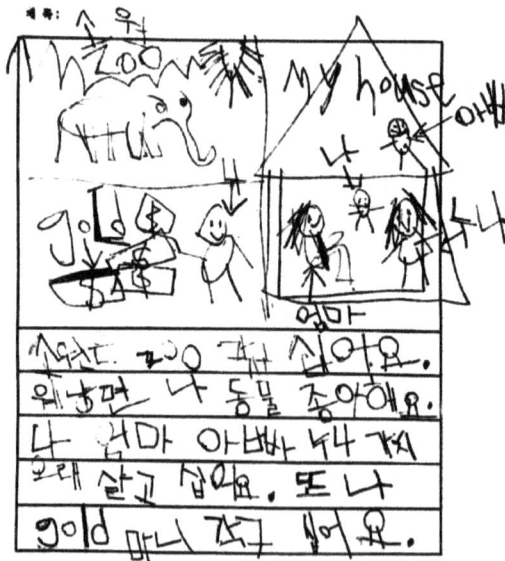

Figure 4.2 Multimodal text creation including trans-semiotizing and translanguaging

Using Korean to refer to his immediate family members was similarly observed when analyzing his oral translanguaging, which was discussed earlier in this chapter and demonstrated his sociocultural understanding. In his drawing, Joon included the US dollar sign ('$') next to the image of gold to explain what he drew was a high-priced object. Joon stated in the interview that 'I drew gold, but they just look like bricks. So, I wrote the dollar sign to show that gold is expensive.' Joon's drawing, featuring the currency symbol and annotated text label, clarifies the message he intended to convey, thereby enhancing the reader's understanding. By using a variety of communication modes (i.e. writing, inserting text labels, drawing and adding symbols), Joon utilized his full linguistic and semiotic resources in his composition to better express his ideas and construct meaning, which appears to be richer and more complex than relying solely on written language.

Figure 4.3 displays one of the third grader's (Suji) multimodal journal entries that accompanied her illustrations capturing her experiences during her family trip to New York City. As displayed, she provided text labels in English around her drawings ('Rockefeller Center', 'Legos', 'Lego Friends' and 'skates'). As shown, the first three English words are proper nouns, and the last one is an English loanword. It is worth noting that Korean speakers are more likely to directly incorporate English proper nouns and English loanwords into their Korean speech when communicating. Although Suji's written text included those English loanword and proper nouns, she wrote them by employing transliteration (i.e. converting the English phonetics of the English loanword and proper

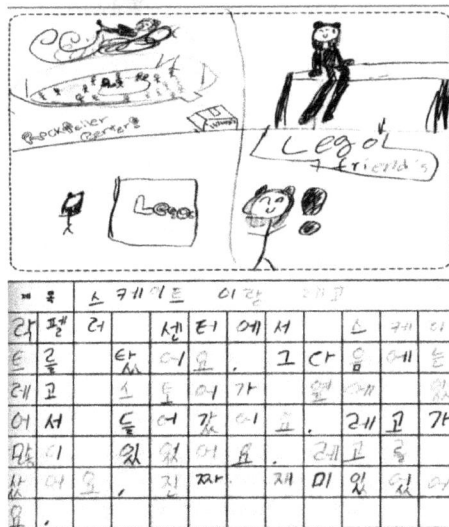

Figure 4.3 Multimodal journal entry using translanguaging and transliteration

nouns to Korean pronunciations to write them using the Korean letter characters). During the interview, Suji explained that she was aware that writing should be completed in Korean, stating: 'I know that I should write my diary in Korean because this is Korean homework. That's why I wrote them (the English loanword and proper nouns) using Korean.' Her statements suggest that she consciously chose her language, being aware of the context in which she should use it and selecting the most appropriate linguistic resources in each situation. Her journal entry, which incorporated both linguistic and visual elements, created a richer narrative as she combined her complex linguistic abilities using transliteration.

Implications for Educational Practice of Empowering Students' Translanguaging Practices

As an increasing number of empirical research has demonstrated that bi/multi/plurilingual students' everyday translanguaging is a natural language process and practice (Li, 2018), this chapter emphasizes that translanguaging was not solely the teacher's pedagogical strategy but also bi/multi/plurilingual learners' normal and natural practices to maximize their communicative potential. The bilingual students' oral and written language use in this chapter insinuates the importance of including literacy instruction to sanction a safe translanguaging space to connect to bi/multi/plurilingual students' full linguistic repertoire, liberate their voices and facilitate their critical thinking (García & Kleifgen, 2019; Sánchez et al., 2018). As the Korean bilingual students' translanguaging performance showcased their bilingual identities and bicultural knowledge, their translanguaging practices suggest that they utilized their bilingual idiolects (Li, 2018) when learning, comprehending and delivering their thoughts both orally and in a written form. Hence, educators must keep in mind that translanguaging is a co-constructed, dialogic approach that involves both teachers and students actively engaging in it, allowing students to move seamlessly between languages to maintain an effective communication flow in learning contexts (Wang, 2019).

As this chapter displayed and discussed the Korean bilingual learners' translanguaging, transmodal and trans-semiotizing practices, educators should be aware that bi/multi/plurilingual learners fully employ the multiple linguistic repertoires and diverse semiotic resources they possess in their complex meaning- and sense-making processes. This implies the importance of not only enhancing the interconnected nature of these various sign systems but also disrupting traditional notions of languages that often exclude incorporating diverse forms of communication (Blommaert et al., 2019). By recognizing the importance of multimodal features for communication, educators are encouraged to design their instructional lessons that integrate diverse semiotic funds and multimodal meaning-making resources, allowing them to understand and document each learner's complex and dynamic translanguaging, transmodal and trans-semiotizing practices.

References

Adamson, J. and Coulson, D. (2015) Translanguaging in English academic writing preparation. *International Journal of Pedagogies and Learning* 10 (1), 24–37. https://doi.org/10.1080/22040552.2015.1084674.

Alamillo, L., Yun, C. and Bennett, L.H. (2017) Translanguaging in a Reggio-inspired Spanish dual-language immersion programme. *Early Child Development and Care* 187 (3–4), 469–486.

Almér, E. (2017) Children's beliefs about bilingualism and language use as expressed in child-adult conversations. *Multilingua* 36 (4), 401–424.

Arizpe, E. (2013) Meaning-making from wordless (or nearly wordless) picture books: What educational research expects and what readers have to say. *Cambridge Journal of Education* 43 (2), 1–14. https://doi.org/10.1080/ 0305764X.2013.767879.

Arreguín-Anderson, M.G., Salinas-Gonzalez, I. and Alanis, I. (2018) Translingual play that promotes cultural connections, invention, and regulation: A LatCrit perspective. *International Multilingual Research Journal* 12 (4), 273–287. https://doi.org/10.1080/19313152.2018.1470434.

Axelrod, Y. (2014) "Ganchulinas" and "Rainbowli" colors: Young multilingual children play with language in head start classroom. *Early Childhood Educational Journal* 45, 103–110. https://doi.org/10.1007/s10643-014-0631-z.

Axelrod, Y. and Cole, M.W. (2018) 'The pumpkins are coming … .Vienen las Calabazas … .that sounds funny': Translanguaging practices of young emergent bilinguals. *Journal of Early Childhood Literacy* 18 (1), 129–153.

Baker, C. (2011) *Foundations of Bilingual Education and Bilingualism* (5th edn). Multilingual Matters.

Barbour, S. (2002) Language, nationalism, and globalism: Educational consequences of changing patterns of language use. In P. Gubbins and M. Holt (eds) *Beyond Boundaries: Language and Identity in Contemporary Europe* (pp. 11–18). Multilingual Matters.

Bauer, E. and Gort, M. (eds) (2012) *Early Biliteracy Development: Images of How Young Bilinguals make Use of their Linguistic Resources*. Routledge.

Bauer, E.B., Presiado, V. and Colomer, S. (2017) Writing through partnership: How emergent bilinguals foster translanguaging. *Journal of Literacy Research* 49 (1), 10–37.

Bergroth, M. and Palviainen, Å. (2017) Bilingual children as policy agents: Language policy and education policy in minority language medium early childhood education and care. *Multilingua* 36 (4), 375–399. https://doi.org/10.1515/multi-2016-0026.

Blommaert, J. and Rampton, B. (2011) Language and superdiversity. *Diversities* 13, 1–20.

Blommaert, J., García, O., Kress, G., Larsen-Freeman, D., Adami, E. and Sherris, A. (2019) Communicating beyond diversity: A bricolage of ideas. In A. Sherris and E. Adami (eds) *Making Signs, Translanguaging Ethnographies: Exploring Urban, Rural and Educational Spaces* (pp. 9–35). Multilingual Matters.

Busch, B. (2012) The linguistic repertoire revisited. *Applied Linguistics* 33 (5), 503–523. https://doi.org/10.1093/applin/ams056.

Canagarajah, A.S. (2011) Codemeshing in academic writing: Identifying teachable strategies of translanguaging. *The Modern Language Journal* 95 (3), 401–417.

Canagarajah, A.S. (2013) Negotiating translingual literacy: An enactment. *Research in the Teaching of English* 48 (1), 40–67.

Crawford, J. (2004) *Educating English Learners. Language Diversity in the Classroom* (5th edn). Bilingual Educational Services, Inc.

Creese, A. and Blackledge, A. (2010) Translanguaging in the bilingual classroom: A pedagogy for learning and teaching? *The Modern Language Journal* 94 (1), 103–115. https://doi.org/10.1111/modl.2010.94.issue-1.

Curiel, L.C. and Ponzio, C.M. (2021) Imagining multimodal and translanguaging possibilities for authentic cultural writing experiences. *Journal of Multilingual Education
Research* 11 (6), 79–102.

Durán, L. (2017) Audience and young bilingual writers: Building on strengths. *Journal of
Literacy Research* 49 (1), 92–114. https://doi.org/10.1177/1086296x16683420.

Durán, L. and Palmer, D. (2014) Pluralist discourses of bilingualism and translanguaging
talk in classrooms. *Journal of Early Childhood Literacy* 14, 367–388. https://doi.org
/10.1177/1468798413497386.

García-Mateus, S. and Palmer, D. (2017) Translanguaging pedagogies for positive identities in two-way dual language bilingual education. *Journal of Language, Identity, &
Education* 6(4), 245–255. Routledge. https://doi.org/10.1080/15348458.2017.1329016.

García, G. and Lee, C. (2022) Case studies of Korean-American first-graders' home
language use and written translanguaging: Pedagogical implications for EFL/ESL
contexts. In Z. Camlibel (ed.) H*andbook of the Development of Skills in English as a
Second/Foreign Language*. Pegem Academy.

García, O. (2011) Educating New York's bilingual children: Constructing a future from
the past. *International Journal of Bilingual Education and Bilingualism* 14, 133–153.

García, O. and Kleifgen, J.A. (2010) *Educating Emergent Bilinguals: Policies, Programs,
and Practices for English Learners*. Teachers College Press.

García, O. and Kleifgen, J.A. (2019) Translanguaging and literacies. *Reading Research
Quarterly* 55 (4), 553–571. https://doi.org/10.1002/rrq.286.

García, O. and Li, W. (2014) *Translanguaging: Language, Bilingualism and Education*.
Palgrave Macmillan Pivot.

García, O., Makar, C., Starcevic, M. and Terry, A. (2011) The translanguaging of Latino
kindergarteners. In K. Potoski and J. Rothman (eds) *Bilingual Youth: Spanish in English Speaking Societies* (pp. 33–55). John Benjamins.

García, O., Johnson, S.I. and Seltzer, K. (2017) *The Translanguaging Classroom: Leveraging Student Bilingualism for Learning*. Caslon.

García, O. and Otheguy, R. (2019) Plurilingualism and translanguaging: Commonalities
and divergences. *International Journal of Bilingual Education and Bilingualism* 23 (1),
17–35. https://doi.org/10.1080/13670050.2019.1598932.

Gort, M. (2012) Code-switching patterns in the writing-related talk of young emergent
bilinguals. *Journal of Literacy Research* 44 (1), 45–75.

Gort, M. and Pontier, R.W. (2012) Exploring bilingual pedagogies in dual language preschool classrooms. *Language and Education* 27. https://doi.org/10.1080/09500782
.2012.697468.

Gort, M. and Sembiante, S.F. (2015) Navigating hybridized language learning spaces
through translanguaging pedagogy: Dual language preschool teachers' languaging
practices in support of emergent bilingual children's performance of academic discourse. *International Multidisciplinary Research Journal* 9 (1), 7–25.

Harman, R. (ed.) (2018) *Bilingual Learners and Social Equity: Critical Approaches to Systemic Functional Linguistics*. Springer.

Hopewell, S. and Abril-Gonzalez, P. (2019) ¿Por qué estamos codeswitching? Understanding language use in a second-grade classroom. *Bilingual Research Journal* 42 (1),
105–120. https://doi.org/10.1080/15235882.2018.1561554.

Hornberger, N.H. (2005) Opening and filling up implementational and ideological spaces
in heritage language education. *The Modern Language Journal* 89 (4), 605–609.

Howard, E.R., Lindholm-Leary, K.J., Rogers, D., Olague, N., Medina, J., Kennedy, B.,
Sugarman, J. and Christian, D. (2018) *Guiding Principles for Dual Language Educa-
tion* (3rd edn). Center for Applied Linguistics, Dual Language Education of New
Mexico, and Santilla.

Hua, Z., Li, W. and Lyons, A. (2017) Polish shop (ping) as translanguaging space. *Social
Semiotics* 27 (4), 411–433.

Jakobson, R. (1960) Closing statement: Linguistics and poetics. In A.S. Thomas (ed.) *Style in Language* (pp. 350–377). The MIT Press.

Jiménez, R.T., David, S., Fagan, K., Risko, V.J., Pacheco, M., Pray, L. and Gonzales, M. (2015) Using translation to drive conceptual development for students becoming literate in English as an additional language. *Research in the Teaching of English* 49 (3), 248–271.

Jönsson, K. (2013). Translanguaging and multilingual literacies: Diary-based case studies of adolescents in an international school. *International Journal of the Sociology of Language* 224, 85–117.

Kiramba, L.K. (2017) Translanguaging in the writing of emergent multilinguals. *International Multilingual Research Journal* 11 (2), 115–130.

Kirsch, C. (2017) Young children capitalising on their entire language repertoire for language learning at school. *Language, Culture and Curriculum* 31 (1), 39–55. https://doi.org/10.1080/07908318.2017.1304954.

Kirsch, C. (2018) Dynamic interplay of language policy, beliefs and pedagogy in a nursery class in Luxembourg. *Language and Education* 32, 444–461.

Kirsch, C. (2020) Opening minds to translanguaging pedagogies. System 92. Special issue. *Translanguaging as a Challenge for Language Teachers* 92, 1–11.

Kirsch, C. and Mortini, S. (2023) Engaging in and creatively reproducing translanguaging practices with peers: A longitudinal study with three-year-olds in Luxembourg. *International Journal of Bilingual Education and Bilingualism* 26 (8), 943–959.

Kress, G. (1997) *Before Writing: Rethinking the Paths to Literacy*. Routledge.

Kress, G. (2003) *Literacy in the New Media Age*. Routledge.

Kress, G. (2010) *Multimodality: A Social Semiotic Approach to Contemporary Communication*. Routledge.

Kress, G. and Van Leeuwen, T. (2001) *Multimodal Discourse: The Modes and Media of Contemporary Communication*. Edward Arnold.

Lee, C. (2020) Functions of translanguaging performed by Korean American emergent bilinguals. *International Journal of Elementary Education* 9 (3), 50–59.

Lee, C. (2021) *Understanding the Oral and Written Translanguaging Practices of Emergent Bilinguals: Insights from a Korean Heritage Language Classroom in the U.S.* Routledge.

Lee, C. (2023a) Using wordless picturebooks to promote bilingual students' translanguaging. *Journal of Research in Childhood Education* 38 (1), 123–144. https://doi.org/10.1080/02568543.2023.2193258.

Lee, C. (2023b) How do children go through a heteroglossic path to becoming bilingual? Comparison of Korean children's translanguaging performance in first and third grades. *International Journal of Bilingual Education and Bilingualism* 27 (4), 612–630. https://doi.org/10.1080/13670050.2023.2232088

Lee, C. and García, G. (2020) Unpacking the oral translanguaging practices of Korean-American first graders. *Bilingual Research Journal* 43 (1), 32–49.

Lee, C. and García, G. (2021) Understanding Korean American first graders' written translanguaging practices. *Linguistic and Education* 66. https://doi.org/10.1016/j.linged.2021.100998.

Lee, A.Y. and Handsfield, L.J. (2018) Code-meshing and writing instruction in multilingual classrooms. *The Reading Teacher* 72 (2), 159–168. https://doi.org/10.1002/trtr.1688.

Li, W. (2011) Moment analysis and translanguaging space: Discursive construction of identities by multilingual Chinese youth in Britain. *Journal of Pragmatics* 43 (5), 1222–1235.

Li, W. (2018) Translanguaging as a practical theory of language. *Applied Linguistics* 39 (1), 9–30.

Lin, A. (2015) Egalitarian bi/multilingualism and trans-semiotizing in a global world. In E. Wayne, B. Sovicheth and G. Ofelia (eds) *The Handbook of Bilingual and Multilingual Education* (pp. 19–37). Wiley-Blackwell.

Lin, A. (2018) Theories of trans/languaging and trans-semiotizing: Implications for content-based education classrooms. *International Journal of Bilingual Education and Bilingualism* 22 (1), 5–16.

Lubis, R. (2018) The progress of students reading comprehension through wordless picture books. *Advances in Language and Literacy Studies* 9 (1), 48–52. https://doi.org/10.7575/aiac.alls.v.9n.1p.48.

Machado, E. and Hartman, P. (2019) Translingual writing in a linguistically diverse primary classroom. *Journal of Literacy Research* 51 (4), 480–503.

Martínez-Roldán, C.M. (2015) Translanguaging practices as mobilization of linguistic resources in a Spanish/English bilingual after-school program: An analysis of contradictions. *International Multilingual Research Journal* 9 (1), 43–58. https://doi.org/10.1080/19313152.2014.982442.

Martínez, R.A., Durán, L. and Hikida, M. (2017) Becoming "Spanish learners": Identity and interaction among multilingual children in a Spanish-English dual language classroom. *International Multilingual Research Journal* 11 (3), 167–183. https://doi.org/10.1080/19313152.2017.1330065.

McCarthey, S., Nunez, I. and Lee, C. (2020) Translanguaging across context. In M. Dressman and R. Sadler (eds) *The Handbook of Informal Language Learning*. Wiley.

Melo-Pfeifer, S. (2015) Multilingual awareness and heritage language education: Children's multimodal representations of their multilingualism. *Language Awareness* 24 (3), 197–215. https://doi.org/10.1080/09658416.2015.1072208.

Mills, C.W. (2015) Global white ignorance. In M. Gross and L. McGoey (eds) *Routledge International Handbook of Ignorance Studies* (pp. 217–227). Routledge. https://doi.org/10.4324/9781315867762-27.

Mora, R.A. (2019) Multimodal texts and tools in preservice methods courses: From consumption to design. In A. Palalas (ed.) *Blended Language Learning: International Perspectives on Innovative Practice* (pp. 359–388). China Central Radio & TV University Press.

Mora, R.A., Tian, Z. and Harman, R. (2022) Translanguaging and multimodality as flow, agency, and a new sense of advocacy in and from the Global South. *Pedagogies: An International Journal* 17 (4), 271–281. https://doi.org/10.1080/1554480X.2022.2143089.

Otheguy, R., García, O. and Reid, W. (2015) Clarifying translanguaging and deconstructing named languages: A perspective from linguistics. *Applied Linguistics Review* 6 (3), 281–307. https://doi.org/10.1515/applirev-2015-0014.

Parmegiani, A. (2022) Translanguaging in a bilingual writing programme: The mother tongue as a resource for academic success in a second language. *Language, Culture and Curriculum* 35 (3), 290–302. https://doi.org/10.1080/07908318.2022.2050742.

Parra, M.O. and Proctor, C.P. (2021) Translanguaging to understand language. *TESOL Journal* 55, 766–794. https://doi.org/10.1002/tesq.3011.

Pennycook, A. (2017) Translanguaging and semiotic assemblages. *International Journal of Multilingualism* 14 (3), 269–282.

Pierson, A.E. and Grapin, S.E. (2021) A disciplinary perspective on translanguaging. *Bilingual Research Journal* 44 (3), 318–334.

Rymes, B. (2010) Classroom discourse analysis: A focus on communicative repertoires. In N.H. Hornberger and S.L. McKay (eds) *Sociolinguistics and Language Education* (pp. 528–546). Multilingual Matters.

Rymes, B. (2014) *Communicating Beyond Language: Everyday Encounters with Diversity.* Routledge.

Sánchez, M.T. (Maite), García, O. and Solorza, C. (2018) Reframing language allocation policy in dual language bilingual education. *Bilingual Research Journal* 41 (1), 37–51.

Sanders-Smith, S.C. and Dávila, L.T. (2019) Progressive practice and translanguaging: Supporting multilingualism in a Hong Kong preschool. *Bilingual Research Journal* 42 (3), 275–290.

Sayer, P. (2013) Translanguaging, TexMex, and bilingual pedagogy: Emergent bilingual learning through the vernacular. *TESOL Quarterly* 47 (1), 63–88.

Schwartz, M., Kirsch, C. and Mortini, S. (2020) Young children's language-based agency in multilingual contexts in Luxembourg and Israel. *Applied Linguistic Review*. https://doi.org/10.1515/applirev-2019-0050.

Seltzer, K. (2019) Reconceptualizing "Home" and "School" language: Taking a critical translingual approach in the English classroom. *TESOL Quarterly* 53 (4), 986–1007.

Seltzer, K. (2020) "My English is its own rule": Voicing a translingual sensibility through poetry. *Journal of Language, Identity & Education* 19 (5), 297–311.

Soltero-González, L. and Butvilofsky, S. (2016) The early Spanish and English writing development of simultaneous bilingual preschoolers. *Journal of Early Childhood Literacy* 16 (4), 473–497.

Song, J., Howard, D. and Olazabal-Arias, W. (2022) Translanguaging as a strategy for supporting multilingual learners' social emotional learning. *Education Sciences* 12 (7), 475. https://doi.org/10.3390/educsci12070475.

Swain, M. (2010) Talking it through: Languaging as a source of learning. In R. Batstone (ed.) *Sociocognitive Perspectives on Language Use and Language Learning* (pp. 112–130). Oxford University Press.

Tai, K.W.H. and Li, W. (2024) The affordances of iPad for constructing a technology-mediated space in Hong Kong English medium instruction secondary classrooms: A translanguaging view. *Language Teaching Research* 28 (4), 1501–1551. https://doi.org/10.1177/13621688211027851.

Tian, Z. (2022) Challenging the 'Dual': Designing translanguaging spaces in a Mandarin-English dual language bilingual education program. *Journal of Multilingual and Multicultural Development* 43 (6), 534–553. https://doi.org/10.1080/01434632.2022.2085732.

Toth, J. and Paulsrud, B. (2017) Agency and affordance in translanguaging for learning: Case studies from English-medium instruction in Swedish schools. In B. Paulsrud, J. Rosén, B. Straszer and Å. Wedin (eds) *New Perspectives on Translanguaging and Education* (pp. 189–207). Multilingual Matters.

Tsai, S.C. (2022) Chinese students' perceptions of using Google Translate as a translingual CALL tool in EFL writing. *Computer Assisted Language Learning* 35 (5/6), 1250–1272.

Turnbull, B. (2019) Translanguaging in the planning of academic and creative writing: A case of adult Japanese EFL learners. *Bilingual Research Journal* 42 (2), 232–251. https://doi.org/10.1080/15235882.2019.1589603.

Valencia, J.A. (2022) Trans-semiotizing and re-sourcing resources in language education. In N. Miranda, A. de Mejía and S. Valencia (eds) *Giraldo Language Education in Multilingual Colombia*. Routledge.

Velasco, P. and García, O. (2014) Translanguaging and the writing of bilingual learners. *Bilingual Research Journal* 37 (1), 6–23. https://doi.org/10.1080/15235882.2014.893270.

Vogel, S. and García, O. (2017) Translanguaging. *Oxford Research Encyclopedia of Education*. Oxford University Press.

Wang, D. (2019) Translanguaging in Chinese foreign language classrooms: Students and teachers' attitudes and practices. *International Journal of Bilingual Education and Bilingualism* 22 (2), 138–149.

5 Embracing Culturally Responsive and Sustaining Pedagogy

Incorporating Multicultural Literature to Provide Equitable and Just Educational Experiences

In a second-grade classroom, the class reads the contemporary realistic fiction book This Next New Year *(Wong, 2000), which portrays Korean traditions and how Koreans celebrate the Lunar New Year (also known as Korean New Year). In the story, the Mexican child says that the Korean New Year is her favorite holiday. Another child in the storyline, who is half French and half German, also mentions that he celebrates the Korean New Year. A student in my class named Juho stated, 'I don't think they know about Korean New Year because I have some friends from Mexico, and they didn't seem to know.' When I responded to him by asking, 'They might have learned in school...?' Juho disagreed and answered, 'We learned about Halloween and Christmas. But, no, we didn't learn anything about Korea. My friends don't know about Korean holidays.' Then, another student, Sky, shared, 'I wish we celebrated the Korean New Year in my American school. It would be great if we did both Korean and American holidays.'*

***

This vignette suggests that Korean American students have insufficient opportunities to learn about their heritage cultures because of the pervasive Eurocentric perspective in their mainstream schools and the absence of Korean or Korean American representation in their school materials. However, according to current projections, the percentage of school-attending children who identify as White is expected to decline steadily, while the proportion of students from each minority ethnic group is projected to increase over time (National Center for Education Statistics, 2024). As schools are experiencing a significant increase in diversity, classroom teachers are now more likely to encounter racially, culturally and linguistically diverse (RCLD) students from a wide range of backgrounds in their classrooms. Thus, it is imperative for educators to design and provide curricula that reflect students' diverse cultural and linguistic backgrounds, ensuring that they see themselves represented in the curriculum and learn about the different cultures around them. Scholars demonstrated the power of asset-based or strengths-based pedagogies to improve student engagement and academic achievement, especially for students from historically marginalized communities. Nevertheless, these pedagogies are still not widely incorporated in practice.

Introduction to the Chapter

The purpose of this chapter is to discuss pedagogical interventions and innovations as a means of supporting equitable and unbiased educational experiences for students, enabling them to continue refining and transforming education. This chapter begins by briefly explaining resource pedagogies and introduces theoretical models of culturally relevant/responsive/sustaining pedagogy. Next, the merits of incorporating multicultural literature into the school curriculum are discussed. Then, the chapter highlights the positive roles of multicultural children's literature by showcasing how Korean American students respond to diverse topics and various social, racial, cultural and political issues from a wide range of perspectives and experiences when engaging in literature discussions and writing activities after reading culturally conscious books. A concluding remark at the end of the chapter highlights some of the teaching implications derived from the theoretical insights and study findings.

Approaches to Pedagogical Interventions and Innovations

In the mid-1990s, educational researchers sought pedagogical interventions and innovations that would embrace linguistic and cultural diversity and establish guidelines for racially, culturally and linguistically marginalized students (i.e. African American, Latino/a and Hispanic American, Indigenous or Native American, Asian American and Pacific Islander American students) (Lee, 1995; McCarty & Zepeda, 1995; Moll & Gonzalez, 1994; Paris, 2012; Valdés, 1996). Scholars sought to resist and disrupt the deficit approaches that viewed language, literacy and cultural practices exclusively based on White, middle-class norms because this deficit view positioned languages and cultures outside the norm as subordinate, unsuitable or ineligible in US schools and society. Paris (2012: 93) pointed out that the goal of deficit approaches in the past was 'to eradicate the linguistic, literate, and cultural practices many students of color brought from their homes and communities and to replace them with what was viewed as superior practices'.

In contemporary education, however, it is crucial to view the linguistic and cultural backgrounds of minority students as equally valuable to the dominant language and culture of the school. Educators must recognize and value the languages and cultural practices brought by students of color, treating them as equally important and relevant as the dominant culture represented in the school. Specifically, marginalized students should be regarded as valuable assets who can significantly contribute to the overall learning experiences, for instance, by bringing different perspectives, unique knowledge and valuable insights gained from their diverse lived experiences that can enrich the classroom environment for all students, rather than viewing them as someone to be assimilated to the dominant culture or blend in with the white social group. It is crucial for educators to create an inclusive learning environment where all students are valued for their diverse backgrounds, unique experiences and different perspectives.

The Benefits of Resource Pedagogies

Resource pedagogies, which are also known as asset-based pedagogies or strengths-based teaching, resist deficit perspectives and honor students' language, literacy and cultural practices as valuable assets (McCarty & Lee, 2014; Reyes & Norman, 2021). As educational researchers and scholars have endeavored to address educational inequities and narrow the opportunity gap between students from the dominant language and culture and those who have been historically marginalized, resource pedagogies have been largely supported in teacher education programs in the US (Goodwin et al., 2014; Henry et al., 2013). When exploring resource pedagogies, linguistic and cultural practices of marginalized groups can be recognized as valuable sources of knowledge and understanding by honoring their funds of knowledge (i.e. resources such as language, community knowledge and cultural heritage) in facilitating their academic learning and enriching their overall emotional, psychological and physical well-being.

By resisting deficit-oriented beliefs, policies and traditional school practices, resource pedagogies take an asset-based perspective of cultural and linguistic differences as they view cultural, linguistic and literacy practices and knowledge of students from diverse communities as key contributors. Hence, educational researchers and scholars have strived to implement resource pedagogies, such as multicultural education, culturally relevant or responsive teaching and culturally sustaining or revitalizing instruction, to address educational inequities and narrow the opportunity gap between students from dominant communities and those from historically marginalized groups.

Recognizing and Valuing Funds of Knowledge

The term 'funds of knowledge' was coined by Luis Moll and his associates (1992: 133), which refers to 'the historically accumulated and culturally developed bodies of knowledge and skills essential for household or individual functioning and well-being'. Funds of knowledge help educators see the rich resources, assets, knowledge and skills that students derive from outside school (e.g. households and communities), and these funds of knowledge can be incorporated into the classroom to support and enhance students' educational experiences (González et al., 2005). Tapping into the funds of knowledge of culturally and linguistically diverse students and families serves as a medium to create more relevant and engaging learning experiences in the classroom by valuing, embracing and capitalizing on students' overall sets of abilities and experiences. Yet, knowledge and skills that students acquire from their households and communities are less likely to be acknowledged or recognized in school if teachers come from different social-cultural backgrounds than their students. Therefore, teachers need to actively seek out, learn about and incorporate students' and their families' funds of knowledge into the classroom to ensure inclusive learning.

The objectives of funds of knowledge are three-fold: (1) to facilitate academic performance of students who are from underrepresented racial, ethnic and cultural groups; (2) to develop relationships with their families by building mutual trust; and (3) to perform curriculum innovation and instructional transformation by incorporating students' assets, knowledge and skills they acquire from outside school within the curriculum and school practice (González et al., 2005; Rios-Aguilar et al., 2011). Educators should know that students' funds of knowledge are essential cultural practices and bodies of knowledge that are embedded in their daily exercises and routines of families. Using a funds of knowledge approach in teaching can establish social relationships with families by learning about the specific knowledge, skills and experiences students possess within their home lives, which need to be used to mediate and support their learning in the classroom.

Culturally and Linguistically Relevant and Responsive Pedagogy

As many teacher education programs are committed to pursuing social justice and equity, their focus has shifted to preparing prospective teachers in ways that support equitable and just educational experiences for all students (Ryan & Grieshaber, 2024). Since multiple terms and different names have been used by scholars and researchers over the past few decades to indicate culturally appropriate instruction, terms like culturally relevant teaching and culturally responsive pedagogy have become ubiquitous when discussing teaching in diverse classrooms (Paris, 2012).

Gloria Ladson-Billings (1994, 1995) formulated a theoretical model of Culturally Relevant Pedagogy (CRP). She proposed a theory of culturally focused pedagogy that can reform curriculum and instructional practices in teacher education. Ladson-Billings (1995: 13) defined CRP as 'a pedagogy that empowers students intellectually, socially, emotionally, and politically by using cultural and historical references to convey knowledge, to impart skills, and to change attitudes'. Ladson-Billings' culturally relevant pedagogy aims to help students achieve academic achievement, demonstrate cultural competence and develop critical consciousness. She highlighted 'cultural competence' as the practice of supporting students in sustaining their cultural heritage and language practices while simultaneously gaining access to the dominant culture. When discussing 'critical consciousness', Ladson-Billings emphasized the ability to challenge the status quo and solve real-world problems by taking a critical stance and praxis-oriented approach.

Geneva Gay (2018) used the term 'culturally responsive pedagogy' to describe 'the use of cultural knowledge, prior experiences, frames of references, and performance styles of ethnically diverse students to make learning encounters more relevant to and effective for them' (2018: 31). Gay's study, which included underachieving African American, Latinx, Asian and Native American students and implemented culturally responsive pedagogy, showed positive student achievement data, which in turn encouraged educators to support and adopt culturally responsive instruction. Gay discovered five key elements of culturally responsive pedagogy; they are (1) developing a knowledge base about cultural diversity, (2) including cultural and ethnic diversity content in the curriculum, (3) demonstrating caring and building learning communities, (4) communicating with ethnically diverse students and (5) responding to ethnic diversity in the delivery of instruction. Similar to what Ladson-Billings (1994, 1995) argued in favor of implementing culturally relevant pedagogy, Gay claimed that teachers need to facilitate the academic achievement and engagement of racially and ethnically diverse students by incorporating students' lived experiences and cultural values that are personally relevant and meaningful into their curricula.

Sharroky Hollie (2012), who accentuated individuals' language aspect beyond their cultural aspect, used the term 'Cultural and Linguistic Responsiveness' (CLR), which refers to 'the validation and affirmation of the home culture and home language for the purposes of building and bridging the student to success in the culture of academia and mainstream society' (2012: 23). According to Hollie, while the term 'culture' encompasses a wide range of elements within a society, one's linguistic identity is often hidden or overlooked; thus, the linguistic aspect should be explicitly included when discussing culturally responsive practices. For Hollie, since language is a crucial aspect of human identity, and linguistic identity plays a pivotal role in identifying one's overall identity, 'the intentionality of the language focus is demonstrated as equal to what we typically consider as culture' (2012: 25). Hollie's CLR encompasses students' cultural and linguistic experiences by emphasizing their unique language identities.

Culturally Sustaining Pedagogy

Django Paris (2012) addressed that although teachers and educational researchers have been inspired by the ideas of culturally relevant and responsive teaching to facilitate students' academic achievement, cultural competence and critical consciousness, the terms 'relevant' and 'responsive' do not ensure retaining of the languages and cultures of RCLD students in the classrooms. According to Paris, making instructional curricula 'relevant' and 'responsive' to students' cultures does not guarantee support for the maintenance of their heritage languages and cultural practices. Paris asserted that culturally relevant or responsive teaching does not sufficiently and adequately promote 'the linguistic and cultural dexterity and plurality' (2012: 95) in this demographically diverse society.

Paris (2012), thus, argued for the need for culturally sustaining pedagogy, which aims to 'perpetuate and foster – to sustain – linguistic, literate, and cultural pluralism as part of the democratic project of schooling' (2012: 95). Paris proposed the term culturally 'sustaining' pedagogy as an alternative because it preserves and maintains the existence of a plurilingual and pluricultural society. For Paris, the meaning of culturally sustaining pedagogy is more than responsive or relevant to the lived experiences and cultural practices of RCLD students, as it supports individuals in sustaining the linguistic competence and cultural practices of their communities while simultaneously providing access to the dominant culture. Paris pointed out that the existing teaching practices and policies in the US were not interested in sustaining the languages and cultures of underrepresented students. Paris viewed that the teaching practices and policies were being pursued from deficit perspectives, such as English-only policies, White privilege, or European imperialism. Consequently, instructional pedagogies explicitly created a monolingual and monocultural society based on Western social orders and cultural norms. Thus, Paris (2012: 96) argued that educators and researchers should not only focus on the relevance or responsiveness of culture and language but also sustain and extend the richness of modern, pluralistic society.

Using Multicultural Literature as Culturally Responsive and Sustaining Practice

One of the culturally (and linguistically) relevant/responsive/sustaining pedagogical practices educators can provide is incorporating multicultural literature into the classroom. Reading a variety of multicultural literature promotes learners' cross-cultural understanding and competence, expands their worldviews and validates their ethnic/cultural identities. Researchers have demonstrated that using multicultural literature has the potential to be culturally relevant, responsive and sustaining if teachers carefully select books and implement relevant class activities during and after reading them (Lee, 2021a, 2021b). Multicultural literature can also be linguistically sustaining if teachers encourage students to read (if available) and discuss the texts using their heritage languages or dialects (McIntyre *et al.*, 2010). It is essential to learn about the definition and characteristics of multicultural literature before exploring the benefits of including multicultural literature in the school curriculum.

Definition and Characteristics of Multicultural Literature

Multiple definitions of multicultural literature have been proposed. For instance, Kruse and Horning (1990: vii) defined it as 'works that focus on people of color'. Yet, it is the narrowest definition as it only covers racial groups. Focusing solely on racial categories has been criticized by other scholars because it endorses racial essentialism that excludes other identity categories (e.g. class, gender, sexual orientation, age, religion, disability, linguistic variation) when understanding the concept of multiculturalism (Cai, 2002). Rochman (1993) stated that multiculturalism does not merely refer to people of color or portray racial issues; rather, it encompasses the coexistence of multiple cultural characteristics and diverse backgrounds, which often extends beyond national and racial borders to embrace the richness of different social and cultural identities.

One of the most inclusive definitions of multicultural literature is 'books other than those of the dominant culture' (Austin & Jenkins, 1973: 50) since it encompasses all existing cultures other than the dominant one. Other scholars' definitions of multicultural literature show varying degrees of inclusion. For Sims Bishop (1992: 39), multicultural literature is 'by and about people who are members of groups considered to be outside the sociopolitical mainstream of the United States'. Harris's (1994: 117) definition includes various aspects of identity categories; she stated that multicultural literature 'feature[s] people of color, the elderly, gays and lesbians, religious minorities, language minorities, people with disabilities, gender issues, and concerns about class'. According to various scholars, multicultural literature encompasses a much broader spectrum than race and ethnicity, including categories like class, gender, language use, sexual orientation, age, religion and disability.

Yet, since the prefix 'multi' indicates as many as possible, scholars regarded multicultural literature as encompassing any culture, including Caucasian cultures. Fishman (1995: 79) indeed insisted that 'all literature is multicultural'. As the trend was toward inclusiveness in multiculturalism in the past, people believed that multicultural literature needed to include the White dominant culture. Shannon (1994) similarly claimed that having a separate category of literature called multicultural literature should not exist because it can perpetuate the notion that the dominant culture is the standard while other cultures are considered alien. Cai (2002: 8), however, argued that a definition of multicultural literature should 'draw a demarcation line between the literature of the dominant mainstream culture and that of marginalized cultures' because if multicultural literature includes literature of mainstream culture, the adjective 'multicultural' loses its meaning; thus, there is no reason to use a distinctive term (i.e. 'multicultural' literature) if multicultural literature could simply refer to any type of literature.

Responding to the raised concern that excluding Caucasian cultures would generate reverse racism, Cai (2002) argued that reading literature about people of color does not exclude the White group because social dominance, inequality, discrimination and/or oppression have been innately perpetrated by Whites and subjected in a White-dominated society. Accordingly, Cai believed that White individuals and their cultures or values are inherently included rather than excluded when people are engaging with stories portraying the cultures and experiences of people of color. Although scholars and researchers have suggested multiple definitions to describe multicultural literature over the past decades, Norton's (1999) definition of multicultural literature, which is 'about racial or ethnic minority groups that are culturally and socially different from the White Anglo-Saxon majority in the United States whose largely middle-class values and customs are most represented in American literature' (1999: 580) is explicit and specific enough thus widely used in the US (Cai, 2002).

Yet, it is important to note that multicultural literature encompasses not only diversity and inclusion but also addresses power dynamics and structures (Boutte *et al.*, 2021; Chaudhri & Teale, 2013; Yoo-Lee *et al.*, 2014). Since the key role of multicultural literature is to decentralize the power and privilege of dominant cultures, the goal of using multicultural literature is to achieve social justice and equity by transforming the existing social order and dismantling systemic inequalities to give voice and authority to the marginalized groups who are deeply entrenched in a given society (Banks, 2016; Cai, 2002; Harris, 2003; Norton, 2013; Sims Bishop, 2003). Accordingly, when providing multicultural literature, we should focus on marginalized individuals, underrepresented social groups or communities and disenfranchised cultures rather than assuming that all human beings or cultures are the same (Norton, 2013; Osorio, 2018; Sims Bishop, 1992, 2016; Yokota, 2009).

Benefits of Using Multicultural Literature

Literature that portrays diverse races, ethnicities and cultures can be a powerful instructional tool in building a culturally inclusive and relevant classroom because multicultural literature supports students in developing an understanding of various social and cultural issues from a wide range of perspectives and experiences (Brinson, 2009; Evans, 2010; Wake & Modla, 2008). Multicultural literature allows readers to reflect on their own culture and gain a broader understanding of the cultures of others by utilizing their funds of knowledge and developing cultural sensitivity through diverse perspectives (Cai, 2002; Lee, 2021a, 2021b). Hence, introducing multicultural literature to students can foster their cultural awareness and broaden their perspectives on diversity in the world (DeNicolo & Fránquiz, 2006; Gopalakrishnan, 2010).

Sims Bishop (1990, 1992) argued that multicultural literature affords readers experiences with stories that serve as 'mirrors, windows, and sliding glass doors', as they can see reflections of themselves, gain insights into the lives of people different from them, and walk into stories that showcase a variety of cultures. According to Sims Bishop, students should read books that not only reflect their own culture and experiences (i.e. literary mirrors) but also learn about the lives and experiences of others (i.e. literary windows). Through the process of seeing themselves reflected in the texts and the world around them, readers can identify similarities and differences between their world and that of others, allowing them to develop an understanding, tolerance and empathy for unfamiliar cultures and different perspectives (Lee, 2021a, 2021b).

According to Cai (2002), multicultural literature can serve as an empowering tool for students from marginalized cultures, as it not only allows them to see themselves or hear their stories reflected in the stories but also validates their experiences and cultural values within a shared cultural narrative. By encountering multicultural literature, students can develop cultural awareness, understanding and appreciation, ultimately facilitating their establishment of values related to justice and equity (Cai & Bishop, 1994). Cai (2002: 7) argued that multicultural literature can 'transform the existing social order to ensure the greater voice and authority to the marginated culture and to achieve social equality and justice among all cultures'. That is, multicultural literature challenges the norm that regards white culture as a golden standard and disrupts the dominant hegemony by addressing existing power relations and social injustices to ensure educational equity for all students (Boutte et al., 2021; Chaudhri & Teale, 2013; Yoo-Lee et al., 2014). Scholars have pointed out that multicultural literature can serve as a vehicle for addressing inequality and achieving social justice by giving voice and authority to historically underrepresented, disadvantaged or vulnerable groups (Sims Bishop, 1992).

Educational researchers advocate the merits of using multicultural literature in the school curriculum (e.g. Banks, 2016; Botelho & Rudman, 2009; Clark & Fleming, 2019; McIntyre et al., 2010; McNair, 2016; Muhammad, 2020; Price-Dennis & Sealey-Ruiz, 2021; Rodríguez, 2018; Rogers & Mosley, 2006; Souto-Manning, 2009; Souto-Manning & Martell, 2016; Steiner et al., 2008; Thomas, 2016; Vlach, 2022). Specifically, studies discovered that encountering multicultural literature encouraged children of minority groups to develop a sense of belonging, positive self-esteem and strong ethnic identities (Brinson, 2009; Hseu & Hetzel, 2000; Norton, 2013), counter inaccurate stereotypes (Evans,

2010; Koss, 2015), promote cross-cultural understanding (Steiner *et al.*, 2008), increase empathy toward others (Evans, 2010; Sarraj *et al.*, 2015; Steiner *et al.*, 2008), broaden perspectives toward diversity and cultural pluralism (Crisp *et al.*, 2016; Lehman, 2017) and identify social (in)justice (Agarwal-Rangnath, 2013; DeNicolo & Fránquiz, 2006; Fain, 2008; Monobe & Son, 2014; Picower, 2011a, 2012a).

Lack of Multicultural Literature about Asian American Protagonists

Despite the merits of using multicultural literature, literature that portrays minority cultures and experiences of people of color has been significantly underrepresented in US school curricula (Chaudhri & Teale, 2013; Crisp *et al.*, 2016; Koss, 2015). Specifically, the number of literature about Asian people or cultures is much more insufficient compared to other demographics, often leaving Asian students without seeing themselves and their culture reflected in their learning materials. According to the 2023 Cooperative Children's Book Center (CCBC) report, the percentage of children's books featuring Asian children as protagonists (10%) lags behind the representation of White characters (28%) and even books with non-human characters, such as animals or objects (20%). In addition, about 18% of children's books published in 2022 featured one Asian author or illustrator, while at least one white author created 71% of the books.

Although the number of literature about and by Asians being published has steadily and gradually increased since 2016 (CCBC, 2023), and the Asian student enrollment in school settings shows a growing percentage (Pew Research Center, 2023), scholars argue that Asian Americans are still significantly underrepresented in children's literature and US school curriculum (An, 2016; Hartlep & Scott, 2016; Lee, 2022, 2024; Rodríguez & Kim, 2018). Hence, Asian Americans are regarded as the most invisible figures among racial/cultural minority groups in the US school curriculum including children's and young adult literature (Loh-Hagen, 2014; Rodríguez & Kim, 2018; Yoo-Lee *et al.*, 2014). Due to the scarcity of multicultural Asian literature from classroom libraries, children of Asian descent have been often exposed to literature that emphasizes the dominant culture but struggled to find accurate portrayals of Asian American literature that deeply explores cultural identity, lived experiences and family dynamics from an Asian American's perspective (Lee, 2021a, 2021b, 2024; Rodríguez & An, 2024).

Korean American students in my Korean heritage language classrooms who attended mainstream schools during the week often reported that they have mainly been exposed to literature that portrays white culture. These students have strongly identified with mainstream culture but have not been given sufficient opportunities to learn about cultural diversity, including their own heritage culture. Unlike children belonging to the dominant social group who can effortlessly find literature that serves as a mirror to their lives, the students in my classroom often have access to stories that display the dominant culture (as their literary windows) but rarely find literature that reflects their cultural heritage, experiences and identities (i.e. literary mirrors) (Sims Bishop, 1990).

Incorporating Multicultural Children's Literature in a Heritage Language Classroom

After recognizing that many Korean American students in heritage language schools have had inadequate opportunities to encounter their heritage cultures and learn about cultural diversity, I conducted two empirical studies (Lee, 2021a, 2021b) with third-grade Korean American students in my classroom. I provided the class with multicultural children's literature to develop the students' understanding of diversity, inclusion and equity and to expand their worldviews through cultural competence by implementing literature discussions and writing activities after reading culturally diverse books (see Table 5.1). Throughout the semester, students were introduced to various types of multicultural picture books that feature diverse racial groups with distinctive cultures and

Table 5.1 Multicultural children's literature with relevant class activities

Title of literature (author, year)	Type and genre of the books	Class activity after reading
The Name Jar (Choi, 2003)	Northeast Asian (Korean); contemporary fiction	Drawing a Venn diagram by providing the similarities and differences between the protagonist and themselves
Moon Watchers: Shirin's Ramadan Miracle (Jalali, 2017)	Western Asian; Muslim contemporary religious fiction	Writing a letter to the protagonist
Four Feet, Two Sandals (Williams & Mohammed, 2007)	Southeast Asian (Afghanistan–Pakistan); contemporary realistic fiction	Creating a T chart by writing their wish and comparing it to that of the protagonists from the book
Friends from the Other Side (Anzaldua, 1993)	Mexican American; contemporary realistic fiction	Writing as if they were making a fictional friend
The Other Side (Woodson, 2001)	African American; historical realistic fiction	Drawing a scene and writing a story in which the protagonists travel out of the book into the present
Separate Is Never Equal (Tonatiuh, 2014)	Mexican American; historical nonfiction biography	Writing a persuasive letter to the superintendent at school from the story
Freedom Summer (Wiles, 2005)	African American; historical realistic fiction	Keeping a diary as if they were the protagonist in the story
I Am Not a Number (Dupuis & Kacer, 2019)	Indigenous People of North America (Indigenous Canadian); historical nonfiction biography	Writing a double entry journal by expressing their reactions and emotions

dynamic life experiences. I closely analyzed the students' oral discourses on diverse topics or issues raised in the stories during book discussions (Lee, 2021a) and then thoroughly examined their written responses to the writing prompts I provided after reading and discussing each literature (Lee, 2021b).

The selected multicultural literature collectively provided students with a valuable tool to deepen their understanding of their heritage culture and provide insight into the cultures, traditions and values of people from different backgrounds. Overall, nine key roles of multicultural literature were identified from both the students' oral discourse during literature discussions and their written responses when participating in in-class writing activities; they are (1) fostering positive self-esteem and identity construction, (2) respecting varied perspectives by avoiding essentialism, (3) developing intercultural awareness and competence, (4) challenging biases and stereotypes, (5) improving self-worth and increasing appreciation and gratitude, (6) developing cross-cultural friendships, (7) promoting critical consciousness and perspectives, (8) supporting strategies to cope with issues in their life and (9) facilitating sympathy and empathy.

Fostering positive self-esteem and identity construction

Multicultural literature featuring characters and experiences that closely resemble the students' cultural background helped them develop positive self-esteem as Korean Americans. When reading the picture book *The Name Jar* (Choi, 2003), which illustrates the Korean immigrant child's experience of moving to the US, the students were able to find themselves by reflecting on their lived experiences from the storyline. For instance, my question based on the story ('Do you agree with what the Korean mother says in the book? The Korean mother says, "we've moved to America doesn't mean we stop eating Korean food."') prompted the class to reflect on and connect with their Korean ethnic identity through the traditional food items.

Specifically, the students commonly stated, 'Although I live in America, I always choose Korean food instead of American food', 'I am Korean American too, but I always prefer to have Korean food' and 'I didn't miss anything when I had to come back to the U.S. after the summer break, but I missed Korean food there a lot'. Responding to my follow-up question ('Do you think food can represent your culture and your identity as Korean?'), the students shared that food can represent their heritage culture by asserting 'food is a part of my culture', 'I see myself as Korean because I eat and enjoy Korean food' and 'I am proud of being Korean because eating very spicy food doesn't make me sweat. It's a part of Asian culture thing'. As displayed, familiar topics and concepts (such as foods that are specific to students' cultural heritage) from this Korean multicultural literature helped the students develop familiarity and understanding, creating a sense of comfort, ease and confidence. As a student named Jay stated that he was 'proud of being Korean', reading books that portray students' heritage cultures can significantly boost their self-esteem and identity construction.

Respecting varied perspectives by avoiding essentialism

As a post-reading activity after reading the literature *The Name Jar* (Choi, 2003), each student was given a Venn diagram worksheet to provide similarities and differences between the Korean protagonist and themselves. When searching for different features, even from the mirror book, the students itemized differences between the protagonist and themselves. The students identified individual distinctiveness and discovered unique personal experiences that set everyone apart from one another although they belong to the same ethnic and cultural group.

Creating the Venn diagram by finding similarities and differences when encountering the mirror book helped them learn about how to respect diverse life experiences and avoid essentialism, which refers to the assumption that 'there is something identifiable ... [and] shared by all members of certain groups' (Nodelman & Reimer, 2003: 171). In other words, multicultural literature can support students to understand the complexity of identities and varied perspectives, preventing them from forming a monolithic idea or single characteristic about people from the same ethnic or cultural group.

Developing intercultural awareness and competence

Engaging in multicultural literature further assists the students in gaining awareness of different cultures and developing their understanding of diverse experiences and practices that exist across various cultural groups. Specifically, when reading the book *Moon Watchers: Shirin's Ramadan Miracle* (Jalali, 2017), the class learned about Ramadan as a religious holiday celebrated by Muslims and explored the Islamic practice of fasting. During the book discussion, the students admitted that they had not learned about other religions (beyond Christianity) or religious holidays and celebrations (except for Easter and Christmas, which are major Christian holidays).

The student named Jase stated, 'We have many kids from Mexico and some Asian kids. So, it would be great if we learned about what they do at home with their families.' Similarly, Jay shared, 'I celebrate both Korean and American holidays, but Korean ones are only at home. No one knows what we [Koreans] are celebrating, so I wish we could celebrate Korean holidays in my American school.' As shown, the students pointed out the lack of diverse cultural curricula in their American schools. The students' critical thinking indicated that they understood the importance of including diverse cultures (e.g. cultural holidays or religious practices) in developing intercultural awareness and competence. This multicultural picture book not only highlights a specific cultural or religious practice but also encourages the students to think critically about marginalized voices, enabling them to identify who is often left out of the narrative.

Challenging biases and stereotypes

Multicultural picture books also offer a crucial space for students to confront stereotypes and prejudices about different cultural and ethnic groups. The book *Four Feet, Two Sandals* (Williams & Mohammed, 2007) illustrates the hardships that refugees face in camps while seeking a safe place. Excerpt 5.1 displays the students' prejudices and stereotypes they had toward refugees before reading the book and further exhibits how their perspectives shifted after reading the story.

Excerpt 5.1 Challenging biases and stereotypes

[When only looking at the book cover before reading the book]

(1) Suzi: I knew people's lives in those camps. They flee from their countries due to wars.
(2) Jena: I watched a movie or something showing people from there.
(3) Jena: I thought that the children there were quite dangerous and fearful because they are from countries where there are wars.
(4) Suzi: I was kind of afraid of them because they looked unsafe and threatening.

[After reading the book]

(5) Jena: I think they are not intimidating at all. The girls in the story were kind to each other.
(6) Suzi: The children there look innocent and harmless to me. They are just unlucky.

Before reading the book, the students used the adjectives 'dangerous', 'fearful', 'unsafe' and 'threatening' to describe refugees (lines 3 and 4), which denotes the students' over-generalized belief and harmful stereotypes toward people in refugee camps. Yet, after reading the book, their word choices when describing refugees have been changed to 'not intimidating', 'kind to each other', 'innocent' and 'harmless' (lines 5 and 6). Encountering this multicultural book had a transformative effect on the students, shifting their initial feelings of nervousness or fearfulness into their curiosity and understanding, which broadened their perspective toward different life experiences and personal desires. The students' responses indicate that reading books about people from varied walks of life and discussing the stories can challenge and dismantle pre-existing biases and stereotypes students might hold toward others.

Improving self-worth and increasing appreciation and gratitude

Multicultural literature further led the students to improve their self-worth and self-value by enhancing appreciation and gratitude in their lives. After the class engaged in reading and discussing the book *Four Feet, Two Sandals* (Williams & Mohammed, 2007), the students were given a T-chart worksheet and asked to provide their wishes in the left column and the wishes of the refugee protagonists from the story in the right column. The students wrote their wishes such as 'having a new computer', 'having a puppy', 'buying a pretty dress' and 'going to Disney World'. Meanwhile, the students speculated the protagonists' wishes as 'finding a new and safe place to live', 'not separating from their family', 'ending the war in their country' and 'finding another pair of shoes'. The students expressed their compassion toward the protagonists by comparing their wishes to those of the characters because the protagonists' lives and situations were qualitatively different from their own. The students addressed, 'I thank you for my parents to have whatever I want to have', 'I thank God to be safe and don't have to worry about wars' and 'I appreciate that I have a house to live safely'. The storybook, along with this writing activity, helped the students improve their self-worth and self-value because comparing and identifying different kinds of wishes or desires heightened their appreciation and gratitude for what they already have in their lives.

Developing cross-cultural friendships

Engaging in multicultural literature also supported the students' development of cross-cultural friendships through their imaginative engagement with the literature as they can envision and foster friendships with people from different ethnic or racial backgrounds. After reading and discussing the African American multicultural book *The Other Side* (Woodson, 2001), which depicts the issue of segregation between White and Black people in town, the class was asked to draw a scene and create a story in which the two literary characters (White and African American girls) time-travel into the present by using their imaginations. Figure 5.1 displays Jena's writing along with her drawing.

As presented, Jena illustrated a scene in which the two protagonists, who live in her neighborhood, become best friends. Veering away from the original storyline but using her imagination, Jena reconstructed the plot by removing the segregated fence that divided the towns for White versus Black people. Jena illustrated a scene in which the three girls (the White and African American protagonists and herself as Asian) play together by holding one another's hands. Her drawing and writing imply that

Imagine the characters time travel into the present

Figure 5.1 Recreating a story in which protagonists travel out of the book into the present

she acknowledged different racial or ethnic backgrounds do not hinder friendship. Instead, she admitted that people of different races can form strong bonds and become best friends in contemporary society. As Jena's writing demonstrates, engaging in a post-reading activity after reading this type of multicultural book can help students develop a cross-cultural understanding by creating a plot of interracial harmony and unity.

Developing cross-cultural friendships

Multicultural picture books further developed the students' critical consciousness and critical eye to identify the existing unfairness, inequality and injustice in our society. The books *Freedom Summer* (Wiles, 2005) and *Separate Is Never Equal* (Tonatiuh, 2014) commonly depict racism, discrimination and segregation toward people of color (African American and Mexican American, respectively). Excerpt 5.2 displays the students' classroom discourse when encountering the scenes of racial inequality and injustice.

Excerpt 5.2 Promoting critical consciousness and perspectives

(1) Ms Lee: Do you think it is fair to treat people differently based on their skin color or race?
(2) Jay: No! It is not fair to treat people differently.
(3) Hanna: No, it is absolutely bad. But sometimes people do because they are mean, or they just think that they are better than others.
(4) Ms Lee: Why do you think people sometimes think they are better or superior to others?
(5) Suzi: We learned about the Civil War and slavery. White people made Blacks slaves at that time. That's why White people still think that they are better than Black um…and Mexican and Asian.

(6) Jena: But I think that is a very bad idea to think that way. People should not be treated differently because we are all equal.
(7) Hanna: I agree too! Actually, some Black people are smarter than White people although Whites believe that they are more intelligent than Blacks.

In this excerpt, I initiated the discussion and raised the issue of racial inequality by asking whether it is fair to treat people differently based on their racial or ethnic backgrounds. During the book discussion, the students not only stated that treating people differently based on their skin color or race was incorrect and unjust (lines 2, 3 and 5) but also argued that people should be treated equally by disagreeing with the idea of White supremacy or privilege (lines 5–7). Suzi specifically indicated how White hegemony can exclude other racial and ethnic groups. As shown, the students demonstrated their understanding of the widespread existence of inequality and injustice through a critical perspective when encountering multicultural picture books. Thus, engaging in multicultural literature can enable students to develop critical consciousness and reflection to redress societal inequities.

The students' writing samples, following their reading of the Mexican American multicultural book *Separate Is Never Equal* (Tonatiuh, 2014), also demonstrated the students' critical consciousness and a critical eye for scrutinizing societal issues. After reading the book, the class was asked to write a persuasive letter to the school superintendent who expressed racial discrimination toward Mexican American children in the storyline. The students' letters reveal that they understood the importance of pursuing equality, fairness and inclusion in school settings. The key arguments in their letters are the following: 'Everyone is equal no matter what', 'It is not fair to tell them that they can't go to the American school' and 'Everyone should be able to go to any school with any skin color and background'. Figure 5.2 displays Ethan's persuasive letter to the school superintendent.

Ethan explained the school superintendent's unfair treatment and discriminating behaviors toward the Mexican American characters by choosing the words 'rude', 'not correct', bad' and 'worst'. Ethan argued the importance of providing an equal opportunity and pointed out the danger of promoting white supremacy by writing, 'They [Mexicans] are the same as white' and 'You are teaching white kids that it is okay to be rude'. Writing a persuasive letter after reading culturally and racially conscious literature can assist students to promote their critical perspectives and develop a critical eye to view unfairness and inequality in society.

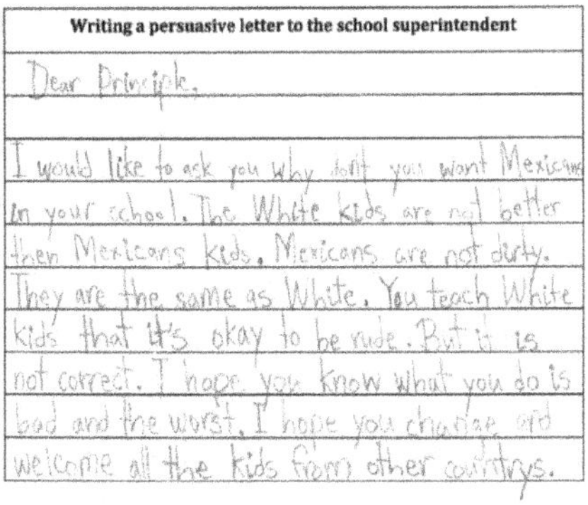

Writing a persuasive letter to the school superintendent

Dear Principle,

I would like to ask you why don't you want Mexicans in your school. The White kids are not better then Mexicans kids. Mexicans are not dirty. They are the same as White. You teach White kids that it's okay to be rude. But it is not correct. I hope you know what you do is bad and the worst. I hope you change and welcome all the kids from other countrys.

Figure 5.2 Writing a persuasive letter to the school superintendent from the story

Supporting strategies to cope with issues in life

Engaging in multicultural literature can also promote students' coping strategies to deal with potential challenges in their lives. After reading the African American multicultural book 'Freedom Summer' (Wiles, 2005), the students were asked to keep diary entries as if they were the African American protagonist in the story. Figure 5.3 displays Jase's diary entry, illustrating his coping strategy for overcoming potential obstacles he may encounter in his life as an African American.

As displayed, Jase criticized the widespread notion of white supremacy by asserting that 'some black people are smarter then [sic] white people' and then listed several African American heroes' names (i.e. Martin Luther King Jr and the former President Obama). Jase then came up with his coping strategy to overcome a possible challenge by stating, 'I will study harder to become a smart person so that no one can ignore or bully me'. This creative writing activity, following the reading of multicultural literature, supported Jase in upholding his coping plan and developing positive coping mechanisms to handle challenges and manage difficult situations that may arise in his life.

Facilitating sympathy and empathy

Multicultural picture books additionally advanced the students' abilities to demonstrate sympathy and empathy toward other racial and cultural groups. The Indigenous Canadian multicultural picture book *I Am Not a Number* (Dupuis & Kacer, 2019) enabled the students to develop empathy for people who are different from themselves. Reading the story from the Indigenous girl's perspective significantly increased the students' understanding and compassion toward the emotions and experiences of the Indigenous children in the story. After reading the book, the students were asked to write a double-entry journal, providing their personal reactions, emotions and connections to the selected scenes. I selected and

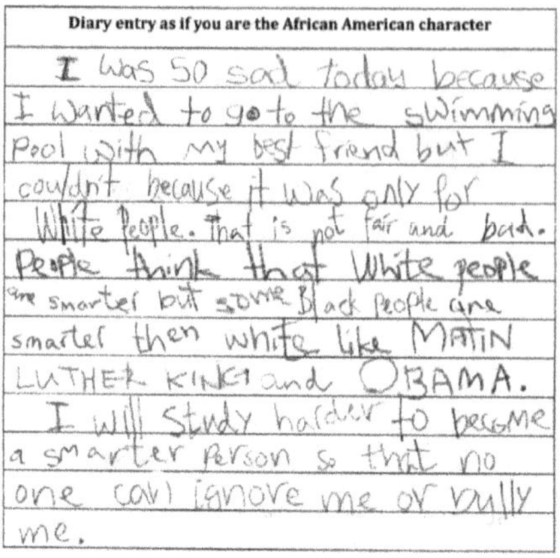

Diary entry as if you are the African American character

I was so sad today because
I wanted to go to the swimming
pool with my best friend but I
couldn't because it was only for
White people. That is not fair and bad.
People think that White people
are smarter but some Black people are
smarter then white like MARTIN
LUTHER KING and OBAMA.
I will study harder to become
a smarter person so that no
one can ignore me or bully
me.

Figure 5.3 Keeping a diary by becoming the protagonist in the story

provided quotes from the harsh scenes in the left column (i.e. when the Indigenous Canadian protagonist is treated inhumanely by the teacher at the residential school), and the students were asked to express their authentic and sincere thoughts and feelings in the right column of their double-entry journal. As an example, Hanna's responses in her double-entry journal are displayed in Figure 5.4.

As presented, Hanna expressed her reactions and empathic responses by writing, 'I am mad and upset', 'My heart really hurts' and 'I actually feel her pain'. It appears that reading the story from the

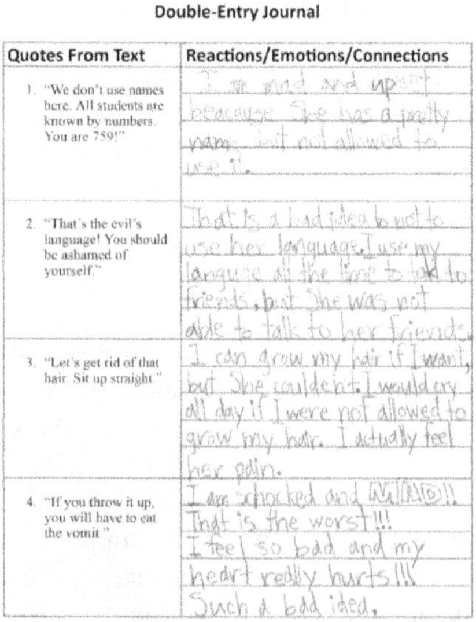

Double-Entry Journal

Quotes From Text	Reactions/Emotions/Connections
1. "We don't use names here. All students are known by numbers. You are 759!"	I am mad and upset because she has a pretty name but not allowed to use it.
2. "That's the evil's language! You should be ashamed of yourself."	That is a bad idea not to use her language. I use my language all the time to talk to friends, but she was not able to talk to her friends.
3. "Let's get rid of that hair. Sit up straight."	I can grow my hair if I want, but she couldn't. I would cry all day if I were not allowed to grow my hair. I actually feel her pain.
4. "If you throw it up, you will have to eat the vomit."	I am shocked and WOW!!! That is the worst!!! I feel so bad and my heart really hurts!!! Such a bad idea.

Figure 5.4 Writing a double-entry journal

protagonist's perspective enhanced Hanna's ability to gauge the literary character's emotions and feelings. Hanna further made personal connections to the main character by connecting to her own life and comparing different daily life experiences. Hanna was able to better grasp the feelings of the Indigenous characters, which led to a greater ability to empathize and show compassion toward people from different racial or cultural backgrounds. Multicultural literature can foster students' sympathy and empathy toward other children, as they come to understand that every child, regardless of their race, ethnicity, language spoken or cultural heritage, deserves respect and appreciation for their unique identities.

Implications for Educational Practice of Implementing Culturally Conscious Multicultural Literature

Many educators and educational researchers actively seek a teaching method that leverages students' diverse social and cultural knowledge and experiences to help them succeed academically and feel affirmed in their identities. It is essential for educators to foster positive social change by actively encouraging students to develop a critical eye and thinking skills that enable them to analyze and challenge existing inequalities, injustices and power dynamics within a society still significantly influenced by white dominance. As this chapter suggested the benefits of adopting and implementing resource pedagogies (or asset-based teaching) for RCLD student groups, educators are expected to consider providing culturally relevant, responsive, sustaining and revitalizing instruction to honor students' language, literacy and cultural practices as valuable assets, resisting deficit-oriented beliefs, policies and traditional school practices.

Specifically, my empirical study findings in this chapter demonstrated that implementing culturally responsive instruction using various collections of multicultural literature acted as a powerful teaching resource and pedagogical tool for the Korean American students, for instance, to develop intercultural competence, cultivate critical consciousness, challenge their biases and stereotypes and facilitate empathy toward others. As demonstrated from the students' oral and written responses, classroom teachers should understand that pairing literature discussions and a variety of writing activities with multicultural books can be beneficial for students to deeply engage with the materials, develop their critical insights and gain a richer understanding of complex issues within our pluralistic society.

Educators also need to acknowledge that they can significantly enhance students' understanding of different cultures and perspectives by carefully and judiciously choosing high-quality multicultural texts and following them up with thoughtful discussions and activities that are well-related and connected to their students' diverse experiences and viewpoints. By incorporating diverse perspectives into their curriculum, implementing social justice-oriented practices in their actual teaching and adopting a critical stance to create engaged classrooms, teachers can foster a more inclusive and equitable classroom environment where all students feel valued and have equal opportunities to participate and thrive. Classroom teachers must consider different cultural, linguistic and literacy experiences and practices students from diverse communities bring with them as rich and valuable funds of knowledge.

Children's Literature Bibliography

Anzaldúa, G., illus. Consuelo Mendez (1993) *Friends from the Other Side. Amigos del otro lado*. Children's Book Press.

Choi, Y., illus. Yangsook Choi (2003) *The Name Jar*. Dragonfly Books.

Dupuis, J. and Kacer, K., illus. Gillian Newland (2019) *I Am Not a Number*. Second Story Press.

Jalali, R., illus. Anne S. O'Brian (2017) *Moon Watchers: Shirin's Ramadan Miracle*. Tilbury House Publishers.

Tonatiuh, D., illus. Tonatiuh Duncan (2014) *Separate Is Never Equal*. Abrams Books for Young Readers.

Wiles, D., illus. Jerome Lagarrigue (2005) *Freedom Summer*. Aladdin Paperbacks.

Williams, K. and Mohammed, K., illus. Doug Chayka (2007) *Four Feet, Two Sandals*. Eerdmans Books for Young Readers.

Wong, J. (2000) *This Next New Year*. Pomelo Books.

Woodson, J., illus. E.B. Lewis (2001) *The Other Side*. Putnam Juvenile.

References

Agarwal-Rangnath, R. (2013) *Social Studies, Literacy, and Social Justice in the Common Core Classroom*. Teachers College Press.

An, S. (2016) Asian Americans in American history: An AsianCrit perspective on Asian American inclusion in state U.S. history curriculum. *Theory & Research in Social Education* 44 (2), 244–276.

Austin, M.C. and Jenkins, E. (1973) *Promoting world Understanding through Literature, K–8*. Libraries Unlimited.

Banks, J.A. (2016) *Cultural Diversity and Education: Foundation, Curriculum, and Teaching* (6th edn). Routledge.

Bishop, R.S. (1990) Mirrors, windows, and sliding glass doors. *Perspectives: Choosing and Using Books for the Classroom* 6 (3), ix–xi. https://scenicregional.org/wp-content/uploads/2017/08/Mirrors-Windows-and-Sliding-Glass-Doors.pdf.

Bishop, R.S. (1992) Children's books in a multicultural world: A view from the USA. In E. Evans (ed.) *Reading against Racism* (pp. 18–38). Open University Press.

Bishop, R.S. (1997) Selecting literature for a multicultural curriculum. In V. Harris (ed.) *Using Multiethnic Literature in the K–8 Classroom* (pp. 1–19). Christopher-Gordon.

Bishop, R.S. (2003) Reframing the debate about cultural authenticity. In D. Fox and K. Short (eds) *Stories Matter: The Complexity of Authenticity in Children's Literature* (pp. 25–40). National Council of Teachers of English.

Bishop, R.S. (2016) A ride with Nana and CJ: Engagement, appreciation, and social action. *Language Arts* 94 (2), 120–123.

Botelho, M. and Rudman, M. (2009) *Critical Multicultural Analysis of Children's Literature: Mirrors, Windows, and Doors*. Routledge.

Boutte, G.S., King, J.E., Johnson, G.L. and King, L.J. (2021) *We Be Lovin' Black Children. Learning to Be Literate about the African Diaspora*. Myers Education Press.

Boyd, F.B. (2003) Experiencing things not seen: Educative events centered on a study of Shabanu. *Journal of Adolescent and Adult Literacy* 46 (6), 460–474.

Brinson, S.A. (2009) African American literature. In N.A. Anderson (ed.) *Elementary Children's Literature: Infancy through Age 13* (pp. 181–185). Allyn & Bacon.

Cai, M. (2002) *Multicultural Literature for Children and Young Adults: Reflections on Critical Issues*. Greenwood Press.

Cai, M. and Bishop, R.S. (1994) Multicultural literature for children: Towards a clarification of the concept. In A.H. Dyson and C. Genishi (eds) *The Need for Story: Cultural Diversity in Classroom and Community* (pp. 57–71). National Council of Teachers of English.

Chaudhri, A. and Teale, W. (2013) Stories of multicultural experiences in literature for children, ages 9–14. *Children's Literature in Education* 44, 359–376.

Clark, A. and Fleming, J. (2019) "They almost become the teacher": Pre-K to third grade teachers' experiences reading and discussing culturally relevant texts with their students. *Reading Horizons: A Journal of Literacy and Language Arts* 58 (3), 23–51.

Colby, S. and Lyon, A. (2004) Heightening awareness about the importance of using multicultural literature. *Multicultural Education* 11, 24–28.

Cooperative Children's Book Center (2023, April 3) 2023 CCBC diversity statistics: Press release and media kit. https://ccbc.education.wisc.edu/literature- resources/ ccbc-diversity-statistics/.

Crisp, T., Knezek, S., Quinn, M., Bingham, G., Girardeau, K. and Starks, F. (2016) What's on our bookshelves? The diversity of children's literature in early childhood classroom libraries. *Journal of Children's Literature* 42 (2), 29–42.

DeNicolo, C. and Fránquiz, M. (2006) 'Do I have to say it?': Critical encounters with multicultural children's literature. *Language Arts* 84 (2), 157–170.

Evans, S. (2010) The role of multicultural literature interactive read-alouds on student perspectives toward diversity. *Journal of Research in Innovative Teaching* 3 (1), 88–100.

Fain, J.G. (2008) "Um, they weren't thinking about their thinking": Children's talk about issues of oppression. *Multicultural Perspectives* 10 (4), 201–208.

Fishman, A.R. (1995) Finding ways in: Redefining multicultural literature. *English Journal* 84 (6), 73–79.

Gay, G. (2018) *Culturally Responsive Teaching: Theory, Research, and Practice* (3rd edn). Teacher Press College.

González, N., Moll, L.C. and Amanti, K. (2005) *Funds of Knowledge: Theorizing Practices in Households, Communities, and Classrooms*. Lawrence Erlbaum Associates.

Goodwin, A., Smith, L., Souto-Manning, M., Cheruvu, R., Tan, M.Y., Reed, R. and Taveras, L. (2014) What should teacher educators know and be able to do? Perspectives from practicing teacher educators. *Journal of Teacher Education* 65 (4), 284–302.

Gopalakrishnan, A. (2010) *Multicultural Children's Literature: A Critical Issues Approach*. Sage Publications.

Harris, V. (1994) Historic readers for African-American children (1868–1944): Uncovering and reclaiming a tradition of opposition. In M.J. Shujaa (ed.) *Too much Schooling, Too Little Education: A Paradox of Black Life in White Societies* (pp. 143–178). Africa World Press.

Harris, V. (2003) The complexity of debates about multicultural literature and cultural authenticity. In D. Fox and K. Short (eds) *Stories Matter: The Complexity of Authenticity in Children's Literature* (pp. 116–134). National Council of Teachers of English.

Hartlep, N. and Scott, D. (2016) *Asian/American Curricular Epistemicide: From Being Excluded to Becoming a Model Minority*. Sense Publishers.

Henry, H., Campbell, S., Thompson, C., Patriarca, L., Luterbach, K., Lys, D. and Covington, V.M. (2013) The predictive validity of measures of teacher candidate programs and performance: Towards an evidence-based approach to teacher preparation. *Journal of Teacher Education* 64 (5), 439–453.

Hollie, S. (2012) *Culturally and Linguistically Responsive Teaching and Learning: Classroom Practices for Student Success.* Shell Education Publishing.

Hseu, M. and Hetzel, J. (2000) *Bridging the Cultural Divide through Multicultural Children's Literature.* http://buddies.org/articles/Literature.html.

Koss, M.D. (2015) Diversity in contemporary picturebooks: A content analysis. *Journal of Children's Literature* 41 (1), 32–42.

Kruse, G.M. and Horning, K.T. (1990) Looking into the mirror. Considerations behind the reflections. In M.V. Lindgren (ed.) *The Multicolored Mirror: Cultural Substance in Literature for Children and Young Adults.* Highsmith.

Ladson-Billings, G. (2014) Culturally relevant pedagogy 2.0: The remix. *Harvard Educational Review* 84 (1), 74–84.

Ladson-Billings, G. (1995) Toward a theory of culturally relevant pedagogy. *American Educational Research Journal** 32 (3), 465–491.

Landt, S.M. (2006) Multicultural literature and young adolescents: A kaleidoscope of opportunity. *Journal of Adolescent & Adult Literacy* 49 (8), 690–697.

Lee, C.D. (1995) A culturally based cognitive apprenticeship: Teaching African American high school students' skills in literary interpretation. *Reading Research Quarterly* 30 (4), 608–631.

Lee, C. (2021a) Exploring multicultural children's literature in a heritage language classroom. *Children's Literature in English Language Education* 9 (1), 32–56.

Lee, C. (2021b) Third-grade students' written responses to multicultural children's literature during post-reading activities. *The Dragon Lode* 39 (2), 14–26.

Lee, C. (2022) How can multicultural children's literature be utilized in the classroom to facilitate transnational students to be border-crossers? *Journal of Multilingual and Multicultural Development* 45 (5), 1717–1731. https://doi.org/10.1080/01434632.2021.2020802.

Lee, C. (2024) Sanctioning a space for literacy practices to promote transnational students' identity development in a HL classroom. *International Multilingual Research Journal* 19 (1), 1–22. https://doi.org/10.1080/19313152.2024.2309695.

Lehman, C.L. (2017) Multicultural competence: A literature review supporting focused training for preservice teachers teaching diverse students. *Journal of Education and Practice* 8 (10), 109–116.

Liang, L., Parsons, L. and Crisp, T. (2017) Diverse children's literature at the university. *Journal of Children's Literature* 43 (1), e5–e10.

Loh-Hagen, V. (2014) A good year for Asian American children's literature. *The California Reader* 47 (3), 40–45.

Louie, B. (2005) Development of empathetic responses with multicultural literature. *International Reading Association* 48, 566–578.

McCarty, T. and Lee, T. (2014) Critical culturally sustaining/revitalizing pedagogy and Indigenous education sovereignty. *Harvard Educational Review* 84 (1), 101–124.

McCarty, T.L. and Zepeda, O. (1995) Indigenous language education and literacy: Introduction to the theme issue. *Bilingual Research Journal* 19 (1), 1–4. https://doi.org/10.1080/15235882.1995.10668587.

McIntyre, E., Hulan, N. and Layne, V. (2010) Reading instruction for diverse populations. In E. McIntyre, N. Hulan and V. Layne *Reading Instruction for Diverse Classrooms: Research-Based, Culturally Responsive Practice* (pp. 1–19). Guilford Publications.

McNair, J.C. (2016) #WeNeedMirrorsAndWindows: Diverse classroom libraries for K-6 libraries. *The Reading Teacher* 70 (3), 375–381.

Moll, L.C. and González, N. (1994) Lessons from research with language-minority children. *Journal of Reading Behavior* 26 (4), 439–456.

Moll, L., Amanti, C., Neff, D. and González, N. (1992) Funds of knowledge for teaching: Using a qualitative approach to connect homes and classrooms. *Theory into Practice* 31, 132–141.

Monobe, G. and Son, E.H. (2014) Using children's literature and drama to explore children's lives in the context of global conflicts. *The Social Studies* 105 (2), 69–74.

Muhammad, G. (2020) *Cultivating Genius: An Equity Framework for Culturally and Historically Responsive Literacy*. Scholastic Teaching Resources.

National Center for Education Statistics (2024) Racial/Ethnic enrollment in public schools. Condition of education. U.S. Department of Education, Institute of Education Sciences. https://nces.ed.gov/programs/coe/indicator/cge.

Nodelman, P. and Reimer, M. (2003) *Pleasures of Children's Literature* (3rd edn). Allyn and Bacon.

Norton, D.E. (1999) *Multicultural Children's Literature: Through the Eyes of Many Children* (1st edn). Allyn & Bacon/Pearson.

Norton, D.E. (2013) *Multicultural Children's Literature: Through the Eyes of Many Children* (4th edn). Pearson.

Norton, D.E. and Norton, S. (2003) *Through the Eyes of a Child: An Introduction to Children's Literature* (6th edn). Pearson.

Osorio, S. (2018) Multicultural literature as a classroom tool. *Multicultural Perspectives* 20 (1), 47–52.

Paris, D. (2012) Culturally sustaining pedagogy: A needed change in stance, terminology, and practice. *Educational Researcher* 41 (3), 93–97. https://doi.org/10.3102/0013189x12441244.

Pew Research Center (2023) Discrimination experiences shape most Asian Americans' lives. https://www.pewresearch.org/race-ethnicity/2023/11/30/discrimination-experiences-shape-most-asian-americans-lives/.

Picower, B. (2011a) Learning to teach and teaching to learn: Supporting the development of new social justice educators. *Teacher Education Quarterly* 38 (4), 7–24.

Picower, B. (2012a) Teacher activism: Enacting a vision for social justice. *Equity and Excellence in Education* 45 (4), 561–574.

Price-Dennis, D. and Sealey-Ruiz, Y. (2021) *Advancing Racial Literacies in Teacher Education: Activism for Equity in Digital Spaces*. Teachers College Press.

Reyes, A. and Norman, T. (2021) Resource pedagogies and the evolution of culturally relevant, responsive, and sustaining education. In M.F. He and W. Schubert (eds) *The Oxford Encyclopedia of Curriculum Studies*. Oxford University Press. .

Rios-Aguilar, C., Kiyama, J.M., Gravitt, M. and Moll, L. (2011) Funds of knowledge for the poor and forms of capital for the rich? A capital approach to examining funds of knowledge. *Theory and Research in Education* 9, 163–184.

Rochman, H. (1993) Against borders. *Journal of Youth Services in Libraries* 6 (4), 420–423.

Rodríguez, N.N. (2018) From margins to center: Developing cultural citizenship education through the teaching of Asian American history. *Theory & Research in Social Education* 46 (4), 528–573.

Rodríguez, N.N. and An, S. (2024) Perspectives on practice: Celebrating AAPI heritage month is not enough: A guide to centering Asian American histories and narratives. *Language Arts* 101 (5), 350–357.

Rodríguez, N.N. and Kim, E. (2018) In search of mirrors: An Asian critical race theory content analysis of Asian American picturebooks from 2007 to 2017. *Journal of Children's Literature* 44 (2), 17–30.

Rogers, R. and Mosley, M. (2006) Racial literacy in a second-grade classroom: Critical race theory, whiteness studies, and literacy research. *Reading Research Quarterly* 41 (4), 462–495. https://doi.org/10.1598/RRQ.41.4.3.

Ryan, S. and Grieshaber, S. (2024) Early childhood teacher education for social justice and equity: A systematic literature review. *International Journal of Early Years Education* 32 (3), 768–790.

Sarraj, H., Bene, K., Li, J. and Burley, H. (2015) Raising cultural awareness of fifth grade students through multicultural education. *Multicultural Education* 22 (2), 39–45.

Shannon, P. (1994) I am the cannon: Finding ourselves in multiculturalism. *Journal of Children's Literature* 20 (1), 1–15.

Short, K. and Fox, D. (2007) Debates about cultural authenticity in books for children. In Y. Goodman and P. Martens (eds) *Critical Issues in Early Literacy* (pp. 219–234). Erlbaum.

Souto-Manning, M. (2009) Negotiating culturally responsive pedagogy through multicultural children's literature: Towards critical democratic literacy practices in a first grade classroom. *Journal of Early Childhood Literacy* 9 (1), 50–74. https://doi.org/10.1177/1468798408101105.

Souto-Manning, M. and Martell, J. (2016) *Reading, Writing, and Talk: Inclusive Teaching Strategies for Diverse Learners, K–2*. Teachers. College Press.

Steiner, S.F., Nash, C.P. and Chase, M. (2008) Multicultural literature that brings people together. *Reading Teacher* 62 (1), 88–92.

Thomas, E.E. (2016) Stories still matter: Rethinking the role of diverse children's literature today. *Language Arts* 94 (2), 112–119.

Valdés, G. (1996) *Con Respeto: Bridging the Distances between Culturally Diverse Families and Schools: An Ethnographic Portrait*. Teachers College Press.

Vlach, S.K. (2022) Elementary literacy teachers change the underlying story through transformative read-aloud curricula. *Journal of Children's Literature* 48 (1), 12.

Wake, D.G. and Modla, V.B. (2008) Using multicultural literature to teach culturally responsive instructional approaches. *College Reading Association Yearbook* 29, 179–200.

Yokota, J. (2009) Learning through literature that offers diverse perspectives: Multicultural and international literature. In D. Wooten and B. Cullinan (eds) *Children's Literature in the Reading Program: An Invitation to Read* (pp. 66–73). International Literacy Association.

Yoo-Lee, E., Fowler, L., Adkins, D., Kim, K. and Davis, H.N. (2014) Evaluating cultural authenticity in multicultural picture books: A collaborative analysis for diversity education. *Library Quarterly: Information, Community, Policy* 84 (3), 324–347.

6 Exploring Transnational and Transcultural Identity Construction in Distinctive Transnational Lifeworld

In a fifth-grade classroom, I developed the Transnational Literacy Unit, which comprizes lessons that integrate reading and writing activities using various types of transnational literature that reflect the dynamics of globalization in storylines, exploring themes that transcend national boundaries, cultures and languages. I consciously select four pieces of literature that align with themes related to transnationalism, allowing me to provide a safe and identity-affirming environment through relevant literature. When the class reads the literature Somewhere Among (Donwerth-Chikamatsu, 2016), I led the discussion by pointing out the scene where the Japanese American protagonist shapes her multiple identities, reading aloud, 'I am one foot here, one foot there between two worlds, Japan and America. Binational, bicultural, bilingual, and biracial.' I ask the class whether they understand what the lines say. A student named Emma responds, 'Yes, I think it describes me. I stand between Korea and America. I live in America but visit Korea often. I travel a lot.' Ben similarly states, 'That's me. I am bilingual and bicultural because I use two languages and celebrate two cultures, Korean and American.' After the class learns that the prefix 'tri' indicates three, Sunny mentions, 'Then, I am "tricultural" and "trilingual". I know Vietnamese culture and how to speak Vietnamese.'

✳✳✳

This vignette demonstrates that students who are bilingual, multilingual or multicultural can construct their multifaceted identities and build a richer understanding of themselves by recognizing, valuing and integrating their diverse linguistic and cultural backgrounds into their overall sense of self. Indeed, a growing body of literature has emerged that explores the educational practices within border regions for transmigrant children, who engage in vibrant living experiences as they negotiate and cultivate their multi-layered identities by reflecting on their transnational and transcultural experiences. Despite an increasing number of transmigrant students, literacy practices focused on transnationalism

– encompassing reading, writing and discussing experiences or discursive practices that cross national borders – are not sustained or endorsed by public schools in the US because literacy in transnational contexts is not emphasized in mainstream curricula and standards. Nevertheless, literacy in cross-cultural contexts is a vital skill in today's interconnected world. Thus, scholars seek to find a way to embrace students' varied experiences, practices and cultures by incorporating diverse perspectives into the curriculum and leveraging students' unique social/cultural backgrounds to develop transnational literacy skills.

Introduction to the Chapter

This chapter begins by reviewing the concepts of transnationalism and transculturalism in a globalized world to understand how students in transnational and transcultural contexts develop the richness and depth of their cultural lifeworld. The chapter discusses the benefits of implementing border pedagogy by including transnational literacies, which illustrate recurring border-crossing experiences and practices of individuals who move across both physical and metaphorical borders. Then, the chapter displays how Korean American transnational students become border-crossers when engaging in transnational children's literature. Next, the literary artifacts of a multi-ethnic Asian American student are explored in more detail toward the end of the chapter to illuminate how an Asian American transnational student constructed and negotiated her dynamic and multifaceted identities.

Globalization and Modern Diasporas in the Contemporary World

The term 'globalization' gained popularity in the 1980s, as technological advances made it easier to conduct international transactions. 'Globalization' is a term used to describe how trade and technology have made the world a more connected and interdependent place. Globalization is the process of increasing interaction and integration between people, companies and governments worldwide, encompassing the economic and social transformations that result from this interconnectedness. As globalization describes 'transcontinental or interregional flows of networks and activity' (Held *et al.*, 2000: 16), it has been amplified by the unimpeded movement of people, goods, services, capital, technology and information across national and cultural borders, facilitating economic interdependence between countries. Due to globalization, culture has become increasingly permeable; therefore, there is no single culture that remains pure. As Beyer (2007: 98) pointed out, 'all people on earth living in a single social space'; these de-territorialized global flows bring people in diaspora communities (i.e. (im)migrants and expatriates) to shape fluid and ambivalent identities (Appadurai, 1996).

Diasporas refer to people who have dispersed from their countries of origin to seek better economic opportunities or due to sociopolitical reasons. International Migration Law (2019: 49) defines diasporas as 'migrants or descendants of migrants, whose identity and sense of belonging have been shaped by their migration experience and background'. Although some diasporas (e.g. the Jewish and Greek diasporas) predated globalization (Cohen, 1996), globalization has strengthened diasporas, leading to a growing number of people identifying as diasporic. Since diasporas have grown in tandem with globalization, diasporas and globalization are responsively related. The vibrant and dynamic aspects of globalization have had an impact on international and multinational movements, and globalization has expanded and embodied the social activities and cultural practices of transnational or transcultural individuals (Elteren, 2011; Morrell, 2008; Robins, 2006). Accordingly, transnationalism and transculturalism became essential aspects of diaspora studies.

Transnationalism and Transculturalism in an Interconnected and Borderless World

Transnationalism refers to the social processes through which transnational immigrants engage in intercultural and sociopolitical activities that connect their homelands and the host country (Giroux, 2005; Lam, 2004; Vertovec, 2001). Schiller *et al.* (1992: 1) defined transnationalism as 'the processes by which immigrants build social fields that link together their country of origin and their country of settlement'. Transnational immigrants refer to individuals who expatriate to or reside in host countries while maintaining close social, cultural, political, economic and/or religious connections with their countries of origin (Guerra, 1998; Hornberger, 2007; Orellana, 2016). Thus, transmigrants sustain connections across national borders by actively participating in social networks that span their country of origin and their host country. Children of immigrant families live in a transnational context as they move across geographical borders to visit their home countries and also traverse social, cultural and linguistic borders to network with their extended families or relatives in their countries of origin (de los Ríos, 2018; Lee, 2022, 2024; Skerrett, 2012).

Transnational practices encompass various forms of direct physical cross-border movements between the country of origin and the host country, as well as ongoing participation through local institutions and communities in the host country (Vertovec, 2001, 2003). Portes (2001: 186) argued that transnational practices embody 'goal-oriented initiatives that require coordination across national borders by members of civil society'. Within this multifarious network, transnational individuals cultivate, reshape and transform their identities through social relations that connect them to multiple societies concurrently (Orellana, 2016).

Transnationalism that establishes sociocultural spheres draws attention to individuals' practices and their relationships that extend national borders (Hannerz, 1998). Hence, the process of transnationalism is not static but inherently in-becoming and continuously evolving (Tedeschi *et al.*, 2022). Scholars in transnational studies have sought to understand 'how everyday practices of ordinary people produce cultural meanings that sustain transnational networks and make possible enduring translocal ties' (Smith, 2003: 468).

According to Vertovec (2009), meaningful and constant border-crossing activities connect six theoretical premises: social morphology (social connections and networks spanning borders), type of consciousness (multiple identities and sense of belonging), mode of cultural reproduction (hybridization of various cultural phenomena), avenue of capital (activities of transnational corporations), site of political engagement (cross-border public participation and political organization) and (re)construction of locality (creation of new social spaces across countries). Vertovec argued that the six aspects of transnationalism are not only interrelated but also transformative, triggering societal changes and bringing about structural renovations. As a result of the movement of people, the flows of information and resources and the influx of ideas and practices, transnationalism has reconstructed the network of interconnected relationships and local communities by changing the way people interact and connect (Rizvi, 2019; Tedeschi *et al.*, 2022; Vertovec, 2004).

The concept of transnationalism inherently includes immigrant adaptation processes (Erdal & Oeppen, 2013; Sanchez & Kusan, 2012) because it recognizes that migrants maintain connections to their home countries while adapting to their new society in the host country, essentially navigating a dual identity and engaging in cross-border activities as part of their integration process. Erdal and Oeppen (2013) noted that transnationalism is not a fixed process; instead, it involves an ongoing negotiation between people who live across national borders, constantly redefining their sense of belonging, embracing or rejecting aspects of different cultures and creating hybrid identities, rather than being strictly tied to one nation-state. Although transnational individuals hold multiple identities related to both their home country and the host country in which they reside (Lucas & Purkayastha, 2007), they are integrated into the society of their current location, as they are required to fully participate in the host country's life in many ways.

Unlike this sociocultural transnationalism that 'recreate[s] a sense of community based on cultural understandings of belonging and mutual obligations' (Itzigsohn & Saucedo, 2002: 767), Beauchemin and Safi (2020) introduced rejection-based transnationalism that is linked to segregation in the host country because it describes a situation where migrants maintain strong ties to their home country only, often due to discrimination, racism or feelings of exclusion in their new society. These social factors can easily lead transnational migrants to interact with people from their ethnic group solely, resulting in segregated communities within the host nation. By rejecting integration into the host society, those transmigrants solidify their original cultural identity by strengthening their sense of belonging to their homeland through close transnational ties. Studies on transnationalism suggest that the dualism between a migrant's country of origin and their host country can be mitigated by allowing individuals to maintain substantial transnational connections through ongoing cross-border interactions, cultural exchange and social networks that bridge the gap between the two countries (Comola & Mendola, 2015; Jones, 2019; Verdery *et al.*, 2018).

By juxtaposing the notion of transnationalism, Welsch (1999) coined the term 'transculturalism' to underscore the transitory and variable nature of culture. According to Welsch, cultures in contemporary society are continually intersecting and profoundly intertwined with one another. Since there are no secluded cultures and uncontacted people in a globalized society, cultures are always interconnected through a flow of people, products and beliefs. These cultural transformations in modern society transcend traditional cultural borders. Transculturalism, in turn, illustrates the social phenomenon that encompasses elements of more than one culture, extending cultural practices and creating new cultural forms (Imbert, 2014; Loh, 2022). Individuals who move across national and cultural borders create dynamic and multifaceted identities shaped by the different life experiences and social activities they participate in within new communities and societies (Jurkova & Guo, 2018; Lange, 2015; Montgomery, 2014).

People in transnational and transcultural contexts build relationships and connections with others by activating flexible and adaptable identities from recurring border-crossing experiences and practices (Giroux, 2005; Kasun & Saavedra, 2014; Sánchez & Kasun, 2012). Transnational individuals who live their lives across borders create distinctive and sophisticated identities from constant social participation and cross-border activities in a new society. In this way, transnationalism provides an opportunity for transnational individuals 'to engage the multiple references that constitute different cultural codes, experiences, and languages' (Giroux, 2005: 22) and to experience a 'synergy of the two cultures' (Anzaldúa, 1987: 63). Sánchez and Kasun (2012) contend that children from transnational families are more likely to develop 'a flexible and adaptable sense of being' (2012: 86) in various surroundings and multiple circumstances as they can employ their 'enhanced identity toolkit' (2012: 86). Accordingly, transnational individuals can envision the power of full potential and a future promise, which are regarded as transnational and transcultural byproducts in a globalized world (de los Ríos, 2018, 2020; Skerrett, 2012).

The Intersection of Translanguaging, Transnationalism and Transculturality

As discussed in previous chapters, translanguaging (see Chapter 3 for translanguaging as an instructional pedagogy and Chapter 4 for dynamic translanguaging practices) describes bi/multi/plurilingual individuals' fluid communicative strategy drawing on their full linguistic and semiotic resources to extend their communicative competence (Cenoz *et al.*, 2022; García *et al.*, 2017; García & Kleifgen, 2019; Lee, 2021, 2023; Solorza, 2019). One of the goals of translanguaging is to endorse and protect minoritized languages, speakers and communities by moving away from hierarchical conceptions of language (Dorner *et al.*, 2023; Lee, 2021; Mendoza *et al.*, 2023; Palmer *et al.*, 2019). Translanguaging disrupts linguistic inequality and the power relations among languages in the classroom (Allard, 2017; Cenoz *et al.*, 2022; Guerrero, 2021; Poza, 2017). In other words, translanguaging recognizes and values the affirmation and sustainability of minoritized languages (Cummins & Persad, 2014; Lee, 2021, 2023) that are often vulnerable and susceptible in the majority language context.

The key purpose of transnational, transcultural and translanguaging studies is to dismantle the national, cultural and linguistic ideologies that draw boundaries between different groups. The integrated notion of the three 'trans-' lenses (Lee, 2025a) provides individuals with a means to move beyond a monolithic and confined ideology by destabilizing static, stagnant and immobile linguistic practices and cultural products (Mahon *et al.*, 2019). Social, cultural and linguistic contact resulting from (im) migration and globalization have significantly influenced and established transnationalism and transculturalism practices in contemporary societies (Canagarajah, 2013). Like bi/multi/plurilingual learners who acquire societal language in addition to their heritage languages, students residing in transnational and transcultural contexts acquire various cultural values by actively engaging with multiple national cultures, allowing them to socially participate across different communities (Lee, 2024).

Researchers, however, warned that transnational and/or transcultural individuals are susceptible to linguistic and cultural assimilation (Guarzino *et al.*, 2003; Smith, 2006) as they are more likely to 'erase or give up all that represents their origin country ... to replace these with the U.S.' (Sánchez, 2009: 53). According to Sánchez, this forced assimilation can easily lead transnational/transcultural students to abandon their heritage language and culture, which would ultimately eradicate their family ties and identities. Therefore, it is imperative for educators to sanction students' translanguaging practices and embrace their transnational and transcultural funds of knowledge (Compton-Lilly *et al.*, 2019; Cuero, 2010; Dabach & Fones, 2016; Kwon, 2022) in the classroom. In addition, incorporating critical tenets of translanguaging, transnationalism and transculturalism into school curricula can challenge dominant discourses that uphold inequitable practices in diverse learning contexts where power dynamics, such as language and cultural hierarchies, are perpetuated (Lee, 2025b).

Exploring Global Flows and Fluid Identities through Transnational Literacies

Scholars have suggested syncretic approaches to learning, which involve the incorporation of culturally inclusive discourses and practices to accelerate the engagement of transnational students by connecting school-based knowledge and home-based discourse (e.g. Gutiérrez, 2014). Specifically, providing a transnational curriculum that is designed to enhance the language and literacy abilities of children of immigrant or transnational families can help students engage with literacy practices that reflect their various social, cultural and linguistic experiences across borders (Brochin & Medina, 2017; Jiménez *et al.*, 2009; Skerrett, 2012, 2015). When engaging with literacy practices that reflect diverse transnational experiences and practices, students can recognize that their lives are valued and appreciated in their school curricula (Dutro & Haberl, 2018; Skerrett & Bomer, 2013). Thus, transnational literacies encourage students to utilize their unique 'in-between' perspectives and validate their dynamic identities, enriching their learning experience, which is often not recognized nor valued in traditional educational settings (Gutiérrez, 2014; Skerrett, 2012, 2015). Educational researchers have pursued ways to integrate transnational students' dynamic life journeys into school curricula (de los Ríos, 2020; Hornberger & Link, 2012) by providing literacies that illuminate their multifarious identities (Compton-Lilly *et al.*, 2019), funds of knowledge (Souto-Manning, 2013) and border-crossing experiences (Lee, 2022, 2024; Sánchez, 2007; Sánchez & Kasun, 2012; Skerrett & Bomer, 2013).

According to Warriner (2007), local literacy practices situated in everyday contexts, such as homes and communities, are influenced by globalization and transnationalism; thus, transnational literacies as social practices are byproducts of globalization and (im)migration. Warriner (2007: 161) pointed out that transnational literacies 'provide a window into global-local interfaces, transmigrant experiences, transnational flows across borders and translocal connections'. Since individuals' lived experiences, life trajectories and dynamic identities are embodied and transformed when bringing practice into everyday life, a careful and close examination of transnational literacies provides insights into the human face of global mobility (Smith, 2006). Warriner (2007) argued that children of transmigrant families can benefit from engaging in transnational literacies because transnational literacies offer a way to understand the experiences and identities of transnational individuals by examining their everyday practices across borders. In this respect, individuals' transnational lives and experiences generate 'theoretical synergy with a view of multiple literacies' (Skerrett, 2012: 368), showcasing the richness and depth of their cultural lifeworld.

By recognizing transnational students' everyday literacies as ongoing, continual and evolving processes of becoming multi-dimensional selves (Skerrett, 2012), researchers have investigated transnational students' literacy practices (e.g. Dutro & Haberl, 2018; Handsfield & Valente, 2016). For instance, Dutro and Haberl analyzed second graders' writing about their experiences of living on the border of the US and Mexico to explore how their compositions entangled with the affective, political and ideological dimensions of borders. Their findings showed that the students expressed their emotional challenges and practical difficulties in maintaining connections across national borders. Similarly, Handsfield and Valente (2016), who analyzed immigrant students' memoirs and testimonies, discovered that students from marginalized countries recounted both joyful and painful experiences in their lives, providing a complex tapestry of their realities through writing. By validating the students' (hi)stories from their narrative writing, Handsfield and Valente documented young immigrant students' intricate and multifaceted experiences in their transnational lifeworld.

Researchers have also reported that the literacy practices of transnational students played a pivotal role in constructing and negotiating their multi-dimensional identities (Canagarajah, 2006; Jiménez *et al.*, 2009; Lam & Warriner, 2012; Skerrett & Bomer, 2013). Studies revealed that transnational students' identity formations and negotiations occurred when participating in meaningful literacy activities, such as reading, writing, drawing, painting and crafting (Compton-Lilly *et al.*, 2017, 2019; Dutro & Haberl, 2018; Machado & Hartman, 2019, 2020; Stewart & Hansen-Thomas, 2016). For instance, Compton-Lilly and her colleagues (2017) investigated how children in immigrant families constructed a wide range of identities by analyzing student-created artifacts. Their findings exhibited that the children actively reflected on their unique identities, ideologies, funds of knowledge, social values and cultural practices to construct and negotiate their identities. Accordingly, the children's intersectional identities created a unique and multifaceted understanding of themselves, contributing to a rich tapestry of their self-perception. In Machado and Hartman's (2020) study, when the second-grade teacher modified his literacy curriculum by positioning students' transnational literacy practices in the center of instruction, the students (re)constructed their identities by reflecting on their border-crossing journeys during their poetry compositions. Their findings suggest the importance of creating a safe space where students feel empowered to express their diverse transnational experiences and sophisticated transnational lifeworld through literacy activities.

Navigating Border Thinking and Border Pedagogy

The dynamics of transnationalism can be understood through the lenses of border thinking (Mignolo, 2000) and border pedagogy (Garza,

2007; Giroux, 1988, 1991; Romo & Chavez, 2006). The concept of border thinking, which originated from decolonial theory, was initially developed by Gloria Anzaldúa (1987) in her book *Borderlands/La Frontera: The New Mestiza*. Then, the concept was further developed by decolonial scholars (most prominently Walter Mignolo, followed by Anibal Quijano, Ramon Grosfoguel, Arturo Escobar and Catherine Walsh) and has subsequently been utilized within the field of decoloniality. Anzaldúa (1987: 3) defined a border as 'a dividing line [that] is a vague and undetermined place created by the emotional residue of an unnatural boundary'. Borders are generally defined as geographical boundaries separating nations, but they are not always restricted to geographical territories between two nations. Borders are defined as both geopolitical and emblematic spaces, and they are demarcated by both geographical distance and epistemic difference (Cervantes-Soon & Carrillo, 2016; Mignolo & Tlostanova, 2006). Although borders indicate the literal demarcation, they not only divide physical space but also represent metaphorical space by classifying groups of individuals 'according to the degree of their belonging to certain racial/ethnic, cultural, and social groups' (Laine, 2021: 747).

Since borders 'elicit a recognition of epistemological, political, social, and cultural boundaries' (Giroux, 1991: 51), they do not exist as fixed or staticentities. Instead, borders are mobile and dynamic social constructions. Borders can be cultural, political or economic boundaries that separate different cultures, ethnicities, religions, languages or social interactions regardless of people's geographical proximity (Cervantes-Soon & Carrillo, 2016; Kazanjian, 2011). Cultural borders, for instance, demarcate metaphorical areas where people share common cultural characteristics. Since border crossers leave their home countries and establish new lives in another country, the process of border crossing is considered 'a perpetual act of cultural understanding and intellectual growth' (Kazanjian, 2011: 374). Accordingly, the borderlands are described as 'the discourse of people who live between different worlds, [which] speaks against dualism, oversimplification, and essentialism' (Elenes, 1997: 53).

The goal of border thinking (Mignolo, 2000) is to understand the importance of perspectives and lived experiences of those on the margins of power structures, particularly those affected by colonialism. It seeks to understand how people navigate and create knowledge outside of the frameworks imposed by dominant systems by creating alternative frameworks.

Decolonial scholars employ border thinking to analyze the colonial matrix of power, which refers to the enduring system of power and domination that continues to shape colonial ideas, structures, practices, relationships and identities. This approach highlights the impact of colonialism on various aspects of society, including knowledge, authority and subjectivity. The concept of border thinking underscores the lived experiences of marginalized groups to disrupt the dominant,

Western-centric narratives and dismantle power structures that perpetuate colonial inequalities by incorporating alternative ways of knowing, thinking, doing and being.

Scholars studied Chicano/as who live between or move across the US and Mexico borders (also known as borderlanders or 'fronterizos [borderers]') contextualized discourses of borders and implemented border pedagogy to examine how they co-construct and reconstruct their fluid identities by incorporating and negotiating the dominant and subordinate cultures (e.g. Powell & Carrillo, 2019; Romo & Chavez, 2006). Specifically, border pedagogy provides an opportunity for learners to engage in 'multiple references that constitute different cultural codes, experiences, and languages' (Romo & Chavez, 2006: 143), which facilitates them to create their identities and transform their beliefs and perspectives. Giroux (1991: 52) similarly noted that border pedagogy embodies cultural integration and transformation as it 'create[s] borderlands in which the diverse cultural resources allow for the fashioning of new identities within existing configurations of power'.

Border pedagogy can empower transnational and transcultural students who transcend both physical and cultural borders to navigate their multiple identities and the complex, vibrant life experiences in the region. Since border pedagogy leads learners to (re)construct, deconstruct and transform their thinking, beliefs and perspectives to connect both sides of the borders from multiple lenses (Giroux, 2005; Powell & Carrillo, 2019; Romo & Chavez, 2006), it informs people to examine the boundaries of ethnicity, race, language, culture and power to gain a deeper understanding of their own identities and the experiences of others by moving beyond traditional social and conceptual barriers (Reyes & Garza, 2005).

Activating Critical Border Pedagogy to Achieve Social and Educational Transformation

Drawing on Mignolo's (2000, 2002) concept of border thinking and Giroux's (1988, 1991) theory of border pedagogy, Cervantes-Soon and Carrillo (2016) conceptualized critical border pedagogy as a radical alternative to the banking system of colonization, patriarchy and neoliberalism, aiming to achieve social transformation. Since borders represent metaphorical space by classifying groups of individuals based on their racial, ethnic, cultural and social belongings and identities (Laine, 2021), students of color are often considered aliens or outliners by the mainstream educational system that overlooks and invalidates their heritage languages, cultures and/or values (Coburn & Gormally, 2017).

Borders are not mere lines of demarcation that signify the separation between two distinctive sovereign or political entities, which indicate territorial borders; instead, they further represent metaphorically peripheral and liminal spaces where subjects are marked as inferior, deviant, subordinate or simply 'Other' in mainstream society (Cervantes-Soon & Carrillo, 2016). The notion of critical border pedagogy goes beyond hybridity or the intermingling of different cultures or perspectives because it 'constitutes a potentially radical way of re-imagining knowledge and educational practices for oppositional social transformation' (2016: 282). Since borders are 'a manifestation of inequality, discrimination, and social injustice' (Laine, 2021: 752), the existence of national borders often reinforces existing global inequalities, such as social, cultural, political, economic and linguistic disparities, by restricting access to opportunities for people from less privileged regions. Thus, critical border pedagogy encourages educators to illuminate and analyze societal disparity, potential emancipation, patterns of domination and the dynamics of power relations within a given context.

Since border regions encompass the ideas of injustice, inequity, power structures and racial/cultural discrimination between the two sides of the border, critical border pedagogy constructs social, political and historical boundaries between hegemonic ideologies of dominance and minority as well as the power structure of centers and margins in our society (Giroux, 2005; Romo & Chavez, 2006). Critical border pedagogy encourages students to actively challenge and re-evaluate their existing beliefs and viewpoints, allowing them to connect with perspectives from diverse cultures and experiences across borders by going beyond a singular view (Carrillo & Karvelis, 2023). Using participatory action research, Dyrness and Sepúlveda III (2020) examined how Latinx diaspora youths critically reflect on belonging, navigate citizenship, experience racism and exclusion and yearn for change, taking into account their transnational identities and transcultural knowledge within the context of contemporary decolonizing citizenship practices. Implementing border pedagogy using critical perspectives not only helped students encompass multiple interpretations and develop their tolerance and ethical sophistication but also promoted their criticality and deeper understanding of complex social issues and power relations.

Critical border pedagogy educators transform their knowledge and skills to attain change through their actions and advocacy (e.g. Carrillo & Karvelis, 2023; Cervantes-Soon & Carrillo, 2016; Romo & Chavez, 2006). For example, Romo and Chavez (2006) investigated how monocultural teacher candidates prepared their lessons to teach in a border region. The pre-service teachers in their study prepared their lessons cognitively to become culturally competent educators by incorporating non-standard classroom resources into their teaching and applying real-life experiences to learning, thereby becoming more culturally relevant and competent educators. The pre-service teachers also identified complexities of their students' identities (i.e. diverse racial, ethnic, national, linguistic, socioeconomic and cultural identities) in a border area, which led them to see widespread racism, sexism, classism and discrimination. Accordingly, the teacher candidates expanded their understanding, attitudes and practical abilities by advocating their students' voices and espousing broad-mindedness to support students from diverse cultural backgrounds.

Through the lenses of Mestiz@ Theories of Intelligences (MTI) (Carrillo, 2013) – an asset-based intelligence framework that values the diverse knowledge systems within subaltern communities – and Chicana feminist thought, which explores how Chicana feminists navigate gender-based conflicts within the Chicano Movement, Cervantes-Soon and Carrillo (2016) demonstrated that teachers' decolonizing border pedagogy for Latin@ students in secondary schools offered pedagogical practices that cultivate personal and educational transformation and foster student agency toward social development. By employing Border Thinking, Reflexivity and Critical Pedagogy as their theoretical frameworks, Carrillo and Karvelis (2023) established a teacher reflexivity framework called Border Thinking Reflexivity, which consists of (1) Strategic Epistemic Disobedience and (2) Curricular and Pedagogical De-Linking (2023: 107), and it became a crucial toolkit for teachers to navigate their identities, actions and everyday practices to make the fundamental transformation of education in a deeply conservative state in the US.

Critical border pedagogy has disrupted traditional perspectives and practices in teaching and learning, suggesting positive alternatives to identify social domination and cultural hegemony (Cook, 2001). Critical border pedagogy can decolonize the curriculum and revitalize the educational system to promote equity and justice for all learners (Cervantes-Soon & Carrillo, 2016). Since critical border pedagogy supports educational transformation by challenging inequitable arrangements such as implicit biases, systemic racism and colonialism, it provides pathways for achieving change in education. When educators utilize critical border pedagogy, students can perceive learning as deeply intertwined with political, social and cultural realities (Giroux, 1988), allowing them to critically analyze power dynamics and social issues of injustice within their learning process. Thus, the practice of border pedagogy, informed by critical perspectives, can promote social justice and foster mutual democracy by encouraging individuals to actively engage in sociocultural negotiation, ultimately creating a more inclusive and equitable society.

The theoretical frameworks introduced in the chapter (i.e. Mignolo's border thinking, Giroux's border pedagogy and Cervantes-Soon and Carrillo's critical border pedagogy) are closely connected to Bhabha's concept of Third Space (see Chapter 2). The Third Space that is understood as a hybrid, liminal and in-between conceptual space underscores spatial politics of inclusion and negotiation for dynamic transformation by navigating different aspects of students' multi-layered identities, embracing their dynamic discursive practices and maintaining counterhegemonic agency, stance and practice (Bhabha, 1994; Soja,

1996). Since the Third Space fosters innovative learning practices that are dynamic, culturally responsive, and student-centered, incorporating authentic and meaningful literacy practices within these Third Spaces can facilitate students' reflection on their unique identities, ideologies, funds of knowledge and social values, enabling them to construct and negotiate their multifaceted identities. Bhabha's Third Space theory intersects with border thinking, as they commonly foster more inclusive and engaging learning environments that embrace diverse voices and experiences. This approach not only validates students' unique perspectives and dynamic identities but also breaks traditional educational norms and conventional methods of teaching.

Crossing Cultural and Inner Borders by Using Transnational Children's Literature

The benefits of using multicultural literature in diverse classroom settings have been discussed in the previous chapter (see Chapter 5). It was discussed that encountering multicultural literature allows readers to accept cultural differences, appreciate cultural diversity and broaden their worldviews. Multicultural literature that specifically portrays transnational children's everyday practices highlights the complex, dynamic and vibrant border-crossing experiences of those children by showcasing their daily routines, cultural negotiations and the richness or challenges of their fluid identities (Sánchez & Landa, 2016). Thus, reading multicultural literature depicting transnational children's lived experiences (i.e. hereafter transnational children's literature) can assist readers to cross cultural borders (Corliss, 1998) by acting as a bridge between different cultures and promoting intercultural awareness because these books provide a platform to explore diverse perspectives, experiences and identities across national boundaries (Boccagni, 2012).

Corliss (1998) discussed three different types of borders – physical, cultural and inner borders. Adopting Corliss' classification of cultural border, Cai (2002) subdivided cultural borders into three categories: physical border, (cultural) difference border and inner border. According to Cai, the inner borders are the most abstract borders as they are marked by deep-rooted biases, harmful prejudices and inaccurate stereotypes, which stem readers from understanding and respecting others. Cai addressed that the inner borders 'have been erected historically by the mainstream culture to isolate and suppress the parallel cultures' (2002: 118).

Since voluminous multicultural children's literature portrays similarities among people of different cultural backgrounds and carries the message of human commonalities, it can help young readers cross cultural borders by creating a close bond (e.g. Rochman, 1993; Sims & Bishop, 1987). For instance, Sims Bishop (1987: 60) claims that 'understanding our common humanity is a powerful weapon against the forces that would divide us and alienate us from one another'. Universal themes in literature can thus serve as a bridge to connect people from different cultural backgrounds. Nonetheless, focusing on books that portray similarities among different cultures hardly questions or challenges the mainstream ideology. Readers encountering those books only often consider the experiences and values of mainstream culture as common and universal in the world. Cai (2002: 122) indeed contends that showing commonalities across cultures by overlooking cultural differences 'oversimplifies the difficulty of crossing cultural borders'. Books focused on common bonds do not disrupt mainstream cultural hegemony and rarely address racial and cultural conflicts in our society. Consequently, readers may not truly cross the inner borders that exist in people's minds.

Since people from minority cultural groups are typically underrepresented and invisible in children's literature, individuals from marginalized groups often learn and know much more about the dominant culture than children from mainstream cultures do about the parallel cultures (Botelho & Rudman, 2009). Scholars reported that authentic and accurate selections of multicultural literature could facilitate students' cultural and inner border crossing because multicultural stories break their biases and stereotypes by assisting them in developing a deeper understanding of others and other cultures through cross-cultural connection and learning (e.g. Banks, 2016; Crisp et al., 2016; Nodelman & Reimer, 2003; Rochman, 1993). As Cai (2002: 130) stated, '[t]rying to ignore differences will not help children cross the cultural borders, especially the inner border'. That is, children need to actively learn about and understand individual and cultural differences to navigate diverse environments and foster inclusivity. Engaging with transnational children's literature can potentially help youngsters cross their cultural and inner borders.

Becoming Border Crossers: Korean American Transnational Students' Stories

It is important to acknowledge that the theme of crossing borders in multicultural children's literature frequently centers on Hispanic heritage, particularly the experiences of Mexican immigrants, as their border-crossing experiences are prevalent and recurring in the US (Rodríguez & Braden, 2018). Nevertheless, themes such as immigration, relocation, colonization, separation, segregation, reunion and inclusion/ exclusion are also frequently explored in books about various ethnic and cultural groups (Lee, 2022). As Kazanjian (2011: 374) stated, border pedagogy is not geographically limited to the US–Mexico border; rather, it is 'applicable to any city, state, or nation that seeks to develop critical thinking among students, regardless of their heritage or geographical proximity'. Considering the learning context and networks in Korean

(2) Jake: It happened to me, oh, many times. People really think that I am Chinese or something because I look like Asian, but I was born in America, and I am American like the others who think that I am Chinese, not even Korean.

(3) Sofia: Me, too. One time when I went to the mall with my older sister and my cousin, the person at the store thought that we didn't speak English and tried to say some words in Chinese, I guess.

(4) Joy: Oh, yes. It happens to me many times. I think that's because people see us ... um, only the outside part of us and then simply judge that we are not from here [America].

(5) Eva: In the book, the boy says, 'nobody on my team or other team, or even anybody in the crowd looked like me.' That's how I felt when I entered the classroom for my first day of school here.

(6) Julie: When I came to the States for the first time, everyone looked different from me. Actually, I felt that from the airport as soon as we landed. I still remember that.

When reading the literature Dreaming of America: An Ellis Island Story (Bunting, 2000), where the protagonist noted her dual racial identities by saying that 'I am Annie Moore of Cork from Ireland. And I am Annie Moore of America,' the students related the content of the story to their own experiences. For instance, the student named Sofia responded that she became more Korean when she was physically in Korea, but her primary identity and sense of belonging remained as American while living in the US. Similarly, Aiden stated that he identified himself as American at his American school but felt more Korean than American at home because of the language and customs he practiced within the family environment. The Korean American transnational students exhibited situational identity, in which they identify with one racial category at one moment in time and then another at other moments depending on social contexts by shifting their racial identification. The students understood that although their biological and genetic composition had not changed over time, their perception and conformation to their racial identity had never been fixed or static, as it had evolved and changed into a dynamic and fluid concept. Since the students lived in an in-between space due to their racial fluidity or flexibility, reading stories about literary characters who shape multifaceted aspects of their identities supported the students to reflect on and negotiate their racial identity construction by navigating and interrogating racial boundaries.

Countering linguistic borders by becoming bilingual

The selected literature includes the presentations of protagonists' heritage language use and learning to some degree. Particularly, the two books The Colour of Home (Hoffman, 2002) and La Frontera: My heritage language schools where transnational US-born children of Korean families attend, I investigated how transnational students can become cognizant border-crossers when they were given curricula focusing on transnational children's literature that portrays diverse border-crossing experiences (Lee, 2022). As a third-grade Korean language teacher, I examined how Korean American transnational students responded to social, cultural, political, linguistic and inner border-crossing narratives to identify whether and how transnational literature facilitated the students' ability to traverse and transcend different kinds of borders.

For that study, I selected transnational children's literature that illustrate people from different racial groups with diverse cultures and dynamic life experiences as border crossers. To have a balanced collection of transnational children's literature from diverse cultural groups, I consciously chose four books about Asian or Asian Americans, four books about Hispanic/Latino Americans, three books from European countries and three stories from Africa countries. Table 6.1 presents a list of literature that portrays transnational children's border-crossing practices. Since the protagonists in the literature confront different borders in their life experiences, reading the collection of books helped the students gain the ability to navigate and understand different perspectives, cultures and life experiences. Below, I display the students' responses

Table 6.1 Transnational children's literature selection portraying border-crossing experiences

Title of literature (author, year)	Ethnic groups	Depicted borders in storylines
Goodbye, 382 Shin Dang Dong (Park, 2002)	Northeast Asian (Korean)	Geographical, racial and linguistic borders
Baseball Saved Us (Mochizuki, 1995)	Northeast Asian (Japanese)	Geographical, political and racial borders
Lailah's Lunch Box (Faruqi, 2015)	Middle Eastern Muslim (The Emirates)	Geographical, racial and religious borders
Four Feet, Two Sandals (Williams & Mohammed, 2007)	Southern Asian (Afghanistan-Pakistan)	Geographical, political, racial and religious borders
When Jessie Came Across the Sea (Hest, 1997)	Eastern Europe	Geographical, political, racial, linguistic and religious borders
The Memory Coat (Woodruff, 1998)	Eastern Europe (Russian)	Geographical, political, racial, linguistic and religious borders
Dreaming of America: An Ellis Island Story (Bunting, 2000)	Western Europe (Irish)	Geographical, political, racial, linguistic and religious borders

to the selected transnational literature that showcases how they came across each border when engaging in dialogues to build upon, reshape and expand their thinking and viewpoints.

Crossing geographical borders by reflecting on transnational experiences

The selected books commonly depict storylines related to immigration, relocation, refugees, separation and/or reunion. Since the Korean American transnational students had experienced physical border crossing between the US and their country of origin (Korea), they easily grasped the concept of geographical borders and identified different physical cross-border movements and practices when reading the stories from the literature. Specifically, the students often made text-to-self connections to the protagonist in the literature *Goodbye, 382 Shin Dang Dong* (Park, 2002), which depicts a Korean child's transnational experience by illustrating her family's immigration stories to the US from South Korea. Since the plot mirrors aspects of the students' life journeys, they were able to see themselves reflected in the story and deeply resonated with the narrative by identifying elements of their life experiences within the situations presented. Encountering a variety of immigration or relocation stories in different literary works powerfully influenced the students to reflect on the shared aspects and unique experiences of various immigrant families who crossed geographical borders.

Confronting political borders by identifying disparity and injustice

As the selected literature presents inequality and injustice in our society, such as corruption, immorality or exploitation, reading the stories helped the students develop a critical eye for analyzing pervasive social and political issues. The students' responses to the books indicated how they situated themselves across political borders, which provided them with a sense of security or belonging, or exclusion and marginalization, and further showed evidence of their political border crossing. For instance, when the class read the Japanese American book *Baseball Saved Us* (Mochizuki, 1995), they addressed the discriminating treatment Japanese Americans experienced after World War II. While reading the scenes depicting the unjust behaviors toward the Japanese protagonist, the students criticized American people's attitudes by stating, 'American people were bad and mean as they called him [the protagonist] Jap' [which is regarded as an ethnic slur to indicate Japanese], and 'He [the protagonist] is American, but Americans blame him because his family is from Japan, and he looks Japanese.' By acknowledging the injustice and inequality toward Japanese Americans during and after World War II, as presented in the story, students developed their critical consciousness

and perspectives, enabling them to encounter political borders and
how to navigate the boundaries that separate different political ent.

Political borders play a significant role for immigrants or tran
tional individuals as they can prevent travelers from other countries f
crossing borders by requiring entry permits such as valid visas or le
documentation. When the students read *Mama's Nightingale: A Story*
Immigration and Separation (Danticat, 2015), which portrays the issu
faced by undocumented immigrants, they acknowledged the significan
of having government documents to belong to a nation. Yet, after readin
other immigration stories from different Hispanic multicultural litera
ture, the students were able not only to recognize the difficult situations
and hardships immigrants face in their home countries but also to understand the difficulty of obtaining official documents to enter and stay in
the US. For instance, when reading *La Frontera: My Journey with Papa*
(Alva & Mills, 2018), the students criticized coyotes (i.e. human smug-
glers) as unreliable guides for immigrants trying to enter the US because
they deceive and abandon immigrants by taking advantage of their eager
needs and desperate situations. As the students learned about the widespread injustice in our society, these books encouraged them to develop
their critical thinking by confronting political borders, which led them
to learn about the different political systems and structures that exist in
regions bordering each other.

Interrogating racial borders by constructing identities through their racial bodies

The Korean American students often negotiated their racial border
crossing because they understood that their races were often conformed
by others' perceptions. The Korean American students who did not
phenotypically fit into the racial majority [White] group were frequently
questioned about their racial and ethnic background because their
appearance seemed unclear or ambiguous to others. Excerpt 6.1 displays
the students' responses when they discussed their identities that were perceived by people around them. As shown, since the students faced social
challenges and confusion about identity due to the mismatch between
their phenotypic race [Asian] and the given nationality [US citizen], they
often negotiated and interrogated the borders of their races.

Excerpt 6.1 Crossing racial borders by constructing and negotiating their
dynamic and fluid racial identities

(1) Ms Lee: Do you have similar experiences to what the Japanese boy
encountered in the story? When people assume that you are an Asian
although you were born in the States...?

Journey with Papa (Alva & Mills, 2018) portray that the protagonists dealt with the English language barrier in their new school in the US. While reading the stories, the students shared their previous experiences in their American schools. As speakers with limited English proficiency, the students went through the same pathway after immigrating to the US. For instance, Eva shared, 'I also had that kind of experience during my preschool year. I only knew "hi" and "thank you".' Aiden and Julie also shared that they were in the same position as the protagonist by stating, 'I did the same thing as Hassan [the protagonist in *The Colour of Home*] did' and 'I was exactly like him', respectively. By reflecting on their language learning journeys, the students further stated that 'I become more American as I became fluent in English' and 'I couldn't speak English well before, but I became a Texan because I feel comfortable living in Texas and using English'. The students' responses indicate that they considered their language proficiency in the host country as a vital component in constructing their identity, as their language use and proficiency had close connections to who they were and became. By learning about other transnational children's language learning adventures, the students were able to see their challenges reflected in the stories and critically think about their experiences tolerating language borders when adapting to a new linguistic environment.

Navigating inner borders by developing empathy toward people from other cultures

Reading and discussing different immigrant or transnational stories helped students bridge the gap between their own culture and others by gaining a deeper understanding of diverse lifestyles and fostering an appreciation for the richness of cultural diversity. Literature that portrays the lives of people from diverse ethnic and cultural backgrounds has significantly helped students cultivate empathy and sympathy toward others by exposing them to different perspectives. Particularly, the selected literature helped the students build their understanding and compassion for literary characters whose lives differ from their own. Excerpt 6.2 illustrates the students' responses to specific scenes from each book, which demonstrate their empathy.

Excerpt 6.2 Crossing the inner border by developing empathy

(1) Julie: [after reading *Mama's Nightingale: A Story of Immigration and Separation*] I was so sad when Saya's mom was arrested by the police because Saya can't live with her mom for a long time. I would cry every day if I were her.
(2) Eva: [after reading *Four Feet, Two Sandals*] It was a heartbreaking moment when Feroza didn't see her name on the list [sending

refugees to America], but Lena's name was there. They had to say goodbye. I would feel so sorry for Feroza if I were Lena.

(3) Sky: [after reading *My Name Is Sangoel*] I was sad when Sangoel said that 'In America, I have lost my name.' It was very touching because he knew that he was losing his name and maybe everything about him...?

(4) Sofia: [after reading *Brothers in Hope: The Story of the Lost Boys of Sudan*] I actually feel the pain when the boys had to drink their urine to get moisture in their bodies.... I feel so hurt inside.

As displayed, the students provided their compassionate empathy by saying, 'I was so sad', 'It was a heartbreaking moment', 'It was very touching', 'I actually feel the pain' and 'I feel so hurt'. Reading stories about people with challenging life experiences that differ from their own helped the students understand the situations from the protagonists' perspectives. The students' responses indicate that they were putting themselves in the literary characters' shoes and expressing their emotions by demonstrating a strong understanding and a deep connection to the narratives, which in turn positively facilitated their empathy. As the students utilized their enhanced ability to understand the literary characters' feelings through empathy, their inner border crossing appeared to be achieved.

The students' responses to transnational children's literature that portrays stories of diverse cultural and life experiences helped Korean American students transcend geographical, political, cultural, linguistic and inner borders. Thus, including those books for immigrant or transnational students can be an influential pedagogical tool to bring the students' experiences of crossing borders between their own cultures and those of others.

Asian American Transnational Students' Identity Construction through Literacy Practices

Since transnational students' everyday practices are constantly developing and changing (Skerrett, 2012), researchers have investigated transnational students' literacy practices to provide insight into how they actively create and navigate their identities as individuals who live and engage with multiple cultures across borders (e.g. Dutro & Haberl, 2018; Handsfield & Valente, 2016). Yet, as discussed earlier in this chapter, much of the literature on transnationalism in the US has focused on Latinx immigrants; still, there is a paucity of research that examines how children of Asian immigrant families engage in transnational practices to build and express their dynamic and multi-layered identities. In response to the lack of studies on Asian groups, one of my studies (Lee, 2024) explored how transnational students from Asian immigrant families shaped their collective identities through authentic and meaningful literacy practices that supported them in reflecting on and making connections to their transnational experiences and stories.

I understood that transnational students who embrace their vibrant living experiences in negotiating and cultivating their multifaceted identities could be benefitted from engaging with literacy practices that reflect transnational experiences both in and out of school. In my fifth-grade classroom, I designed the Transnational Literacy Unit, which reflected diverse transnational experiences and practices of different Asian American groups. This unit aimed to validate and enrich their learning journey by illuminating their multifaceted identities and transnational funds of knowledge within their transnational lifeworld. For this curriculum unit, which consisted of lessons that integrated reading, writing, drawing, painting and crafting, I consciously chose transnational literature of diverse Asian ethnic groups for upper elementary graders in which themes are aligned with transnationalism (e.g. stories of immigration, cross-border movements and racial/cultural dynamics). After reading and discussing each story, the class was asked to create artifacts in writing. The fifth graders were provided with culturally authentic and personally relevant writing prompts, allowing them to reflect on their unique life experiences and multiple identity constructions (see Table 6.2 for the literacy activity, along with writing and drawing prompts).

For this particular study (Lee, 2024), I paid attention to two focal students who lived in a transnational context by transcending social, cultural and linguistic borders to network with extended families and relatives in their home countries to seek how they engaged in transnational practices in various ways as they embraced their vibrant living experiences in negotiating and cultivating their multi-dimensional identities. In this chapter, I focus on a student (named Sunny) who was a mixed-ethnic child as she was born in the US to a Korean mother and a Vietnamese father. Sunny established multiple (i.e. biological, national, cultural, racial/ethnic and linguistic) identities as a multilingual, multicultural and transnational learner. She biologically identified as half Korean and half Vietnamese, racially identified as Asian and nationally and linguistically identified as American. Sunny was a learner of two different heritage languages: Korean and Vietnamese. Sunny shared her dynamic transnational practices both on physical and metaphorical levels (see Lee, 2022) as she has traveled back to her parents' countries of origin regularly (i.e. during summer break). Sunny's artifact creations, which illuminate how she constructed and negotiated her collective and hybrid identities through multi-dimensional border-crossing experiences (i.e. her self-portrait and 'I Am' poem), are presented and discussed below.

Table 6.2 Transnational children's literature selection and literacy activities promoting students' transnational identity development

Title of literature (author, year)	Ethnic group; type and genre of literature	Literacy activity Drawing and writing prompt
Cooper's Lesson (Shin, 2015)	Korean American; bilingual picture book/ realistic fiction	Creating an identity web "Write a self-identity essay based on your identity web."
Inside Out and Back Again (Lai, 2013)	Vietnamese American; historical fiction with free verse	Creating a life graph and an autobiography "Draw your life graph by thinking about positive and negative moments/events in your life." "Write an autobiography using the data from your positive and negative life graph."
Somewhere Among (Donwerth-Chikamatsu, 2016)	Japanese American; free verse poetry	Drawing a self-portrait and writing a poem "Provide a visual representation of your racial, cultural and linguistic identities by investigating your races, languages and cultures." "Compose an 'I Am' poem by describing special things about yourself."
The Great Wall of Lucy Wu (Shang, 2013)	Chinese American; contemporary realistic fiction	Participating in a cultural iceberg activity "Create an iceberg by portraying visible (surface level) and hidden (deeper level) cultures." "Write a letter to a new friend by introducing you and your culture using the features you have on your cultural iceberg."

Challenging racial boundaries as an individual who holds both aspects of identity

Sunny openly explored and addressed the different aspects of her racial identities in her poem (see Figure 6.1 for Sunny's 'I Am' poem). Although she regarded herself as half Korean and half Vietnamese (Stanza 1; line 3), she identified with her Asian identity on a biological level due to her genetic makeup. Sunny acknowledged that her Asian identity was shaped by her 'gene', 'DNA' and 'blood' (line 4), but she navigated her American identity by stating, '[a]lthough I don't look like American, I was American. I am American. I will be American' (Stanza 4; lines 3–4). During the interview, Sunny stated, 'Since I don't have white skin and have dark hair, people may not consider me American. But I know that there are dark skin Americans. I am not White, but I can still be American because I am a citizen here.' Her response suggests that a

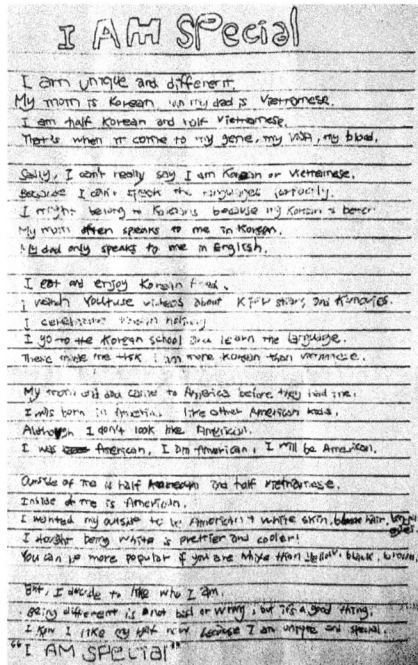

Figure 6.1 Sunny's autobiographical ('I Am') poem

person's phenotype or physical appearance may not always accurately reflect their national identity, as national identity is a complex combination of cultural, historical and personal factors that extend beyond physical characteristics.

Similarly, Sunny illustrated herself with a Vietnamese face on the left side and a Korean face on the right side when drawing her self-portrait (see Figure 6.2 for Sunny's self-portrait), but she indicated her body was closer to American than Asian due to her frequent use of American body language and gestures. Sunny shared that she habitually used common American hand gestures, for instance, using the so-so gesture (i.e. by tilting the hand back and forth horizontally with the palm facing down) to indicate something is mediocre but does not particularly impressive and air quotes (i.e. making virtual quotation marks using the index and middle fingers) to express satire, sarcasm or irony. Sunny stated, 'I always use American body language and gestures, but I do not use Asian body language, which made me think that my body is more like American.' Sunny encountered racial boundaries due to the mismatch between how people perceived her (i.e. Asian, given her Asian phenotype on a biological level) and how she understood herself (i.e. a US citizen, due to her citizenship and American ways of her body language). By addressing

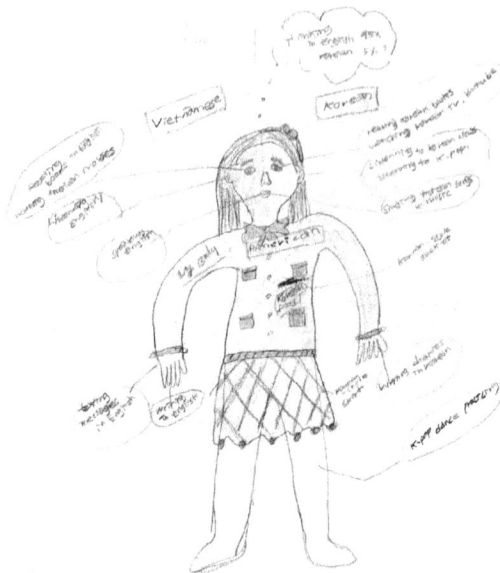

Figure 6.2 Sunny's self-portrait drawing

challenges related to her race, Sunny confronted the complexities of navigating multiple identities in society.

Tolerating linguistic boundaries to belong to two ethnic groups

Although Sunny depicted her facial features in her self-portrait as being partially Vietnamese, she saw herself communicating primarily in English and Korean. In her self-portrait, Sunny did not illustrate her using the Vietnamese language. During the interview, Sunny responded that she used Korean with her mother at home because the mother is a first-generation immigrant from Korea and used Korean as much as possible when talking to Sunny. Yet, Sunny barely used Vietnamese at home because her father, who is a second-generation Vietnamese American, primarily used English and barely spoke Vietnamese. Thus, Sunny's home languages were English and Korean only. During the interview, Sunny stated, 'The Vietnamese side of me became American, but the Korean side of me still kept me as Korean.' Her self-portrait displayed that the left side of her (which she depicted as Vietnamese) was learning and using English. In contrast, the right side of her (which she illustrated as Korean) was continuing to learn the Korean language. Sunny shared that her ability to speak Korean and her continuous use of it made her feel more Korean than Vietnamese. In her poem, Sunny also wrote that attending the Korean heritage language school reinforced her connection to the Korean identity (Stanza 3; lines 4–5). What Sunny shared in her poem and self-portrait, along with her interview responses, indicates the essential role of linguistic borders in belonging to a particular ethnic and cultural group.

Sustaining Cultural Border Crossing to Build a Strong Transnational Identity

Sunny was closely connected to Korean culture through food, entertainment activities, holidays/celebrations and clothing/fashion, which helped her sustain cultural border crossing to build a strong identity as Korean. Sunny illustrated in her self-portrait that her eyes were for watching Korean TV programs (beyond reading English books and watching American movies), her ears were for listening to Korean pop music (beyond listening to English) and her hands were for practicing Korean pop dance (beyond writing and text messaging in English). By elaborating on her preference for Korean food and Korean-style clothing to US food and US-style apparel, Sunny additionally depicted Korean foods in her stomach and drew herself wearing Korean-style outfits. Similarly, Sunny's poem showcased a deep connection to Korean culture as she listed her enjoyment of Korean cuisine, active participation in Korean entertainment and celebration of Korean holidays (Stanza 3; lines 1–3). Although Sunny has maintained her life across borders between Korea and the US, she continued to cross cultural borders to build a strong identity as Korean, which led her to see herself as Korean American rather than Vietnamese American. Consequently, Sunny was able to create distinctive and sophisticated identities through different social and cultural participation while residing in the US.

Enduring inner borders by shifting perspectives to draw positive self-image

Even though Sunny admitted that she looked Asian, she wrote: 'inside of me is American' in her poem (Stanza 5; line 2) because of the unconscious understanding and awareness of cultural norms and behaviors she absorbed through her everyday experiences and interactions while growing up in the US. Sunny wrote in her poem that she wanted her outside to appear White American by listing the White phenotype features 'white skin', 'blonde hair' and 'bigger eyes' (Stanza 5; line 3) and used the adjectives 'prettier' and 'cooler' (line 4) by comparing the White phenotypic characteristics to other racial groups (i.e. Asian, African-American and Latinx). Sunny then shared her notion of White privilege and hegemony by affirming that 'you can be more popular if you are white than yellow, brown, [or] black' (line 5).

Sunny, however, later crossed the inner border, which denotes the boundaries of her attitudes and mindsets (Cai, 2002) by breaking negative stereotypes and combating unconscious biases from her notion of White-skin privilege. In the last stanza, Sunny shared how her viewpoint had shifted; she came to believe that being different was 'not bad or wrong', instead it was 'a good thing' (Stanza 6; line 2), and she made a conscious choice to accept and love herself and embrace her true self because she was 'unique' and 'special' (line 3). Sunny shared during the interview, 'I didn't like myself before because I was different and strange to others. But now I know being different is something special. When others have one language and culture, I can have two or three at the same time. That means I am lucky and rich, not like rich rich but mentally rich.' Although Sunny initially had low self-esteem due to her belief that Whiteness is the standard of beauty, her view and perspective had been changed. Hence, Sunny successfully crossed the inner border by overcoming negative stereotypes and unconscious biases, which led her to like the unique self of her being and appreciate her multifaceted identities. By moving across the inner border that existed in her mind (Cai, 2002), Sunny not only gained a deeper understanding of diverse forms of physical beauty but also appreciated the unique life journey that made her feel valued and special in her own right. Overall, Sunny identified that her identities (i.e. race, nationality, language skills, social participation and cultural knowledge) largely shaped her perception of who she is and where she belongs in the context of her transnational identity construction.

Implications for Educational Practice of Implementing Transnational Literacies

Considering the ever-changing student demographics in US public schools, this chapter suggests classroom teachers create a space for transnationalism within their existing curricula by including literature that portrays unique border-crossing stories and the resilience of transnational families who live in between and across national borders. As shown by the two empirical studies in this chapter, educators can incorporate transnational children's literature into their curriculum, allowing students to share their unique perspectives and utilize their transnational funds of knowledge to develop multi-dimensional selves. By doing so, classroom teachers can educate transnational students about how to cultivate and negotiate their dynamic and fluid identities by adopting multiple perspectives and critical lenses. Implementing literacy activities that embrace transnationalism and transculturalism can thus be an entry point to starting discussions and providing opportunities for students to reflect on their richly diverse lived experiences and construct their collective identities, making sense of their transnational lifeworld.

As displayed from the findings that transnational students traversed and transcended different levels of metaphorical borders (e.g. racial, cultural, linguistic, emotional, inner borders) beyond their geographical boundaries, educators should consider their role as facilitators of border crossings in the classroom by offering a space for mutual engagement of different life experiences and cultural practices so that cultural and inner border crossings can be smooth transitions for the students (Lee, 2022). Since crossing borders through narrative storytelling significantly helps transnational students broaden their perspectives, educators are responsible for implementing intentional teaching practices that embrace and explore diverse border-crossing experiences, practices and perspectives. Educators play a crucial role in fostering a culturally sensitive classroom by guiding students to understand perspectives beyond their own and to critically examine their personal biases, thereby promoting a more inclusive and empathetic learning environment. In doing so, educators can facilitate students' development as culturally aware, sensitive and responsible citizens.

Children's Literature Bibliography

Alva, A. and Mills, D. (2018) *La Frontera: My Journey with Papa*. Barefoot Books.

Anzaldúa, G. (1987) *Borderlands: The new mestiza: La frontera* [Borderlands: The New Mestiza: The Border]. Spinsters/Aunt Lute.

Bunting, E. and Stahl, B. (2000) *Dreaming of America: An Ellis Island Story*. Troll Communications.

Danticat, E. (2015) *Mama's Nightingale: A Story of Immigration and Separation*. Dial Books for Young Readers.

Donwerth-Chikamatsu, A. (2016) *Somewhere Among*. Atheneum/Caitlyn Dlouhy Books.

Faruqi, R. (2015) *Lailah's Lunch Box*. Tilbury House Publishers.

Hest, A. (1997) *When Jessie Came Across the Sea*. Candlewick.

Hoffman, M. (2002) *The Colour of Home*. Frances Lincoln Publishers Ltd.

Lai, T. (2013) *Inside Out and Back Again*. HarperCollins.

Mochizuki, K. (1995) *Baseball Saved Us*. Lee & Low Book.

Park, F. and Park, G. (2002) *Goodbye, 382 Shin Dang Dong*. National Geographic Society.

Pérez, A.I. (2013) *My Diary: From Here to There*. Lee & Low Books.

Shang, W.W. (2013) *The Great Wall of Lucy Wu*. Scholastic Press.

Shin, S.Y. (2015) *Cooper's Lesson*. Children's Book Press.

Williams, K.L. and Mohammed, K. (2007) *Four Feet, Two Sandals*. Eerdmans.

Williams, K.L. and Mohammed, K. (2009) *My Name Is Sangoel*. Eerdmans Books for Young Readers.

Williams, M. and Christie, G. (2005) *Brothers in Hope: The Story of the Lost Boys of Sudan*. Lee & Low Books.

Woodruff, E. (1998) *The Memory Coat*. Scholastic Press.

References

Allard, E. (2017) Re-examining teacher translanguaging: An ecological perspective. *Bilingual Research Journal* 40 (2), 116–130.

Anzaldúa, G. (1987) *Borderlands: The new mestiza: La frontera* [Borderlands: The New Mestiza: The Border]. Spinsters/Aunt Lute.

Appadurai, A. (1996) *Modernity at Large: Cultural Dimensions of Globalization*. University of Minnesota Press.

Banks, J. (2016) *Cultural Diversity and Education: Foundation, Curriculum, and Teaching* (6th edn). Routledge.

Beauchemin, C. and Safi, M. (2020) Migrants' connections within and beyond borders: Insights from the comparison of three categories of migrants in France. *Ethnic and Racial Studies* 43 (2), 255–274.

Beyer, C. (2007) Non-governmental organizations as motors of change. *Government and Opposition* 42 (4), 513–535.

Bhabha, H.K. (1994) *The Location of Culture*. Routledge.

Boccagni, P. (2012) Rethinking transnational studies: Transnational ties and the transnationalism of everyday life. *European Journal of Social Theory* 15 (1), 117–132.

Botelho, M.J. and Rudman, M.K. (2009) *Critical Multicultural Analysis of Children's Literature: Mirrors, Windows, and Doors*. Routledge.

Brochin, C. and Medina, C.L. (2017) Critical fictions of transnationalism in Latinx children's literature. Bookbird. *A Journal of International Children's Literature* 55 (3), 4–11.

Cai, M. (2002) *Multicultural Literature for Children and Young Adults: Reflections on Critical Issues*. Greenwood Press.

Canagarajah, A.S. (2006) The place of world Englishes in composition: Pluralization continued. *College Composition and Communication* 57, 586–619.

Canagarajah, S. (2013) *Translingual Practice: Global Englishes and Cosmopolitan Relations*. Routledge.

Carrillo, J.F. (2013) I always knew I was gifted: Latino males and the Mestiz@ Theory of Intelligences (MTI). *Berkeley Review of Education* 4 (1), 69–95.

Carrillo, J.F. and Karvelis, N. (2023) Border thinking reflexivity in city schools: Possibilities for teaching in historically red states. *Critical Education* 14 (4), 96–112. https://doi.org/10.14288/ce.v14i4.186782.

Cenoz, J., Leonet, O. and Gorter, D. (2022) Developing cognate awareness through pedagogical translanguaging. *International Journal of Bilingual Education and Bilingualism* 25 (8), 2759–2773.

Cervantes-Soon, C.G. and Carrillo, J.F. (2016) Toward a pedagogy of border thinking: Building on Latin@ students' subaltern knowledge. *The High School Journal* 99 (4), 282–301.

Chang, R.S. (1999) *Disoriented: Asian Americans, Law, and the Nation-State*. New York University Press.

Coburn, A. and Gormally, S. (2017) A critical border pedagogy for praxis. *Counterpoints* 483, 155–174.

Cohen, R. (1996) Diasporas and the nation-state: From victims to challengers. *International Affairs (Royal Institute of International Affairs 1944-)* 72 (3), 507–520.

Comola, M. and Mendola, M. (2015) Formation of migrant networks. *The Scandinavian Journal of Economics* 117 (2), 592–618. https://doi.org/10.1111/sjoe.12093.

Compton-Lilly, C., Kim, J., Quast, E., Tran, S. and Shedrow, S. (2019) The emergence of transnational awareness among children in immigrant families. *Journal of Early Childhood Literacy* 19 (1), 3–33.

Compton-Lilly, C., Papoi, K., Venegas, P., Hamman, L. and Schwabenbauer, B. (2017) Intersectional identity negotiation: The case of young immigrant children. *Journal of Literacy Research* 49 (1), 115–140.

Cook, V. (2001) Using the first language in the classroom. *Canadian Modern Language Review* 57 (3), 402–423.

Corliss, J.C. (1998) *Crossing Borders with Literature of Diversity*. Christopher-Gordon.

Crisp, T., Knezek, S., Quinn, M., Bingham, G., Girardeau, K. and Starks, F. (2016) What's on our bookshelves? The diversity of children's literature in early childhood classroom libraries. *Journal of Children's Literature* 42 (2), 29–42.

Cuero, K.K. (2010). Artisan with words: Transnational funds of knowledge in a bilingual Latina's stories. *Language Arts* 87 (6), 427–436.

Cummins, J. and Persad, R. (2014) Teaching through a multilingual lens: The evolution of EAL policy and practice in Canada. *Education Matters* 2, 3–40.

Dabach, D.B. and Fones, A. (2016) Beyond the "English learner" frame:Transnational funds of knowledge in social studies. *International Journal of Multicultural Education* 18 (1), 7–27.

de los Ríos, C.V. (2018) Toward a corridista consciousness: Learning from one transnational youth's critical reading, writing, and performance of Mexican corridos. *Reading Research Quarterly* 53 (4), 455–471.

de los Ríos, C.V. (2020) Translingual youth podcasts as acoustic allies: Writing and negotiating identities at the intersection of literacies, language and racialization. *Journal of Language, Identity, and Education* 21, 1–15.

Dorner, L., Palmer, D., Cervantes-Soon, C., Heiman, D. and Crawford, E. (2023) *Critical Consciousness in Dual Language Bilingual Education: Case Studies on Policy and Practice*. Routledge.

Dutro, E. and Haberl, E. (2018) Blurring material and rhetorical walls: Children writing the border/lands in a second-grade classroom. *Journal of Literacy Research* 50 (2), 167–189.

Dyrness, A. and Sepúlveda III, E. (2020) *Border Thinking: Latinx Youth Decolonizing Citizenship*. University of Minnesota Press.

Elenes, C.A. (1997) Reclaiming the borderlands: Chicana/o identity, difference, and critical pedagogy. *Educational Theory* 47 (3), 359–375. https://doi.org/10.1111/j.1741-5446.1997.00359.x.

Elteren, M. (2011) Cultural globalization and transnational flows of things American. In P. Pachura (ed.) *The Systemic Dimension of Globalization*. IntechOpen. https://doi.org/10.5772/732.

Erdal, M.B. and Oeppen, C. (2013) Migrant balancing acts: Understanding the interactions between integration and transnationalism. *Journal of Ethnic and Migration Studies* 39 (6), 867–884.

Favell, A., Feldblum, M. and Smith, M.P. (2006) The human face of global mobility: A research agenda. In M.P. Smith and A. Favell (eds) *The Human Face of Global Mobility* (pp. 1–25). Transaction Press.

García, O. and Kleifgen, J. (2019) Translanguaging and literacies. *Reading Research Quarterly* 55 (4), 553–571.

García, O., Johnson, S. and Seltzer, K. (2017) *The Translanguaging Classroom: Leveraging Student Bilingualism for Learning*. Caslon.

Garza, E. (2007) Becoming a border pedagogy educator. *Multicultural Education* 14 (3), 1–7.

Giroux, H.A. (1988) Border pedagogy in the age of postmodernism. *Journal of Education* 170 (3), 162–181.

Giroux, H.A. (1991) Border pedagogy and the politics of postmodernism. *Social Text* (28), 51–67.

Giroux, H.A. (2005) *Border Crossings: Cultural Workers and the Politics of Education*. Routledge.

Guarzino, L., Portes, A. and Haller, W. (2003) Assimilation and transnationalism: Determinants of transnational political action among contemporary migrants. *American Journal of Sociology* 6, 1211–1248.

Guerra, J.C. (1998) *Close to Home: Oral and Literate Practices in a Transnational Mexicano Community*. Teachers College Press.

Guerrero, M. (2021) Gauging the adequacy of translanguaging allocation policy in two-way immersion programs in the U.S. *Journal of Latinos and Education* 22 (4), 1427–1441.

Gutiérrez, K. (2014) Integrative research review: Syncretic approaches to literacy learning. Leveraging horizontal knowledge and expertise. In P. Dunston, L. Gambrell, K. Headley, S. Fullerton and P. Stecker (eds) *63rd Literacy Research Association Yearbook*. (pp. 48–61). Literacy Research Association.

Handsfield, L.J. and Valente, P. (2016) Momentos de cambio: Cultivating bilingual students' epistemic privilege through memoir and testimonio. *International Journal of Multicultural Education* 18 (3), 138–158.

Hannerz, U. (1998) *Transnational Connections: Culture, People, Places*. Routledge.

Held, D., McGrew, A., Goldblatt, D. and Perraton, J. (2000) Global transformations: Politics, economics and culture. In C. Pierson and S. Tormey (eds) *Politics at the Edge*. Political Studies Association Yearbook Series. Palgrave Macmillan.

Hornberger, N.H. (2007) Biliteracy, transnationalism, multimodality, and identity: Trajectories across time and space. *Linguistics and Education* 18, 325–334.

Hornberger, N.H. and Link, H. (2012) Translanguaging in today's classrooms: A biliteracy lens. *Theory Into Practice* 51, 239–247.

Imbert, P. (2014) Linking transculturality and transdisciplinarity. *Semiotica* 202, 571–588.

Itzigsohn, J. and Saucedo, S.G. (2002) Immigrant incorporation and sociocultural transnationalism. *International Migration Review* 36 (3), 766–798. https://doi.org/10.1111/j.1747-7379.2002.tb00104.x.

Jiménez, R.T., Smith, P.H. and Teague, B.L. (2009) Transnational and community literacies for teachers. *Journal of Adolescent & Adult Literacy* 53 (1), 16–26.

Jones, R.C. (2019) The decline of migrant transnationalism with time abroad. *Ethnic and Racial Studies* 43 (15), 2685–2704. https://doi.org/10.1080/01419870.2019.1685117.

Jurkova, S. and Guo, S. (2018) Connecting transculturalism with transformative learning: Toward a new horizon of adult education. *Alberta Journal of Educational Research* 64 (2), 173–187.

Kasun, G.S. and Saavedra, C.M. (2014) Crossing borders toward young transnational lives. In J. Keengwe and G. Onchwari (eds) *Cross-Cultural Considerations in the Education of Young Immigrant Learners* (pp. 200–216). IGI Global.

Kazanjian, C.J. (2011) The border pedagogy revisited. *Intercultural Education* 22 (5), 371–380.

Kwon, J. (2022) *Understanding the Transnational Lives and Literacies of Immigrant Children*. Teachers College Press.

Laine, J.P. (2021) Beyond borders: Towards the ethics of unbounded inclusiveness. *Journal of Borderlands Studies* 36 (5), 745–763. https://doi.org/10.1080/08865655.2021.1924073.

Lam, W.S.E. (2004) Border discourses and identities in transnational youth culture. In J. Mahiri (ed.) *What they don't Learn in School: Literacy in the Lives of Urban Youth* (pp. 79–98). Peter Lang.

Lam, W.S.E. and Warriner, D.S. (2012) Transnationalism and literacy: Investigating the mobility of people, languages, texts, and practices in contexts of migration. *Reading Research Quarterly* 47, 191–215. https://doi.org/10.1002/RRQ.016.

Lange, E. (2015) Transformative learning and concepts of the self: Insights from immigrant and intercultural journeys. *International Journal of Lifelong Education* 34 (6), 623–642.

Lee, C. (2021) *Understanding the Oral and Written Translanguaging Practices of Emergent Bilinguals: Insights from a Korean Heritage Language Classroom in the U.S.* Routledge.

Lee, C. (2022) How can multicultural children's literature be utilized in the classroom to facilitate transnational students to be border-crossers? *Journal of Multilingual and Multicultural Development* 45 (5), 1717–1731. https://doi.org/10.1080/01434632.2021.2020802.

Lee, C. (2023) How do children go through a heteroglossic path to becoming bilingual? Comparison of Korean children's translanguaging performance in first and third grades. *International Journal of Bilingual Education and Bilingualism* 27 (4), 612–630. https://doi.org/10.1080/13670050.2023.2232088.

Lee, C. (2024) Sanctioning a space for literacy practices to promote transnational students' identity development in a HL classroom. *International Multilingual Research Journal* 19 (1), 1–22. https://doi.org/10.1080/19313152.2024.2309695.

Lee, C. (2025a) Teaching through the lens of the transformative stance: Envisioning teachers' "trans" perspective in diverse classrooms. *International Journal of Multilingual Education* 27 (1), 29–53.

Lee, C. (2025b) Using Asian Americans' counter-narratives for social justice and equity. *Journal of Literacy Research* 57 (2), 192–216.

Loh, S.H. (2022) The continued relevance of multiculturalism: Dissecting interculturalism and transculturalism. *Ethnic and Racial Studies* 45 (3), 385–406.

Lucas, S. and Purkayastha, B. (2007) "Where is home?" Here and there: Transnational experiences of home among Canadian migrants in the United States. *GeoJournal* 68 (2/3), 243–251.

Machado, E. and Hartman, P. (2019) Translingual writing in a linguistically diverse primary classroom. *Journal of Literacy Research* 51 (4), 480–503.

Machado, E. and Hartman, P. (2020) "It took us a long time to go here": Creating space for young children's transnationalism in an early writers' workshop. *Reading Research Quarterly* 56 (4), 693–714.

Mahon, K., Heikkinen, H. and Huttunen, R. (2019) Critical educational praxis in university ecosystems: Enablers and constraints. *Pedagogy, Culture, and Society* 27 (3), 463–480.

Mendoza, A., Hamman-Ortiz, L., Tian, Z., Rajendram, S., Tai, K.W.H., Ho, W.Y.J. and Sah, P.K. (2023) Sustaining critical approaches to translanguaging in education: A contextual framework. *TESOL Quarterly*. https://doi.org/10.1002/tesq.3240.

Mignolo, W.D. (2000) *Local Histories/Global Designs: Coloniality, Subaltern Knowledges, and Border Thinking*. Princeton University Press.

Mignolo, W.D. (2002) *The Many Faces of Cosmo-polis: Border Thinking and Critical Cosmopolitanism*. Duke University Press.

Mignolo, W.D. (2013) Geopolitics of sensing and knowing: On (de)coloniality, border thinking, and epistemic disobedience. *Confero* 1 (1), 129–150.

Mignolo, W.D. and Tlostanova, M.V. (2006) Theorizing from the borders: Shifting to geo- and body-politics of knowledge. *European Journal of Social Theory* 9 (2), 205–221.

Montgomery, C. (2014) Transnational and transcultural positionality in globalised higher Education. *Journal of Education for Teaching* 40 (3), 198–203.

Morrell, G. (2008) *Globalisation, Transnationalism and Diaspora*. ICAR.

Nodelman, P. and Reimer, M. (2003) *Pleasures of Children's Literature* (3rd edn). Allyn and Bacon.

Orellana, M.F. (2016) *Immigrant Children in Transcultural Spaces: Language, Learning, and Love*. Routledge.

Palmer, D., Cervantes-Soon, C., Dorner, L. and Heiman, D. (2019) Bilingualism, biliteracy, biculturalism and critical consciousness for all: Proposing a fourth fundamental goal for two-way dual language education. *Theory Into Practice* 58 (2), 121–133.

Portes, A. (2001) Introduction: The debates and significance of immigrant transnationalism. *Global Networks* 1, 181–194. https://doi.org/10.1111/1471-0374.00012.

Powell, C. and Carrillo, J.F. (2019) Border pedagogy in the new Latinx South. *Equity & Excellence in Education* 52 (4), 435–447. https://doi.org/10.1080/10665684.2019.1668314.

Poza, L. (2017) Translanguaging: Definitions, implications, and further needs in burgeoning inquiry. *Berkeley Review of Education* 6 (2), 101–128.

Reyes, M. and Garza, E. (2005) Teachers on the border: In their own word. *Journal of Latinos and Education* 4 (3), 153–170.

Rizvi, F. (2019) Global mobility, transnationalism and challenges for education. In M. Drinkwater, F. Rizvi and K. Edge (eds) *Transnational Perspectives on Democracy, Citizenship, Human Rights and Peace Education* (pp. 27–50). Bloomsbury Publishing.

Robins, K. (2006) *The Challenge of Transcultural Diversities*. Council of Europe.

Rochman, H. (1993) *Against Borders: Promoting Books for a Multicultural World*. American Library Association.

Rodríguez, S.C. and Braden, E.G. (2018) Representation of latinx immigrants and immigration in children's literature: A critical content analysis. *Journal of Children's Literature* 44 (2), 46–61.

Romo, J. and Chavez, C. (2006) Border pedagogy: A study of preservice teacher transformation. *The Educational Forum* 70 (2), 142–153.

Sánchez, P. and Kasun, G.S. (2012) Connecting transnationalism to the classroom and to theories of immigrant student adaptation. *Berkeley Review of Education* 3, 71–93.

Sánchez, P. and Landa, M. (2016) Cruzando fronteras: Negotiating the stories of Latino immigrant and transnational children. In E.R. Clark *et al.* (eds) *Multicultural Literature for Latino Bilingual Children: Their Eords, their Worlds* (pp. 69–82). Rowman & Littlefield.

Sánchez, P. (2007) Cultural authenticity and transnational Latina youth: Constructing a metanarrative across borders. *Linguistics and Education* 18, 258–282.

Sánchez, P. (2009) Even beyond the local community: A close look at Latina youths' return trips to Mexico. *The High School Journal* 92 (4), 49–66.

Schiller, N.G., Basch, L. and Blanc-Szanton, C. (1992) Transnationalism: A new analytic framework for understanding migration. *Annals of the New York Academy of Sciences* 645 (1), 1–24.

Sims Bishop, R. (1987) Extending multicultural understanding through children's books. In B.E. Cullinan (ed.) *Children's Literature in the Reading Program* (pp. 60–67). International Reading Association.

Skerrett, A. (2012) Language and literacies in translocation: Experiences and perspectives of a transnational youth. *Journal of Literacy Research* 44, 364–395.

Skerrett, A. (2015) *Teaching Transnational Youth: Literacy and Education in a Changing World*. Teachers College Press.

Skerrett, A. and Bomer, R. (2013) Recruiting languages and lifeworlds for border-crossing compositions. *Research in the Teaching of English* 47, 313–337.

Smith, M.P. (2003) Transnationalism, the state, and the extraterritorial citizen. *Politics and Society* 31 (4), 467–502.

Smith, R. (2006) *Mexican New York: Transnational Lives of New Immigrants*. UC Press.

Solorza, C.R. (2019) Trans + Languaging: Beyond dual language bilingual education. *Journal of Multilingual Education Research* 9 (15) 99–112.

Soja, E. (1996) *Thirdspace: Journeys to Los Angeles and Other Real-and-Imagined Places*. Oxford: Blackwell.

Souto-Manning, M. (2013) Teaching young children from immigrant and diverse families. *Young Children* 68 (4), 72–80.

Stewart, M.A. and Hansen-Thomas, H. (2016) Sanctioning a space for translanguaging in the secondary English classroom: A case of a transnational youth. *Research in the Teaching of English* 50 (4), 450–472.

Tedeschi, M., Vorobeva, E. and Jauhiainen, J. (2022) Transnationalism: Current debates and new perspectives. *GeoJournal* 87, 603–619.

Verdery, A.M., Mouw, T., Edelblute, H. and Chavez, S. (2018) Communication flows and the durability of a transnational social field. *Social Networks* 53, 57–71.

Vertovec, S. (2001) Transnationalism and identity. *Journal of Ethnic and Migration Studies* 27 (4), 573–582.

Vertovec, S. (2003) Migration and other modes of transnationalism: Towards conceptual cross-fertilization. *International Migration Review* 37 (3), 641–665.

Vertovec, S. (2004) Migrant transnationalism and modes of transformation. *International Migration Review* 38 (3), 970–1001.

Vertovec, S. (2009) *Transnationalism*. Routledge.

Warriner, D.S. (2007) Transnational literacies: Immigration, language learning, and identity. *Linguistics and Education* 18, 201–214.

Welsch, W. (1999) Transculturality—the puzzling form of cultures today. In M. Featherstone and S. Lash (eds) *Spaces of Culture: City, Nation, World* (pp. 194–213). Sage.

7 Implementing Social Justice-Oriented Practices to Achieve Equity and Justice

In my fifth-grade classroom, when the class is reading the book Boys in the Back Row (Jung, 2020), a student named Grace points out the scene when Kenny [a White boy] keeps calling Matt [the Korean American protagonist] Wang in a mocking tone even though Matt tells Kenny that his last name is Park many times. Another student, Henry, emotionally says, 'Kenny is a racist. He said that "I am talking to the Chink." That is a racial slur. I know people say Ching Chang Chong to Asians or to people they believe Asians.' By directly quoting what Kenny said to Matt, the class criticizes the derogatory and pejorative terms Kenny uses when describing the Asian protagonist in the storyline. On a different day in the same classroom, a student named Bella shares that her older sister, who is in eighth grade, reads the novel Eleanor & Park (Rowell, 2013), which portrays the power of human connection between a Caucasian and a Korean American high school student. Bella and her sister think that the title of the book is ridiculous and inaccurate because Park is a common Korean last name, but it is used as the literary character's first name. After listening to Bella's story, another student, Noah, shares a similar experience. Noah says, 'A few of my classmates called me Kim. But that's my last name. My first name [in Korean] is difficult. Kim is used as a first name for Americans. So I had to teach them my first name.'

***

The two stories in this vignette indicate that Asian American students recognize that they have been negatively discriminated against and significantly underrepresented in media, often depicted as nameless, faceless and/or voiceless foreign figures, leading to a sense of their absence within mainstream narratives. The invisibility of Asian Americans in the US school curriculum remains a concern. Accordingly, Asian American children in the US are less likely to encounter accurate stories and authentic illustrations from a broader range of Asian American perspectives. Moreover, at the height of the COVID-19 pandemic, hate crimes and incidents against Asian or

Asian Americans increased considerably in the US (Pew Research Center, 2023). This racist belief that Asians are accountable for causing COVID-19 has led to deleterious effects on Asian students' mental, emotional, psychological and behavioral health and well-being. Hence, elucidating racial and social inequality toward Asian Americans and confronting the invisibility of anti-Asian racism remain as crucial and urgent as ever.

Introduction to the Chapter

By acknowledging that intersectionality (Crenshaw, 1989) and multiple forms of oppression (such as race, class, gender, sexual orientation, ethnicity, language and immigration status) pervasively exist in society, this chapter discusses AsianCrit, which is a critical race framework that draws on the principles of Critical Race Theory to analyze and understand the unique experiences of Asian Americans within a racialized society. The chapter also focuses on critical literacy and counter-narratives as powerful pedagogical tools that interrogate racial injustice and advocate for social change through narratives to challenge dominant perspectives. The discussion in this chapter narrows the gap in the literature by demonstrating how critical literacy instruction that incorporates Asian American counter-narratives can facilitate educational transformation, equity and social justice by enabling Asian American students to challenge hegemony, stereotypes and racism.

The Role of Race and Racial Identity in Society

Race is a social, cultural and political reality that remains unfixed due to the role of social institutions and contemporary society (Winant, 2000). Since racial categories classify people based on physical features such as skin color or hair texture, race is subsumed in society as a social fabrication. According to Omi and Winant (1994: 68), race is 'an unstable and decentered complex of social meanings'. Race is not just a mode of representation but also an articulation of social structure; a social construct divides people into distinct groups based on racial categories, ethnic classification and/ or physical appearance. Thus, race actively shapes the underlying power dynamics and inequalities within a social system, influencing how people are positioned and treated based on their racial identity.

As society not just defines but also controls racial formation (O'Brien, 2017), scholars found race to be a valuable tool in identifying how racial boundaries shape and change social dynamics in various ways. Both historical and contemporary societies use race and racial ideology to establish, justify and perpetuate systems of power and oppression. As individuals or groups are bestowed opportunities, power and privileges depending on their racial identities, it is vital to understand how the ideology of race in society and the racial worldview has shaped our identities and experiences.

While there is no biological reality to the concept of race at a genetic level, the social construct of race still holds significant power and impact on people's lives, shaping societal structures and experiences of privilege or discrimination based on perceived racial categories. Since race is not biological, and one's racial identity is not static but fluid, people consciously make choices to assimilate or fit into prevailing norms of a larger or dominant group that holds the most power and influence. The notion of race is intimately connected to and closely shaped by human lives. Individuals' racial identities not only significantly impact their lived experiences, opportunities and overall life trajectory but also become fundamental factors affecting how people navigate the world around them.

The Importance of Studying Racial Formations and Racial Discourse

Omi and Winant (1994: 61) defined racial formation as 'the process by which social, economic, and political forces determine the content and importance of racial categories'. Racial formation describes how race is created, represented, deployed, institutionalized, transformed and destroyed. That is, racial formation highlights how race is not a fixed attribute but a social construct that changes over time and across different contexts. According to Omi and Winant, a racial formation perspective views race as 'an autonomous field of social conflict, political organizations, and cultural/ideological meaning' (1994: 52). The racial formation perspective emphasizes that race is a social and political construction that operates at both the micro- (i.e. individuals' everyday interactions) and macro-levels (i.e. broader societal forces or collective social structures, such as laws or policies). The two levels interact and cooperate to shape racial politics and social changes when individuals are organized to actively address racial discrimination and inequalities that exist in a larger societal structure. In other words, racial social movements are generated when people on a micro-level are galvanized to bring significant alterations and make changes due to deeply ingrained and institutionalized patterns of systemic racism occurring at the macro level.

Omi and Winant (1994) emphasized that racial projects not only aim to interpret and examine various aspects of racial dynamics in society but also reorganize and redistribute resources and opportunities to challenge racial disparities and promote equity. This involves analyzing how society provides advantages or preferential treatment to certain racial groups that have been historically disadvantaged. The recognition of the importance of examining racial discourse has resulted in a substantial and growing body of literature in ethnic and racial studies (Dixon & Levine, 2012). Research has examined the role of race in specific situations by focusing on how races created hierarchical systems and constructed power relations in different social contexts, which in turn shaped individuals' social and discursive practices based on their racial identities (Augoustinos & Every, 2007; Back & Zavala, 2019; Bonilla-Silva 2002; Condor et al., 2006; Condor & Figgou, 2012; Every & Augoustinos, 2007; Figgou & Condor, 2006; Gibson, 2020; Goodman et al., 2017; Sleeter & Zavala, 2020; Whitehead, 2015). By taking race as its key topic, racial discourse examines how race is formed and perpetuated through social practices and ideological processes by centering power dynamics and cultural representations that shape people's understanding of race within society.

Identifying Critical Race Theory: An Academic Theoretical Framework

Critical Race Theory (CRT) acknowledges intersectionality, which explains multiple forms of oppression and interlocking systems of inequality due to race, ethnicity, gender, class, sexual orientation and/or disability (Crenshaw, 1989), pervasively exist in society (Crenshaw et al., 1995; Delgado, 2011). CRT centers race as the primary lens for examining the political enactment of laws and legislation (Chapman, 2007). According to McNair (2008b: 7), racism is 'embedded into the fabric of our everyday lives and often appears natural, instead of abnormal'. CRT scholars explored how racism has played and continues to play a dominant role in determining inequity in the US by viewing that race and racism have a significant impact on the US legal system (e.g. Brown, 2014; Crenshaw et al., 1995; DeCuir & Dixson, 2004; Donnor, 2018; Gillborn, 2006; Ladson-Billings, 2014; Solorzano & Yosso, 2002; Tate, 1997; Vaught & Castagno, 2008). Since CRT recognizes that racism is largely embedded in institutional laws and policies, CRT scholars seek to understand how structural racism has shaped public policy that upholds and exacerbates racial inequalities and inequity.

As racism is deeply rooted in history and exists in a natural way in people's lives as a permanent fixture in society (Museus & Iftikar, 2014: 20, italics in original), proponents of CRT acknowledge that the concept of race is a socially constructed phenomenon (Delgado & Stefancic, 2001; Willis et al., 2008). CRT scholars believe in a regime of White supremacy with its subordination of people of color (Museus & Iftikar, 2014; Solórzano & Yosso, 2002). CRT helps us identify and criticize social oppression and racial subordination by analyzing experiential knowledge marginalized groups have gained. CRT scholars are committed to eliminating racism and other forms of oppression in society by challenging racial hegemony, phenotypical inequality and color blindness to establish social justice and equity, which is the ultimate goal of CRT (DeCuir & Dixson, 2004; Delgado, 2011; Delgado & Stefancic, 2012; Ladson-Billings, 2013; Solorzano & Yosso, 2002). CRT scholars call for a thorough examination and ongoing monitoring of political, economic and social institutions to ensure they do not continue to 'allocate the privileging of Whites and the subsequent Othering of people of color in all arenas, including education' (DeCuir & Dixson, 2004: 27).

Critical Race Pedagogy as a Teaching Approach Rooted in CRT

CRT has been used by scholars in higher education as a framework of legal analysis to challenge white privilege, dominant belief and color blindness (Delgado & Stefancic, 2013) and to analyze how race and racism function to oppress people of color (Museus *et al.*, 2018; Poon, 2014; Solorzano, 1998; Solorzano & Yosso, 2002). Educational researchers who have adopted the CRT framework identified that race and racism intertwine with other forms of social inequality and subordination, such as class, gender, sexuality and ability, which shape the social construct of oppression (Delgado & Stefancic, 2013; Solorzano *et al.*, 2000). CRT elucidates multifaceted tenets, which refer to the idea that racism is not simply a matter of individual prejudice but is deeply embedded within social structures, systems and institutions, creating a complex web of interconnected inequalities.

Through multifaceted, interconnected tenets, CRT encourages a deep understanding of how systemic racism perpetuates racial inequity by unveiling power structures that maintain disparities based on race across multiple dimensions of life. As one of the tenets of CRT, 'interest convergence' indicates that the advancement of civil rights movements for people of color is often proclaimed and more likely to happen when the interests of those in power (i.e. the White group) align with the interests of people of color (Delgado & Stefancic, 2012), suggesting that the progress is not solely motivated by the genuine desire of marginalized groups, but also by the self-interest of privileged individuals or groups who benefit from participating in these movements.

A central tenet of CRT is to actively deconstruct and challenge the dominant narratives that serve to normalize, obscure and conceal racial inequalities and inequities within institutions and systems. According to Compton-Lilly (2009), CRT exposes the importance of literacy among people of color which involves the acknowledgment of race, culture, language and abilities that non-Whites or marginalized groups use and hold. Thus, CRT includes narratives that 'foreground the voice, experience, and realities that inform the consciousness of people of Color' (Willis *et al.*, 2008: 36) by acknowledging racialized people as multifaceted individuals with valuable perspectives who are essential to dismantle dominant narratives and promote social justice collectively (Delgado & Stefancic, 2012). Since racism is 'a system of privileges that works to the advantages of whites and to the detriment of people of color' (McNair, 2008b: 26), it is embedded and deeply ingrained within the structures and systems of American society (Bell, 1992). CRT aims to use literature as a tool to analyze systemic racism, thereby motivating social protests and political movements against racial injustice by examining issues through a critical race lens (Delgado & Stefancic, 2012, 2013).

Using critical race pedagogy from CRT, educators can foster diverse community recognition to value minority races, cultures and languages that social organizations and institutions have undermined (Poon, 2014). Critical race pedagogy seeks an active transformation to increase students' sense of self-efficacy and resilience (Sleeter, 2017). Proponents of critical race pedagogy recognize the silence of internalized racism (Ladson-Billings & Tate, 1995; Solórzano & Yosso, 2002). Scholars have notably claimed that multicultural literature should be used to counter dominant hegemonic narratives and eschew harmful stereotypes of minority groups prevalent in contemporary society (Pak & Ravitch, 2021). In other words, critical race pedagogy can challenge dominant myths of racism and amplify the voices of people of color by challenging the use of language, literacy and power that normalize and universalize whiteness (Delgado & Stefancic, 2012; Dixson & Rousseau, 2005; Gangi, 2008; Willis *et al.*, 2008).

Asian Critical (AsianCrit) Theory in Education

Museus and Iftikar (2014) addressed the limitations of CRT when examining Asian or Asian Americans' experiences of racial injustice and oppression because CRT disproportionately pays attention to African American populations. Museus and Iftikar thus proposed 'Asian critical (AsianCrit) theory' as a critical race framework that employs the principles of CRT to analyze and understand the unique experiences of Asian Americans in a racialized society. Although AsianCrit is grounded in CRT, it offers a critical lens to explore racial prejudice, ethnic disparities and structural racism experienced specifically by Asian Americans that perpetuate systems of dominance and White supremacy (Iftikar & Museus, 2018; Museus & Iftikar, 2013, 2014). By resonating with original CRT tenets, AsianCrit includes seven tenets – (1) Asianization, (2) Transnational Context, (3) (Re)Constructivist History, (4) Strategic (Anti)Essentialism, (5) Intersectionality, (6) Story, Theory and Praxis and (7) Commitment to Social Justice.

Specifically, *Asianization* defines the reality where racism and racial ideologies toward Asian Americans are persistent in the White society. According to Museus and Iftikar (2013: 23), Asianization '(re)shape[s] laws and policies that affect Asian Americans and influence Asian American identities and experiences'. The second tenet of *Transnational Context* refers to the analysis of Asian experiences and identities not just within the borders of a single Asian country but also considers the interconnectedness and shared experiences across different Asian nations as part of a larger network, both within and outside of Asia. This tenet focuses on how (im)migration, transnationalism, transculturalism and colonialism shape the experiences and identities of Asian diaspora communities. *(Re)constructive History* refers to the process and practice of actively restructuring and retelling historical narratives to include the voices, experiences and contributions of Asian Americans who have been invisible and voiceless in mainstream historical accounts. It aims to create an inclusive understanding of Asian American history, centering Asian American perspectives and voices in combating the invisibility of Asian American stories within the dominant narrative.

Intersectionality is a concept that can be used to examine the complex ways that race, gender, sexuality, class and other identities interact with systems of oppression to affect individuals, but Intersectionality from AsianCrit explains how different identities intersect and overlap inside the Asian American communities and how systems of oppression and exploitation mutually shape within the field of Asian American studies. Since White supremacy views all Asians as a monolithic group and homogenizes their unique histories, experiences and identities, *Strategic (Anti)Essentialism* disrupts the notion that Asian Americans are all the same and strives to scrutinize diversity and heterogeneity in Asian Americans.

The Story, Theory and Praxis tenet centers on Asian Americans' perspective by concentrating on the voices and stories of Asian American communities (Museus & Iftikar, 2013). This tenet challenges Eurocentrism (i.e. Euro-Western dominance of worldview) by offering an alternative epistemology that focuses on Asian American people's experiences, practices and values (Iftikar & Museus, 2018). *Commitment to Social Justice* not only combats racism and imperialism but also prioritizes social changes to make equity and justice for Asian Americans. AsianCrit is committed to actively ending all forms of oppression and exploitation directed toward Asian Americans, aiming to eradicate systems that dehumanize them. AsianCrit, thus, essentially seeks to critically analyze and dismantle the specific racialized experiences of Asian Americans within broader societal structures (Iftikar & Museus, 2018). Since AsianCrit focuses explicitly on the unique racial and historical features that shape the lives of Asian Americans, it is fundamental and essential to exploring the stories and experiences of Asian Americans.

Examining the Powerful Role of Critical Literacy

Educational researchers who have adopted the CRT framework consider critical literacy as a powerful tool for social protest and political activism against racism by giving voice to marginalized communities, exposing the realities of racial injustice and advocating for change through narratives that challenge dominant perspectives (Delgado & Stefancic, 2013; Ladson-Billings, 2014; Rodríguez, 2018). Critical literacy was rooted in the social justice pedagogy by Brazilian educator and theorist Paulo Freire (1972). According to Freire, critical literacy is an instructional approach that promotes the use of critical perspectives toward text. Freire (1978) claimed that reading the word critically and the world consciously supported the transformation of power imbalances, structured systems of domination and hierarchical forms of oppression within society.

As Freire (1978: 11) argued, 'reading always involves critical perception, interpretation, and re-writing what is read'. Critical literacy encourages readers to actively engage with texts by questioning assumptions, identifying biases and analyzing the power structures present in both narratives and real life. Hall (1980) indeed claimed that readers engage with a text by encoding it in three ways by accepting the intended meaning, negotiating (i.e. partially accepting and modifying) the meaning to fit their own experiences and viewpoints, or rejecting the intended meaning and creating their interpretation. In other words, readers' construction, deconstruction or reconstruction of knowledge empowers them to critically identify the unequal status quo to social structures and prejudiced power relations (Freire & Macedo, 1987; Lankshear & McClaren, 1993; Morrell, 2004).

Critical literacy teaches readers how to combat the social injustices that perpetuate marginalized social groups in their communities. Reading from a critical perspective involves thinking beyond the text to understand social issues and power dynamics by analyzing how power is distributed and exercised within a society (McLaughlin & DeVoogd, 2004). Hence, critical literacy scholars contended that readers need to actively engage with the text and analyze the systemic inequalities in underlying messages by adopting a critical approach and continuously interrogating implicit assumptions (Jowallah, 2015; McLaughlin & DeVoogd, 2010; Shor, 1999). Since texts are socially constructed from certain perspectives, and no text is neutral (Freire & Macedo, 1987), readers who adopt a critical literacy lens can question things that are taken for granted or assumed to be normal in the world. Critical literacy practices use literature by closely examining texts to identify and challenge embedded messages that perpetuate prejudiced power relations, which often generate Eurocentric norms and unequal status quo (Freire & Macedo, 1987; Hull, 1993; Lankshear & McClaren, 1993). Proponents of critical literacy emphasize the importance of taking an active stance toward language use when reading and interpreting texts to examine the correlation between language and power, to deconstruct the core messages conveyed in the text and to challenge underlying biases that perpetuate inequality (Knoblauch & Brannon, 1993; Lewison et al., 2002).

Freirean critical literacy is regarded as a means of sanctioning and empowering marginalized populations against oppression, coercion and compulsion. As critical literacy indicates 'the process of becoming conscious of one's experience as historically constructed within specific power relations' (Anderson & Irvine, 1993: 82), critical literacy pedagogy identifies racial inequities and societal problems caused by the unequal power structure in society. Critical literacy practices further encourage readers to develop critical thinking and advocate for social action and political movements to bring about social and political change against systemic inequality and structural racism (Ladson-Billings, 2014). Thus, critical literacy serves as a powerful tool in eradicating hierarchical forms of oppression and reinforcing the transformation of the power dynamics by assisting readers to take concrete social action to transform unjust systems and change biased structures within contemporary racialized society (Ellis & Eberly, 2015; Ladson-Billings, 2014; Lewison *et al.*, 2002; Morrell, 2004; Willis *et al.*, 2008).

An Educator's Role in Critical Literacy Instruction

Many educators and classroom teachers found critical literacy to be beneficial and transformative for students (e.g. Borsheim-Black *et al.*, 2014; Clark & Whitney, 2009; Ellis & Eberly, 2015; Kim & Hsieh, 2021; Lee, 2021a, 2021b, 2024; Riley, 2015; Schiera, 2019; Williams, 2022). Critical literacy goes beyond basic reading comprehension as it focuses on deeper analysis considering the underlying social context and potential biases embedded within the text. Critical literacy encourages readers to deeply analyze, acutely evaluate and critically question the information within a given text, particularly the messages that are related to power dynamics and societal problems. The use of critical literacy instruction thus prompts students to think judiciously and take appropriate action to address specific issues by developing a deeper understanding of social concerns and thoughtfully examining power structures within texts.

Educators can incorporate a critical literacy approach into their instruction to help students become actively involved in the reading process through questioning, interrogating or disputing the commonplace and inequities that are present in the text (McLaughlin & DeVoogd, 2010). By employing a critical literacy lens, educators can assist students to become more analytical and critical consumers of text by helping them identify whose stories are (not) often told and heard and whose voice is included or missing in narratives. Educators' critical literacy instruction approach can further inspire students to enact positive social change for themselves, their community and society (Ellis & Eberly, 2015).

Classroom teachers should examine and analyze how children's or young adult literature contains messages of power and privilege according to one's race, ethnicity, culture, language use, gender and/or socioeconomic status. After a close examination of the text, teachers can create lessons that are connected to social action projects by tapping into students' critical thinking and understanding of different perspectives. For instance, teachers can encourage students to discuss how the story could differ if the protagonist were from a different racial/ethnic background or if the story took place in a different part of the world. By doing so, teachers can educate students to take a critical stance toward literature and make their curriculum more transparent and socially just.

A curricular framework for teaching critical literacy can be through using Lewison, Flint and van Sluys's (2002) four dimensions of critical literacy: (1) disrupting the commonplace, (2) interrogating multiple viewpoints, (3) focusing on sociopolitical issues and (4) taking action and promoting social justice. Their framework indicates that critical literacy encourages readers to question and challenge preconceived notions and taken-for-granted assumptions, explore multiple viewpoints and diverse perspectives, examine complex ways in which power is distributed and exercised in society and take deliberate actions for positive social transformation. These four dimensions of critical literacy offer a valuable framework to help students develop into critical thinkers, readers and consumers. Lewison *et al.* (2002) suggest that people cannot take action against racism or achieve social justice without learning about current disparities within a historical and social context. Hence, educators should actively guide their students in developing their knowledge and understanding, and fostering critical thinking by using different viewpoints and perspectives to create a holistic learning experience.

The Characteristics and Role of Counter-Narratives

Counter-narratives are stories that portray the lived experiences of racial, ethnic or cultural groups who have been historically oppressed, excluded and silenced in society (DeCuir & Dixson, 2004; Delgado & Stefancic, 2001; Solórzano & Yosso, 2002). Martinez (2014) noted that counter-stories depict marginalized groups by centering their experiences and embodied knowledge so that their voices, perspectives, experiences and practices can be included, embraced and valued. The Minnesota Humanities Center (2018) characterized counter-narratives as 'absent narratives' because the lived experiences of minority groups are often 'left out, overwritten, [and] absented by a dominant story' (2018: 1). That is, counter-narratives assist students in interrogating societal issues and challenge deficit perspectives toward people of marginalized groups and their communities (Ellison & Solomon, 2019; Martinez, 2018).

Counter-narratives oppose widely accepted dominant narratives by interpreting stories from non-dominant viewpoints, which are often distorted or suppressed in traditional curricula materials (Cheruvu *et al.*, 2015; Heidt *et al.*, 2023; Miller *et al.*, 2020; Milner & Howard, 2013). Since counter-narratives lead readers to criticize 'normalized dialogues that perpetuate racial stereotypes' (DeCuir & Dixson, 2004: 27), they empower readers to reveal societal inequality and injustice and disrupt biased attitudes and prejudiced behaviors from the traditionally marginalized groups' standpoints to bring potential transformation (Solórzano & Yosso, 2002).

Counter-Narratives as a Key Component of CRT and Critical Literacy

Counter-narratives, also known as counter-storytelling (Delgado & Stefancic, 2001) or counter-stories (Matsuda, 1995), are an essential element of CRT. Counter-storytelling is described as 'a method of telling a story that aims to cast doubt on the validity of accepted premises or myths, especially ones held by the majority' (Delgado & Stefancic, 2001: 144). Matsuda (1995: 63) argued that counter-stories illustrate experiences of people who have been marginalized and discriminated against 'with a special voice to which we should listen'. Thus, counter-stories offer a perspective that 'help[s] us understand what life is like for others, and invite the reader into a new and unfamiliar world' (Delgado & Stefancic 2001: 41). CRT scholars believe that counter-narratives provide a voice to marginalized or less privileged individuals and groups. Counter-narratives validate the life circumstances and experiences of underrepresented groups by providing alternative stories that directly challenge and subvert the dominant narratives often held by privileged individuals.

Counter-narratives incorporate each feature of critical literacy because critical readers and writers recognize that texts are never neutral (Freire & Macedo, 1987; Gee, 2012). By analyzing what messages are conveyed and why certain language is used in the story, readers can go beyond the literal meaning of words to examine how language is used to maintain or disrupt the status quo and further investigate an unequal society that perpetuates the power structures (DeCuir & Dixson, 2004; Delgado & Stefancic, 2013; Solórzano & Yosso, 2002). The use of counter-storytelling as a tool of critical literacy instruction can challenge dominant hegemony and widespread stereotypes by learning about the (hi)stories of marginalized and oppressed people (Delgado & Stefancic, 2013). When encountering counter-narratives, readers can uncover and criticize injustice issues in a racialized society where the experiences of minority groups are eradicated and perpetuated. Being immersed in counter-narratives brings an educational outcome of critical literacy pedagogy, and opening spaces and creating opportunities for deep discussion can be advisable ideas to achieve educational equity and justice (Lee, 2026).

Pursuing the Goals of AsianCrit Using Asian American Counter-Narratives

The goal of AsianCrit is not just to inform people that racial inequities toward Asians exist in society but also to educate people to achieve social equality and justice by centering Asian American voices, stories, experiences and perspectives in combating the invisibility of

Asian American stories within the dominant narrative (Iftikar & Museus, 2018). Yet, former critical race theorists argued that reflection itself is not enough to bring significant change or societal transformation; rather, taking concrete actions based on those reflections is strongly required for transformative learning and social impact (Ladson-Billing & Tate, 1995; Mezirow, 2000). According to Freire (1972), reflection without taking any concrete actions becomes mere 'verbalism', while performing action without critical reflection becomes 'pure activism'. Thus, the ideal approach to achieve social transformation is combining reflection and action (i.e. thinking and doing), which Freire defined as 'praxis' that signifies 'reflection and action upon the world in order to transform' (1972: 52). Since praxis suggests taking responsive and accountable actions based on critical thinking and thoughtful reflections, praxis can generate transformation to work toward social justice. Critical race theorists and critical literacy scholars have emphasized the inseparable elements of an indivisible relationship between reflection and social action to promote educational equity (Liu & Ball, 2019). Critical literacy scholars strongly advocate for using counter-narratives as instructional resources to examine societal issues and actively challenge deficit perspectives often directed toward marginalized groups, ultimately aiming to pursue equity and justice (DeCuir & Dixson, 2004; Delgado & Stefancic, 2013; Solórzano & Yosso, 2002).

Past studies have discovered how counter-narratives promoted students to criticize majoritarian stories that immortalize racial stereotypes and racism (e.g. Cammarota, 2014; Cammarota & Romero, 2011; Ellison & Solomon, 2019; Godley & Loretto, 2013; Heidt et al., 2023) by recognizing how ingrained systems of power and inequality are often considered normal and neutral in everyday life. These studies documented that counter-narratives encouraged marginalized students to adopt multiple perspectives, critiquing the power structures that function as societal norms by raising awareness of how these structures benefit certain groups at the expense of others. When encountering counter-narratives, the students in earlier studies confronted biases, inequalities and injustice issues in a racialized society where the experiences of minority populations were eradicated and perpetuated. The findings showed that the use of counter-narratives not only highlighted the existence of a dominant hegemony and the persistence of racism but also underscored different forms of subordination and (hi)stories of oppressed groups through voices from the margins of society (Delgado & Stefancic, 2013; Martinez, 2014, 2018).

Although studies have correspondingly exhibited the central role of using counter-narratives to interrogate majoritarian narratives by centering marginalized individuals' voices and experiences (Miller et al., 2020), most studies included Latinx (e.g. Buchanan & Hilburn, 2016; Cammarota, 2014; Cammarota & Romero, 2011; Salinas et al., 2016) and African American student groups (e.g. Ellison & Solomon, 2019;

Flennaugh *et al.*, 2017; Motha & Varghese, 2018). Hence, we have little understanding of how Asian American students engage in analyzing counter-narratives to discover, analyze and/or critique issues of injustice in traditional curricula materials. In addition, few studies have investigated how teachers incorporate Asian American counter-narratives into their instruction to bring the lived experiences of Asian Americans, whose stories and voices are often underrepresented in traditional curricula materials, to the forefront.

Using Asian American Counter-Narratives in a Heritage Language Classroom

After recognizing the absence of literature portraying Asian Americans as protagonists from the public school curricula where Korean American students attended in my heritage language classroom, I advocated for the use of counter-narratives as a medium for promoting liberation and equality from a social justice approach. My studies (Lee, 2026, 2025a) narrowed the gap in the literature by demonstrating how my (as a teacher) critical literacy instruction that included Asian American counter-narratives achieved educational transformation, equity and social justice (Lee, 2026), and how literature discussions based on Asian American counter-narratives helped fifth-grade Korean American students learn to disrupt hegemony, stereotypes and racism (Lee, 2025a).

For these studies, I purposefully selected five literary works about Asian American individuals that depict their unique lived experiences and the challenges or obstacles they faced in certain events. Each piece of literature portrays different Asian ethnic groups with diverse genres (see Table 7.1 for the list of Asian American counter-narratives). I used the chosen literature as my curricular counter-narratives to question hegemonic discourse and deconstruct traditionally accepted narratives that had been prevalent in the students' mainstream school programs. I anticipated that including Asian American counter-narratives in my curriculum would be a powerful praxis that achieves educational equity and yields a social justice outcome in pursuit of the goals of AsianCrit in the classroom. The following section displays how I, as a fifth-grade teacher, implemented a transformational approach using the Asian American counter-narratives (as my critical literacy pedagogy) to create an equitable classroom space for Korean American students to articulate their critical perspectives through profound conversations during their literature discussions.

Employing a transformational approach in a curriculum

All the selected literature depicts (hi)stories and experiences of traditionally ostracized Asian American individuals. Reading and discussing the stories led the students to identify the existing biases and

Table 7.1 Asian American counter-narratives selection

Title of literature (author, year)	Ethnic group	Story synopsis
The Boys in the Back Row (Jung, 2020)	Korean American	The story is laced with Asian-racism but also portrays how the Korean American protagonist overcomes challenges by standing up for himself
Amina's Voice (Khan, 2017)	Pakistani American and Korean American	The Pakistani American and Korean American protagonists are mocked by their White classmates and deal with different forms of racism and hate crimes, but they overcome challenges, heal and re-establish their identities
Inside Out and Back Again (Lai, 2011)	Vietnamese American	The Vietnamese-born protagonist faces bullies and discrimination at school after her family fled to America. The story depicts how she overcomes the differences and challenges as she adjusts to a new country, culture and language
'Ten Things You Should Know about Being an Asian from the South' (Yamazawa, 2022)	Japanese American	Having grown up in the US South, Japanese American poet Yamazawa explains how he had to deal with racial stereotypes and biases due to his Asian racial identity
'Remembering Linsanity' (Wang, 2022)	Taiwanese American	This graphic memoir depicts Jeremy Lin, the first American-born NBA player of Taiwanese descent, who fights for race-based discrimination due to stereotypes toward Asian American athletes in professional sports

widespread stereotypes toward Asians or Asian Americans living in the US. Although the class easily identified negative stereotypes and harmful prejudice toward Asian American protagonists because they were obvious and apparent in the storylines, I led the class to discern and identify implicit biases toward certain racial groups, which are involuntarily formed in people's subconscious minds and thus impact their perceptions and behaviors without conscious awareness and recognition.

Excerpt 7.1 illustrates how I initiated the book discussion after reading the graphic memoir 'Remembering Linsanity' (Wang, 2022), which depicts Jeremy Lin's (a Taiwanese American basketball player) journey to the NBA, highlighting his struggles and hardships due to his Asian identity. I led the class to critically analyze and discuss implicit racial biases toward Asians in the literature.

Excerpt 7.1 Examining hidden stereotypes and implicit biases

(1)   Ms Lee: What do you think about when the White boy said 'That kid's good. I mean, for an Asian guy' when describing Jeremy Lin?

(2)   Noah: I thought that it was praise because he said Jeremy was good, but I know that it is not a compliment. If he said, 'That kid's good'

and a period, it can be a compliment, but he additionally said, 'for an Asian guy'.

(3) Emma: Yes, I can see that the boy initially thought that Asians were not good at basketball because he automatically thought Asians were shorter or weaker than Americans.

(4) Liam: That's bad. But I think that's better to hear than 'pancake' or 'yellow monkeys'.

(5) Ms Lee: Why do you think this comment is better than the words like 'pancake' or 'yellow monkeys'?

(6) Liam: Because 'pancake' and 'yellow monkeys' are very insulting words. They are very direct, directly targeting Asians looking at the appearances only.

(7) Ms Lee: That makes sense because the words you mentioned were very explicit and visible, but I also want you all to think about hidden or unseen biases. The White boy didn't say that 'Asians were poor basketball players', rather he said, 'That Asian kid is good… for an Asian guy'. Although the boy did not use the word 'bad' or 'poor', his comment included his assumption regarding Asian basketball players.

(8) Liam: I also thought that the white boy did not have bad intentions. When people say you are a yellow monkey, they definitely have a bad intention to insult you. But he may not even remember what he said.

(9) Ms Lee: That is a great point to mention. Sometimes people say it without intention or even awareness, but we still need to be careful and avoid those biases and stereotypes as they still affect our behaviors, judgments and attitudes toward others.

(10) Ava: I have heard the same thing in the past. Someone told me that I was pretty for an Asian girl. I did not know what that meant at that time because I was younger. But now I know that it was not a compliment. I would be actually mad and feel bad if I heard that now.

(11) Henry: Now I remember one of my neighbors once told me that I was taller for an Asian guy. I don't think I am supposed to be short because I am Asian. That's ridiculous. I have a few Asian guy friends who are taller than the White kids.

(12) Ms Lee: Ava and Henry, thank you for sharing your experiences. Yes, when people tell you that you are pretty and tall, those can be good compliments. But the phrase 'for Asian people' would make you feel bad because they already have certain perceptions about us as Asians, for example, Asians are not pretty enough, or Asians are not tall enough.

(13) Emma: Sometimes I have certain beliefs about other people. For instance, Black people are noisy and violent. I think that's okay if I don't say that loud and just think that in my head. But, even

thinking that way is actually detrimental because it will lead me to believe that.

When I asked the class to analyze the remark ('That kid's good. I mean, for an Asian guy') made by one of the Caucasian boys when describing Lin's basketball performance (line 1), Noah responded that he initially thought the statement was a compliment, but later he recognized that it was not a complimentary comment due to the phrase 'for an Asian guy'. Emma pointed out that the Caucasian boy held an inherent bias toward Asian sports players. Yet, when Liam pointed out much more direct, intimidating and negative referents ('pancake' and 'yellow monkeys') to describe Asians (lines 4, 6 and 8), I taught the concepts of explicit versus implicit biases to the class and then explained that implicit biases could be dangerous and harmful as they would ultimately affect people's judgments, attitudes and actions toward others (lines 7 and 9).

Both Ava and Henry identified that the comments they heard before ('pretty for an Asian girl' and 'taller for an Asian guy', respectively; lines 10 and 11) were due to others' implicit or inherent biases. By honestly sharing her belief about a particular racial group, Emma acknowledged the lesson she had learned (i.e. the danger of having implicit or overgeneralized racial bias and the negative consequences of holding them) after participating in the class discussion (line 13). My critical perspective, as a teacher of Asian American students, supported the students to explore implicit or inherent biases and challenge oppressive ideologies depicted in the storyline.

I further discovered that positive stereotypes are also depicted in the literature. I initiated the discussion for the students to examine the pervasiveness of positive stereotypes and their detrimental impacts. Excerpt 7.2 presents the class discussion about the consequences of holding positive stereotypes after reading the poem 'Ten Things You Should Know about Being an Asian from the South' (Yamazawa, 2022), which illustrates a Japanese American poet's experiences while growing up in the South of the US.

Excerpt 7.2 Analyzing negative consequences of positive stereotypes

(1) Ms Lee: What do you all think about when it says, 'Asians are supposed to be good with numbers?'
(2) Noah: I think that is true. Asian parents tend to spend a lot of time with their children on math.
(3) Grace: Asians learn how to do multiplication from a very early age.
(4) Emma: But I would worry that I might not get perfect scores or good grades in math if people already think that I am good at math.
(5) Ms Lee: That's a good point. Some stereotypes are positive because people talk about something people are good at or famous for.

That's why it is different from negative stereotypes. However, sometimes even positive stereotypes can have negative effects on people.

(6) Noah: Is it because not all Asian children are good at math? There are Asian kids who are not good at math or numbers. Then, it [the positive stereotype] will affect those kids quite badly.

(7) Ava: So … positive stereotypes sound better than negative stereotypes, but what we think is positive might not be positive for some people.

(8) Ms Lee: Exactly! A positive stereotype represents a 'positive' evaluation of a group. Thus, it may be considered a form of compliment or praise. However, as I said, even positive stereotypes can affect people negatively. Emma mentioned that she would worry if she didn't get perfect scores in math because people already assumed she was good at math as an Asian. What other positive stereotypes can we think of that people might perceive as compliments, but not always?

(9) Henry: When we say black kids run very fast. But not all black people are fast runners.

(10) Noah: Another example is when people usually think that men are stronger than women. But some women are stronger than men, right?

When I asked the class to analyze the sentence 'Asians are supposed to be good with numbers', the students agreed with the statement, as they had a certain perception of Asians' performance in mathematics (lines 2–3). Yet, Emma raised concern as she understood the possible negative impact of that statement despite its positive implication (line 4). After I explained how the perception of positive stereotypes differs from that of negative stereotypes (line 5), Noah and Ava understood why positive stereotypes could lead to negative consequences and perpetuate harmful generalizations (lines 6–7). Henry and Noah then shared the prevalent stereotypes people have toward different racial and gender groups (lines 9–10). The ongoing dialogue and conversation following the reading of this counter-narrative encouraged the class to approach positive, stereotypical beliefs with a critical eye. This dialogic discussion alarmed the possible harmful consequence of holding positive stereotypes toward certain ethnic, cultural or gender groups because even positive stereotypes can bring negative effects on individuals' emotional and psychological well-being.

Based on my transformational approach using critical literacy pedagogy, I examined how the counter-narratives of Asian Americans helped fifth-grade students articulate their analytical perspectives through profound conversations that disrupted existing stereotypes, dominant hegemony and systemic racism. These two excerpts showcase how classroom teachers can encourage their students to critically examine their own assumptions and challenge implicit biases they may hold toward a specific group of people by fostering a shift in their perspectives and beliefs through verbal interaction. The following section further illustrates the Korean American students' dialogic responses to the Asian American counter-narratives.

Students' responses to the Asian American counter-narratives

Since the selected Asian American counter-narratives reveal issues of power asymmetries and structural inequities, analyzing the students' dialogic responses to the characters, plots and/or issues from each piece of literature exhibited their critical stances, voices and perspectives toward the literary work and the world around them. As the students engaged in critical conversations about Asian Americans' lived experiences and discursive practices during their dialogic discussions, I scrutinized the students' reflexive reactions and authentic responses to societal power imbalances, dominant ideologies and systematic racism that are presented in literature and observed in contemporary society. The following section illustrates how the counter-narratives helped students transform their perspectives by critiquing the Eurocentric worldview on linguistic norms and challenging the pedagogic hegemony in their American school curriculum.

Challenging the Eurocentric Worldview on Linguicism. The literature discussion assisted the class in disrupting Western-Eurocentric epistemologies that are prevalent in the stories they encountered. For instance, the book *Amina's Voice* (Khan, 2017) illustrates a scene where the Pakistan American and Korean American protagonists are blamed by White classmates for the fact that they teach each other their heritage languages (Urdu & Korean, respectively). Excerpt 7.3 presents the students' responses to reading that scene, which reveal their critiques of the Eurocentric worldview on English hegemony.

Excerpt 7.3 Criticizing the linguistic hegemony of English

(1) Ms Lee: When Amina and Soojin were teaching each other's languages, Emily and Julie scoffed at them and said, 'Speak English, you're in America'. Why don't we talk about the scene here?

(2) Henry: I think Emily and Julie are wrong. Since Amina speaks Urdu and Soojin speaks Korean, they can teach each other's languages. That's what I do with my friends.

(3) Emma: Maybe Emily and Julie are jealous of their language talents because they already speak two languages, and they are learning another one. Sometimes people are jealous of me because I speak two languages – Korean and English. But I have a right to use both.

(4)   Noah: Hmmm... I don't think they have to speak English only. They have the freedom to use whatever language they want to speak.

(5)   Liam: Some of my classmates are from Mexico so they speak Spanish during recess. But I don't mind because I often speak Korean with Korean people.

(6)   Ava: Oh, last year we had a Korean kid from Korea. He couldn't speak English, so I helped him [speak] English. We often spoke in Korean in the classroom. I was glad that I could help him, and he thanked me. So what Emily and Julie said to Amina and Soojin is rude and offensive.

(7)   Bella: I know people sometimes think that English is the most important language or the only language people need to use because this is America. But that's a selfish idea.

(8)   Henry: We should not tell people that they need to speak English only. Even though they live in America, they can freely use their languages. We need to accept different languages as we have many people from different countries.

The class analyzed the scene when the protagonists (Amina and Soojin) are reprimanded by their White classmates (Emily and Julie) for not using English. Henry and Emma criticized the White literary characters' behaviors by stating that speaking languages other than English is a normal practice and fundamental right for bilingual speakers (lines 2–3). Specifically, Noah rejected the idea of English hegemony; he believed that bilingual individuals have the freedom to use their heritage or home languages (line 4). Both Liam and Ava as bilingual speakers shared their own experiences of using their two languages in different learning contexts (lines 5–6). Ava similarly reflected on the positive experience she had with a newcomer from Korea in her class and criticized the literary characters' disrespectful behaviors toward Amina and Soojin (line 6). Bella pointed out that language practice has been predominantly framed by Eurocentric epistemologies, which set standards that require people to speak English only while living in the US (line 7). Henry correspondingly acknowledged the danger of the pervasive English hegemony and further supported the notion of linguistic pluralism (line 8). Reading and discussing the literature not only led the students to challenge the hegemony of a monolingual English ideology but also helped them value fluid translanguaging practices by speakers who use more than two languages.

Interrogating Academic Hegemony in the Mainstream Curriculum. The literature discussion also led the students to interrogate academic hegemony that does not include cultural diversity in their school curriculum. Excerpt 7.4 presents the class discussion based on a stanza from the poem 'Ten Things You Should Know about Being an Asian from the

South' (Yamazawa, 2022), which highlights Americans' limited general knowledge about Asian countries and people.

Excerpt 7.4 Advocating multicultural curriculum and education

(1)   Ms Lee: Why don't we think about the stanza here? [read aloud] 'One day a classmate asked me what I was. When I told her I was Japanese, she said, Oh, I thought you was [sic] Asian.'
(2)   Henry: That is so funny. I wonder if she really doesn't know Japanese are Asian.
(3)   Noah: She should read books and study something like geography.
(4)   Ms Lee: Well... What type of education does your school provide to learn about other countries such as their locations, cultures and people?
(5)   Henry: My school does not do a lot to learn about others' cultures. We celebrated Black History Month and learned about a few Black heroes. But I think that was it.
(6)   Liam: My school has many students from Mexico, so we once learned about Cinco de Mayo and read fiction where the main character was from Mexico, but not much about Asian culture.
(7)   Ava: No Asian stuff in my school.
(8)   Emma: Correct. I have never been taught Asian people, history and culture.
(9)   Ava: Our schools should teach Asian American history, people and cultures so that Americans know and understand who Asians are, where we are coming from, why we are living here and what we do and celebrate.
(10) Daisy: Right. Because we are different from Chinese, and Chinese people are different from Vietnamese. Vietnamese are different from Japanese. Not all Asians are not the same.

While reading the stanza (see line 1) from the poem, the students denounced the American literary character's ignorance as he did not know Japanese were Asians (lines 2–3). Responding to Noah's statement, I asked the class if they had learned about the geographical features or cultures of other countries in their American schools (line 4). Although the students shared that they learned about African American and Hispanic cultures when celebrating Black History Month and Cinco de Mayo, respectively (lines 5 and 6), they reported that Asian histories and cultures were not included in their school curricula (lines 7 and 8). By acknowledging the lack of Asian American studies in her American school, Ava criticized a heavy emphasis on mainstream culture and advocated for the inclusion of Asian American history and cultures in US school programs (line 9). Daisy notably claimed the danger of classifying people of Asian descent as a monolithic group because it disregards the diversity and heterogeneity among the Asian groups (line 10). Reading and analyzing this literary piece empowered the students to actively interrogate the pedagogic hegemony in their mainstream curriculum by highlighting the absence of Asian representation and a lack of inclusivity.

The classroom discourses in these excerpts demonstrate how the students expressed their voices and criticality by interrogating and challenging the linguistic and cultural hegemony prevailing in their American schools. Reading and discussing the counter-narratives of Asian Americans helped students articulate their analytical perspectives through engaging in in-depth discussions, which cultivated their critical consciousness and supported them in transforming their perspectives into those of informed and cognizant citizens. Unlike dominant narratives that perpetuate racial stereotypes, counter-narratives served as a vehicle for the students to identify issues of widespread structural racism against Asian American populations and communities by bringing their Asian American views and values.

Implications for Educational Practice of Implementing Critical Literacy Instruction

It is important to note that educators encounter several challenges when employing critical literacy pedagogy because many school curricula are deeply rooted in traditional teaching methods, which often focus on information transmission and passive learning. These traditional education systems, with standardized curricula, can be resistant to the transformative approach of critical literacy and limit the freedom educators must implement in their critical literacy instruction. Educators need to advocate for changes in policy and practice to support transformative instruction by seeking resources and training on critical literacy pedagogy to enhance their understanding and teaching practices. By doing so, classroom teachers can reevaluate and move away from traditional 'banking' models of education to foster a more interactive, meaningful and student-learning environment.

As the empirical study in this chapter showed, the implementation of critical literacy praxis using Asian American counter-narratives worked as a powerful pedagogical tool for the Korean American students because the students were able to share their understanding and interpretations of the counter-stories by integrating their critical thinking, unique voices, personal experiences, different perspectives and genuine and powerful testimonials. This chapter demonstrates how the essential enactment of literacy pedagogy, incorporating Asian American counter-narratives from an AsianCrit perspective, can contribute to social justice in eradicating racial inequality and social oppression. Educators can effectively implement critical literacy practices by utilizing different types of counter-narratives as a pedagogical platform to counterdominant, hegemonic narratives and approaches prevalent in students' everyday school experiences.

It is crucial for educators to include Asian American voices and perspectives in the school curriculum because it can assist students in gaining a more comprehensive understanding of American (hi)stories, cultures and values by promoting inclusivity and combating biases or stereotypes. If educators wish to help Asian American students elevate their Asian voices to fight against injustice and racism, they are required to carefully design a curriculum using literature portraying Asian Americans as protagonists and guide them to interpret narratives using a critical eye to uncover any discriminating attitudes or behaviors toward Asian American characters.

Educators need to understand that creating a space for students to identify racial inequality and social oppression through discussions should be an initial step before encouraging them to take social justice action to achieve educational transformation and promote educational equity. Classroom teachers of students from racially, culturally and/or linguistically diverse backgrounds can indeed create transformative, inclusive, unbiased and equitable classroom environments by actively including students' perspectives, experiences and identities in their teaching, ensuring that all students feel seen, valued and empowered to participate fully in their education. When implementing critical literacy (e.g. incorporating critical counter-narratives) in diverse learning communities, educators are required to actively listen to students' experiences and intentionally incorporate diverse perspectives into the curriculum to build meaningful connections and foster cultural humility, thereby enhancing the learning experiences of historically underrepresented students.

Children's Literature Bibliography

Jung, M. (2020) *The Boys in the Back Row*. Levine Querido.

Khan, H. (2017) *Amina's Voice*. Simon & Schuster Books for Young Readers.

Lai, T. (2011) *Inside Out and Back Again*. HarperCollins.

Rowell, R. (2013) *Elena & Park*. St. Martin's Griffin.

Wang, P. (2022) Remembering linsanity. In J. Yang, P. Yu and P. Wang (eds) *Rise: A Pop History of Asian America from the Nineties to Now* (pp. 322–325). HarperCollins.

Yamazawa, G. (2022) Ten things you should know about being an Asian from the South. In S. Pak (ed.) *My Life: Growing up Asian in America* (pp. 154–157). MTV Entertainment Books.

References

Anderson, G.L. and Irvine, P. (1993) Informing critical literacy with ethnography. In C. Lankshear and P.L. McLaren (eds) *Critical Literacy: Politics, Praxis, and the Postmodern* (pp. 81–104). SUNY Press.

Augoustinos, M. and Every, D. (2007) The language of "race" and prejudice: A discourse of denial, reason, and liberal-practical politics. *Journal of Language and Social Psychology* 26, 123–141.

Back, M. and Zavala, V. (2019) *Racialization and Language: Interdisciplinary Perspectives from Peru*. Routledge.

Bell, D. (1992) *Faces at the Bottom of the Well*. Basic.

Bonilla-Silva, E. (2002) The linguistics of color blind racism: How to talk nasty about blacks without sounding "racist." *Critical Sociology* 28 (1/2), 41–64.

Borsheim–Black, C., Macaluso, M. and Petrone, R. (2014) Critical literature pedagogy: Teaching canonical literature for critical literacy. *Journal of Adolescent & Adult Literacy* 58 (2), 123–133.

Brown, K.D. (2013) Trouble on my mind: Toward a framework of humanizing critical sociocultural knowledge for teaching and teacher education. *Race Ethnicity and Education* 16 (3), 316–338.

Buchanan, L.B. and Hilburn, J. (2016) Riding la Bestiá: Preservice teachers' responses to documentary counter-stories of U.S. immigration. *Journal of Teacher Education* 67 (5), 408–423.

Cammarota, J. (2014) Challenging colorblindness in Arizona: Latina/o students' counter-narratives of race and racism. *Multicultural Perspectives* 16 (2), 79–85.

Cammarota, J. and Romero, A. (2011) Participatory action research for high school students: Transforming policy, practice, and the personal with social justice education. *Educational Policy* 25 (3), 488–506.

Chapman, T.K. (2007) Interrogating classroom relationships and events: Using portraiture and critical race theory in education research. *Educational Researcher* 36 (3), 156–162.

Cheruvu, R., Souto-Manning, M., Lencl, T. and Chin-Calubaquib, M. (2015) Race, isolation, and exclusion: What early childhood teacher educators need to know about the experiences of pre-service teachers of color. *The Urban Review* 47 (2), 237–265.

Cho, H. and Song, K. (2023) *Korean as a Heritage Language from Transnational and Translanguaging Perspectives*. Routledge.

Clark, L. and Whitney, E. (2009) Walking in their shoes: Using multiple-perspective texts as a bridge to critical literacy. *Reading Teacher* 62 (6), 530–534.

Compton-Lilly, C. (2009) What can new literacy studies offer to the teaching of struggling readers? *The Reading Teacher* 63 (1). https://doi.org/10.1598/RT.63.1.10

Condor, S. and Figgou, L. (2012) Rethinking the prejudice problematic: A collaborative cognition approach. In J. Dixon and M. Levine (eds) *Beyond Prejudice: Extending the Social Psychology of Conflict, Inequality and Social Change* (pp. 200–221). Cambridge University Press.

Condor, S., Figgou, L., Abell, J., Gibson, S. and Stevenson, C. (2006) 'They're not racist.' Prejudice, denial, mitigation and suppression in dialogue. *British Journal of Social Psychology* 45, 441–462.

Crenshaw, K. (1989) Demarginalizing the intersection of race and sex: A black feminist critique of antidiscrimination doctrine, feminist theory and antiracist politics. *The University of Chicago Legal Forum* 140, 139–167.

Crenshaw, K., Gotanda, N., Peller, G. and Thomas, K. (1995) *Critical Race Theory: The Key Writings that Formed the Movement*. New Press.

Cruickshank, K., Bianco, J. and Wahlin, M. (2024) *Community and Heritage Languages Schools Transforming Education*. Routledge.

DeCuir, J.T. and Dixson, A.D. (2004) "So when it comes out, they aren't that surprised that it is there": Using critical race theory as a tool of analysis of race and racism in education. *Educational Researcher* 33 (5), 26–31.

Delgado, R. (2011) Rodrigo's reconsideration: Intersectionality and the future of critical race theory. *Iowa Law Review* 96, 1247–1288.

Delgado, R. and Stefancic, J. (2001) *Critical Race Theory: The Cutting Edge* (2nd edn). Temple University Press.

Delgado, R. and Stefancic, J. (2012) *Critical Race Theory: An Introduction*. NYU Press.

Delgado, R. and Stefancic, J. (2013) *Critical Race Theory: The Cutting Edge* (3rd edn). Temple University Press.

Dixon, J. and Levine, M. (2012) *Beyond Prejudice: Extending the Social Psychology of Conflict, Inequality and Social Change*. Cambridge University Press.

Dixson, A. and Rousseau, C. (2005) And we are still not saved: Critical race theory in education ten years later. *Race Ethnicity and Education* 8 (1), 7–27.

Donnor J.K. (2018) *Cowan*, Whiteness, resistance to *Brown*, and the persistence of the past. *Peabody Journal of Education* 93 (1), 23–37.

Ellis, A. and Eberly, T.L. (2015) Critical literacy: Going beyond the demands of common core. *Illinois Reading Council Journal* 43 (2), 9–15.

Ellison, T.L. and Solomon, M. (2019) Counter-storytelling vs. deficit thinking around African American children and families, digital literacies, race, and the digital divide. *Research in the Teaching of English* 53 (3), 223–244.

Every, D. and Augoustinos, M. (2007) Constructions of racism in the Australian parliamentary debates on asylum seekers. *Discourse and Society* 18, 411–436.

Figgou, L. and Condor, S. (2006) Irrational categorization, natural intolerance and reasonable discrimination: Lay representations of prejudice and racism. *British Journal of Social Psychology* 45, 219–243.

Flennaugh, T.K., Howard, T.C., Malone, M., Tunstall, J., Keetin, N. and Chirapuntu, T. (2017) Authoring student voices on college preparedness: A case study. *Equity & Excellence in Education* 50 (2), 209–221.

Freire, P. (1972) *Pedagogy of the Oppressed*. Penguin.

Freire, P. (1978) *Pedagogy in Process: The Letters to Guinea-Bissau*. The Seabury Press.

Freire, P. and Macedo, D. (1987) *Literacy: Reading the Word and the World*. Bergin & Garve.

Gainer, J.S. (2010) Critical media literacy in middle school: Exploring the politics of representation. *Journal of Adolescent & Adult Literacy* 53, 364–373. https://doi.org/10.1598/JAAL.53.5.2.

Gangi, J. (2008) The unbearable whiteness of literacy instruction: Realizing the implication of the proficient reader research. *Multicultural Review* 17 (1), 30–35.

Gee, J. (2012) The old and the new in the new digital literacies. *The Educational Forum* 76, 418–420. https://doi.org/10.1080/00131725.2012.708622.

Gibson, S. (2020) Accusations and denials of racism in dialogical context. In M.A. Demasi, S. Burke and C. Tileagă (eds) *Political Communication: Discursive Perspectives* (pp. 35–62). Palgrave Macmillan.

Gillborn, D. (2006) Rethinking white supremacy: Who counts in 'WhiteWorld'. *Ethnicities* 6 (3), 318–340.

Godley, A.J. and Loretto, A. (2013) Fostering counter-narratives of race, language, and identity in an urban English classroom. *Linguistics and Education* 24 (3), 316–327.

Goodman, S., Sirriyeh, A. and McMahon, S. (2017) The evolving (re)categorisations of refugees throughout the "refugee/migrant crisis". *Journal of Community and Applied Social Psychology* 27, 105–114.

Hall, S. (1980) Encoding/Decoding. In S. Hall, D. Hobson, A. Lowe and P. Willis (eds) *Culture, Media, Language* (pp. 63–87). Hutchinson.

Harvard EdCast (2022, April) The need for Asian American history in schools. Harvard EdCast. See https://www.gse.harvard.edu/ideas/edcast/22/04/need-asian-american-history-schools.

Heidt, M.A., French, M. and Miller, H. (2023) Graphic novels as curricular counternarratives for English language learners and emergent bilinguals. *Multicultural Perspectives* 25 (2), 116–125.

Hull, G. (1993) Critical literacy and beyond: Lessons learned from students and workers in a vocational program and on the job. *Anthropology and Education Quarterly* 24 (4), 308–317.

Iftikar, J.S. and Museus, S.D. (2018) On the utility of Asian critical (AsianCrit) theory in the field of education. *International Journal of Qualitative Studies in Education* 31 (10), 935–949.

Jowallah, R. (2015) Awakening students through critical literacy: Implications for teaching and learning within contemporary education. *International Journal of Literacies* 21 (3/4), 17–27.

Kagan, O., Carreira, M. and Chik, C.H. (2017) *Handbook of Heritage Language Education from Innovation to Program Building*. Routledge.

Kim, J. and Hsieh, B. (2021) *The Racialized Experiences of Asian American Teachers in the US: Applications of Asian Critical Race Theory to Resist Marginalization*. Routledge.

Knoblauch, C.H. and Brannon, L. (1993) *Critical Teaching and the Idea of Literacy*. Heinemann.

Ladson-Billings, G. (2014) Culturally relevant pedagogy 2.0: The remix. *Harvard Educational Review* 84 (1), 74–84.

Ladson-Billing, G. and Tate, W.F. (1995) Toward a critical race theory of education. *Teachers College Record* 97 (1), 47–68.

Lankshear, C. and McClaren, P. (1993) *Critical Literacy: Radical and Postmodernist Perspectives*. SUNY Press.

Lee, C. (2021a) Exploring multicultural children's literature in a heritage language classroom. *Children's Literature in English Language Education* 9 (1), 32–56.

Lee, C. (2021b) Third-grade students' written responses to multicultural children's literature during post-reading activities. *The Dragon Lode* 39 (2), 14–26.

Lee, C. (2024) Sanctioning a space for transnational literacy practices in a HL classroom. *International Multilingual Research Journal* 19 (1), 1–22. https://doi.org/10.1080/19313152.2024.2309695.

Lee, C. (2025a) Using Asian Americans' counter-narratives for social justice and equity. *Journal of Literacy Research* 57 (2), 192–216.

Lee, C. (2025b) Teaching through the lens of the transformative stance: Envisioning teachers' "trans" perspective in diverse classrooms. *International Journal of Multilingual Education* 27 (1) 29–53.

Lee, C. (2026) Critical literacy in a Korean heritage language classroom: Implementing social justice-oriented practices for Asian American students. In K. Lê, Z. Tian, A. Nguyen and T. Morita-Mullaney (eds) *Asian Americans in Bilingualism and Bilingual Education: The Long Overdue Voice* (pp. 196–215). Multilingual Matters.

Lewison, M., Flint, A.S. and van Sluys, K. (2002) Taking on critical literacy: The journey of newcomers and novices. *Language Arts* 79 (5), 382–392.

Liu, K. and Ball, A.F. (2019) Critical reflection and generativity: Toward a framework of transformative teacher education for diverse learners. *Review of Research in Education* 43 (1), 68–105.

Martinez, A.Y. (2014) A plea for critical race theory counterstory: Stock story versus counterstory dialogues concerning Alejandra's "fit" in the academy. *Composition Studies* 42 (2), 33–55.

Martinez, A.Y. (2018) The responsibility of privilege: A critical race counterstory conversation. *Peitho Journal* 21 (1), 212–233.

Matsuda, M. (1995) Looking to the bottom: Critical legal studies and reparations. In K. Crenshaw, N. Gotanda, G. Peller and K. Thomas (eds) *In Critical Race Theory: The Key Writings that Formed the Movement* (pp. 63–79). The New Press.

McLaughlin, M.K. and DeVoogd, G.L. (2004) Critical literacy as comprehension: Expanding reader response. *Journal of Adolescent & Adult Literacy* 48, 52–62. https://doi.org/10.1598/JAAL.48.1.5.

McLaughlin, M.K. and DeVoogd, G.L. (2010) *Critical Literacy as Comprehension*. Routledge.

McNair, J.C. (2008a) Yes, it'll be me: A comparative analysis of the Brownies' Book and contemporary African American children's literature written by Patricia C. McKissack. In W. Brooks and J. McNair (eds) *Embracing, Evaluating and Examining African American Children's Literature* (pp. 3–29). Scarecrow.

McNair, J.C. (2008b) Innocent though they may seem . . . A critical race theory analysis of Firefly and Seesaw Scholastic book club order forms. *Multicultural Review* 17 (1), 24–29.

Mezirow, J. (2000) *Learning as Transformation: Critical Perspectives on a Theory in Progress*. Jossey Bass.

Milner, H.R.IV. and Howard, T.C. (2013) Counter-narrative as method: Race, policy and research for teacher education. *Race Ethnicity and Education* 16 (4), 536–561.

Miller, R., Liu, K. and Ball, A.F. (2020) Critical counter-narrative as transformative methodology for educational equity. *Review of Research in Education* 22, 269–300.

Minnesota Humanities Center (2018) Increase engagement through absent narratives. See https://www.mnhum.org/program/increase-engagement-through-absent-narratives.

Morrell, E. (2004) *Becoming Critical Researchers: Literacy and Empowerment for Urban Youth*. Peter Lang.

Motha, S. and Varghese, M.M. (2018) Rewriting dominant narratives of the academy: Women faculty of color and identity management. *Race Ethnicity and Education* 21, 503–517.

Museus, S.D. and Iftikar, J. (2013) An Asian critical theory (AsianCrit) framework. In M.Y. Danico and J.G. Golson (eds) *Asian American Students in Higher Education* (pp. 18–29). Routledge.

Museus, S.D. and Iftikar, J. (2014) Asian critical race theory (AsianCrit). In M.Y. Danico and J.G. Golson (eds) *Asian American Society* (pp. 96–98). Sage Publications and Association for Asian American Studies.

Museus, S.D., Yi, V. and Saelua, N. (2018) How culturally engaging campus environments influence sense of belonging in college: An examination of differences between White students and students of color. *Journal of Diversity in Higher Education* 11 (4), 467–483.

O'Brien, E. (2017) Racial formation. In K. Korgen (ed.) *The Cambridge Handbook of Sociology: Specialty and Interdisciplinary Studies* (pp. 5–11). Cambridge University Press.

Omi, M. and Winant, H. (1994) *Racial Formation in the United States: From the 1960s to the 1990s* (2nd edn). Routledge.

Pak, K. and Ravitch, S.M. (eds) (2021) *Critical Leadership Praxis: Leading Educational and Social Change*. Teachers College Press.

Pew Research Center (2023) Discrimination experiences shape most asian americans' lives. See https://www.pewresearch.org/race-ethnicity/2023/11/30/discrimination-experiences-shape-most-asian-americans-lives/.

Poon, O. (2014) "The land of opportunity doesn't apply to everyone": The immigrant experience, race, and Asian American career choices. *Journal of College Student Development* 55 (6), 499–514.

Riley, K. (2015) Enacting critical literacy in English classrooms: How a teacher learning community supported critical inquiry. *Journal of Adolescent & Adult Literacy* 58 (5), 417–425.

Rodríguez, N.N. (2018) From margins to center: Developing cultural citizenship education through the teaching of Asian American history. *Theory & Research in Social Education* 46 (4), 528–573.

Salinas, C.S., Fránquiz, M.E. and Rodríguez, N.N. (2016) Writing Latina/o historical narratives: Narratives at the intersection of critical historical inquiry and LatCrit. *Urban Review* 48 (2), 264–284.

Schiera, A.J. (2019) Justice, practice and the 'real world': Pre-service teachers' critically conscious visions for teaching amid the complexities and challenges of learning to teach. *International Journal of Qualitative Studies in Education* 32 (7), 929–946. https://doi.org/10.1080/09518398.2019.1609125.

Sethy, M. and Mishra, R. (2020) An integrated approach to deal with mental health issues of children and adolescent during COVID-19 pandemic. *Journal of Clinical and Diagnostic Research* 14 (9), SE01–SE03.

Shor, I. (1999) What is critical literacy? *Journal of Pedagogy, Pluralism, and Practice* 1 (4), 2.

Sleeter, C.E. (2017) Critical race theory and the whiteness of teacher education. *Urban Education* 52 (2), 155–169.

Sleeter, C.E. and Zavala, M. (2020) *Transformative Ethnic Studies in Schools: Curriculum, Pedagogy, and Research*. Teachers College Press.

Solorza, C.R. (2019) Trans + Languaging: Beyond dual language bilingual education. *Journal of Multilingual Education Research* 9 (15), 99–112.

Solorzano, D. and Yosso, T. (2002) Critical race methodology: Counter-storytelling as an analytical framework for education research. *Qualitative Inquiry* 8 (1), 23–44.

Solórzano, D., Miguel, C. and Yosso, T. (2000) Critical race theory, racial micro aggressions, and campus racial climate: The experiences of African American college students. *The Journal of Negro Education* 69 (1/2), 6073.

Tate, W. (1997) Critical race theory and education: History, theory, and implications. *Review of Research in Education* 22, 195–247.

Vaught, S.E. and Castagno, A.E. (2008) "I don't think I'm a racist": Critical race theory, teacher attitudes, and structural racism. *Race Ethnicity and Education* 11 (2), 95–113.

Whitehead, K.A. (2015) Everyday antiracism in action: Preference organization in responses to racism. *Journal of Language and Social Psychology* 34, 374–389.

Williams, O.A. (2022) Critical literacy in practice: How educators leverage supports and overcome challenges to enact critical literacy pedagogy in their classrooms. *Literacy Research: Theory, Method, and Practice* 71 (1), 323–340.

Willis, A., Montavon, M., Hall, H., Hunder, C., Burke, L. and Herrera, A. (2008) *Critically Conscious Research*. Teachers College Press.

Winant, H. (2000) Race and race theory. *Annual Review of Sociology* 26, 169–185.

Yoo, H.C., Gabriel, A. and Okazaki, S. (2021) Advancing research within Asian American psychology using Asian critical race theory and an Asian Americanist perspective. *Journal of Humanistic Psychology* 62 (4), 563–590.

8 (Re)constructing and Negotiating Ethno-Racial and Linguistic Identities from Raciolinguistic Ideologies

(1) *When people see me, I am an Asian kid.*
(2) *People think that I can speak perfect Korean.*
(3) *Because I look like Korean.*
(4) *I am not fluent enough to be Korean.*
(5) *I am not white enough to be American.*

***

The above excerpt is from Kenny's 'I Am' poem (see Figure 8.1 for the entire poem), in which he identifies himself as an Asian American. Although Kenny understands that his racial phenotype plays a major role in constructing his identity (see line 3 above), later in the poem, he highlights that language skills and linguistic competence play a much more essential role than racial positioning in his life. Kenny understands that people more easily discern his race than his language competence because his racial phenotype is readily apparent and detectable. In contrast, his language use or abilities are comparatively invisible and imperceptible at first glance. Kenny states that sharing a language can make it easier to build friendships with people of different racial or ethnic backgrounds. Still, it is challenging to maintain a close connection with someone who does not share the same language, even if they belong to the same ethnic group.

Due to the increased global migration and the growing recognition of linguistic and cultural diversity, it is becoming increasingly evident to see and meet students like Kenny in our schools and communities today. Like Kenny, many immigrant or transnational students may identify a close relationship between race and language by understanding how their phenotypic traits and their language proficiency describe who they are when constructing and enriching their collective social identity. A part of Kenny's poem exhibits that raciolinguistic ideologies, which examine

I am Komerican

When people see me, I am an Asian kid.
When people hear me, I am an American kid.

I can be Asian, but I can also be American.
I can fit into two groups.
Maybe I can't fit in either group.
I am not fluent enough to be Korean.
I am not white enough to be American.

People think that I can speak perfect Korean.
because I look like Korean.
But I say "Sorry I don't speak Korean well..."
I am probably closer to American than Korean
because I am fluent in English.

I am more Korean at home.
My father and grandparents are Korean.
I eat Korean food almost every day.
I see me as Korean.

I am more American at school.
I was born in America.
I am fluent in English.
I see me as American.

I feel more safe and secure living here.
I make more American friends and
use more English as time goes by.
My home is here.

I visit Korea to see my relatives.
Korea is far from here.
There are 14 hrs difference.
I wish it was closer.
I wish I could go there more often.
Then I could be more Korean.

I asked myself.
"Can I really be a good Korean?"
Hmmm... Maybe not.
When I traveled to Korea, I felt like I didn't belong there.
Although I enjoyed all the food there,
I still felt awkward, and I was a stranger.

Maybe I can be a better Korean in the future.
I become fluent in Korean.
That's why I come to Korean school.
My grandparents would be proud of me
once I am good at Korean.
I want to make them happy.
I want to make them feel proud of their grandson.

I am still somewhere in the middle.
I am Komerican "Korean-American".

Figure 8.1 Kenny's autobiographical ('I Am') poem

how language is used to build race and how ideas of race influence language and language use, play a pivotal role in students' (like Kenny) lived experiences and shape the course of their lives.

The previous chapter discussed how race is constructed in society as a social fabrication, dividing people into distinctive groups primarily based on their racial categories or ethnic classifications (see Chapter 7). It is, however, important to understand that both race and language constitute large areas of scholarship in the field of education (Brayboy *et al.*, 2007; Chaparro, 2019), because not only individuals' racial background but also their language practices play pivotal roles in describing the way contemporary societies are organized. That is, both an individual's racial and linguistic identities significantly influence social interactions and identity formation within a society. We, therefore, need to understand the intertwined relationship between race and language in describing the way contemporary societies are structured (i.e. raciolinguistics) (Alim *et al.*, 2016). Still, race-centered scholarships often overlook the fundamental role of language in identifying the notion of racialization, and linguistic research has paid attention to the process or product of individuals' language use without contemplating their racial identities (Lee, 2025; Lo, 2020).

Introduction to the Chapter

The discussion in this chapter begins by reviewing the importance of studying language and power, linguistic (in)justice and language ideologies that influence cultural notions about language. By claiming the interlaced connection between race and language, this chapter explores the concept of raciolinguistic ideologies that explain how race can be constructed or deconstructed through language. The chapter focuses on the racial and linguistic anthropological analysis of Asian American students to examine how raciolinguistic hierarchies can destabilize Asian American students' racial identity, emasculate their social positioning and undermine their linguistic abilities. Close analyses of Asian American students' stories of resilience and their life experiences are presented using the lens of raciolinguistics. This chapter concludes by offering implications for disrupting raciolinguistic hierarchies and suggestions for promoting educational justice and equity.

Linguistic Identities and Language Ideologies

Since one's race is readily discernible and apparent to others just by looking at them, individuals' phenotypic traits can be the prevailing marker of their perceived identity. While one's language use or abilities are not immediately observable and can only be detected through conversation. Unlike racial phenotype, one's language competence is comparatively unseen at first glance and imperceptible on the surface. According to Wolfram (2023), identity features such as race, ethnicity, class, gender, sexual orientation and religion are considered when discussing diversity. However, linguistic differences are often not traditionally included in this conversation, indicating that language variations are frequently neglected dimension of diversity. Yet, Wolfram claimed that language 'intersect[s] with all of the themes in the canonical catalog of diversity issues' (2023: 37). Since an individual uses language or other linguistic resources to express their race, ethnicity and/or nationality and to show solidarity with the same social and cultural group (Alim *et al.*, 2016), one's language use and linguistic abilities are 'critical component[s] in the extant canon of diversity' (Wolfram *et al.*, 2023: 7), which should not be disregarded or diminished. In this regard, Rosa and Burdick (2017: 109) indicated that 'language actively participates in the construction, reproduction, and transformation of identity', suggesting that language is not just a tool for communication but also a dynamic and powerful force that largely shapes and influences how individuals express and perceive their identities.

Linguistic anthropologists and sociolinguistic researchers (Gal & Woolard, 1995; Irvine, 1990; Irvine & Gal, 2000) discussed the notion of 'language ideologies'. Silverstein (1979: 346) defined linguistic ideologies as 'sets of beliefs about language articulated by users as a rationalization or justification of perceived language structure and use', which underscores the role of speakers' linguistic awareness. Irvine's (1989: 255) definition displays sociocultural emphasis; she argued that language ideologies are 'the cultural system of ideas about social and linguistic relationships, together with their loading of moral and political interests'. For Rumsey (1990: 346), language ideology refers to 'shared bodies of commonsense notions about the nature of language in the world'. Kroskrity (2004) problematized Rumsey's definition because it promoted an overly homogeneous view of language ideologies by accentuating a static, uniformly shared culture without considering other ideological variations (e.g. age, gender, class). Meanwhile, Errington (2001: 110) indicated that language ideologies specify 'the situated, partial and interested character of conceptions and uses of language', which suggests how people use language is deeply influenced by their specific social structure and context.

Language ideologies in different scholars' definitions are viewed as multiple, circumstantial and contextual as they recognize that people's beliefs about language are not singular or universal; instead, they vary depending on the different social and political environments. Kroskrity (2004: 497) stated that language ideologies are 'a more ubiquitous set of diverse beliefs ... used by speakers of all types as models for constructing linguistic evaluations and engaging in communicative activity'. That is, language ideologies directly and largely influence 'the cultural ideas about language' (Irvine, 1989: 255). To further explore the notion of language ideologies, Kroskrity (2004) considered the five levels of language ideologies as (1) **group or individual interests**, indicating language use is constructed and held by a specific social or cultural group, (2) **multiplicity of ideologies**, denoting language ideologies are best understood as being multiple because different social groups hold diverse perspectives on language use, (3) **awareness of speakers**, suggesting individuals have different levels of understanding and knowledge about how language is used around them, (4) **mediating functions of ideologies**, meaning that people's language ideologies act as a bridge between the broader social structures they live in and the specific ways they speak and (5) **role of language ideology in identity construction**, implying people's beliefs and attitudes about language fundamentally contribute to the formation and expression of various social and cultural identities (2004: 501).

Kroskrity (2010: 192) defines language ideologies as the 'beliefs, feelings, and conceptions about language structure and use which often index the political, economic interests of individual speakers, ethnic and other interest groups, and nation-states'. According to Kroskrity's definition, a language-ideological perspective is used to understand the complex ways in which individuals, groups and society use languages to shape, navigate and transform their sociocultural worlds (Kroskrity, 2018, 2021). The idea of language ideologies shapes speakers' attitudes, identities and positionalities 'in direct relation to racialized (linguistic) hierarchies and associated discursive practices' that highlights the close analysis of the 'subliminal interplay of language and racism' (May, 2023: 655). Since language ideologies 'locate the meaningfulness of linguistic signs in relation to other signs in particular historical, political-economic, and sociocultural contexts' (Rosa & Burdick, 2017: 103), they play a pivotal role in shaping one's racial/ethnic identities and authenticity, which connect certain groups with shared linguistic features, while others lacking such shared linguistic characteristics or patterns are seen as others or outsiders (Chun, 2011). In this regard, Urciuoli (2011) claimed that the dynamic relationship between social, cultural, racial and linguistic markedness ('others') and unmarkedness ('normal') is a distinguishing feature and a key attribute in racialized discourses.

Linguistic (In)justice and the Study of Language and Power

Scholars have recently called for linguistic justice (Baker-Bell, 2020; Valdes, 2023), extending beyond racial justice by elucidating concepts such as linguistic racism (Kroskrity, 2020), White language supremacy (Caldera & Babino, 2020) and linguistic hierarchization (May, 2023). According to May, the processes of language hierarchization have long been evident and documented by linguists and education researchers. In the past, Pierre Bourdieu (1991) highlighted the dangers of insisting on a single standard of the common language or one correct form of a language, as a codified version of the language threatens linguistic diversity by prioritizing particular dialects and unfairly constraining speakers' access to language opportunities and rights.

Baker-Bell (2020: 7) defined linguistic justice as 'an antiracist approach to language and literacy education'. By emphasizing that standard English reinforces the language patterns of White, male, upper or middle-class speakers, Baker-Bell argued that the idea of one correct way of speaking English is 'a myth that normalizes white ways of speaking English and is used to justify linguistic discrimination on the basis of race' (2020: 99). Thus, linguistic justice recognizes that the English language naturally varies across different regional and social group. It values the richness of diverse ways people speak and communicate by honoring various language practices and treating bi/multi/plurilingual speakers with equal respect and dignity without prioritizing one standard language structure over others.

A considerable number of scholars have contributed to the study of language and power (e.g. Austin, 1962; Bourdieu, 1991; Fairclough, 1989; Goffman, 1974; Halliday, 1975; Wodak, 1996). By criticizing traditional approaches to language, the scholars argued that language should be understood as a medium of power (through which people pursue their own goals and interests and demonstrate their abilities and competence within a social context) rather than only as a tool for communication. Individuals and groups can exert influence, control and dominance over others through the words they select and the language they use. Hence, language acts as a powerful tool to establish and maintain power dynamics in society by reinforcing social hierarchies and asserting dominance because the way people speak or the language they use can reflect and influence their social status and power within a community.

Bourdieu (1991) examined the social implications of language use and its relationship to power dynamics within society. He addressed that linguistic expressions should be understood as the outcome of the relationship between a linguistic market, which represents the social context where different forms of language are assigned and valued, and a linguistic habitus, which refers to an individual's ingrained patterns of language use and linguistic dispositions that are shaped by their sociocultural backgrounds. That is, speakers adapt their language use according to the social context or cultural environment they are in (i.e. linguistic market), and at the same time, they utilize their collective linguistic resources by drawing from their entire linguistic toolkit (i.e. linguistic habitus). Speakers' communication style is significantly influenced by the social environment in which they live and the linguistic patterns they have absorbed from their past social interactions and experiences.

Identifying Linguistic Racism by Examining Everyday Language of Racism

As we understand that speakers' communication is shaped both by the social context they are in and their own internalized linguistic patterns (Bourdieu, 1991), scholars have examined how language is used and how individuals' discursive practices have changed over time based on the dynamic sociopolitical contexts they navigate and the diverse sociocultural experiences they encounter (Blommaert, 2005; Fairclough, 1992, 2003; Gee, 2007; Schiffrin, 1995; van Dijk, 2006, 2009, 2011). Acknowledging that language not only reveals and maintains power but also challenges and disrupts existing dominance, linguistic scholars (e.g. Austin, 1962; Bourdieu, 1991; Fairclough, 1989; Goffman, 1974; Halliday, 1975; Wodak, 1996) who had contributed to the study of language and power utilized critical literacy perspectives and employed critical discourse analysis (Reisigl & Wodak, 2001; van Dijk, 1993, 2009; Wodak & Richardson, 2013). Their work explored how language is used to exert, maintain and perpetuate power and social hierarchies, for instance, by constructing specific narratives, suppressing opposing opinions, controlling discourse with carefully selected word choices, silencing dissenting views or voices or utilizing different forms of address. Past studies that sought to understand organizational power structures in society have helped us comprehend racist discourses in everyday conversation by analyzing how power manifests in different sociopolitical contexts.

As Austin (1962) claimed that people 'do things with words', individuals' speech acts suggest that their language is used to do things beyond merely making verbal assertions. In this sense, racism is not a simple matter of linguistic practice (Wetherell & Potter, 1992); rather, it is 'a specific form of discursive exclusion' (Herzog & Porfillio, 2022: 3) and intricately systematized through diverse discursive practices. Thus, racism must be scrutinized through the analysis of discourse, paying close attention to language use, choices and structure, which elucidates the underlying power dynamics in given contexts. Researchers have employed critical discourse analysis to scrutinize speech acts and verbal actions, extending beyond mere interpretation of written words to understand the underlying social implications embedded within a message and to reveal hidden ideologies and power structures embedded in communication (Angermuller, 2014; Beetz & Schwab, 2017; Herzog, 2016).

Wetherell and Potter (1992) indicated that examining systemic racism must focus on social structures and institutional practices. By claiming that the examination of racism is intertwined with the study of linguistic discourse, Wetherell and Potter inspected the White speakers' discourse patterns and their discursive practices of 'everyday racism' (Essed, 1991) toward an indigenous group by paying attention to their discriminatory social actions and behaviors. Hill (2008) similarly studied everyday White racist discourses by analyzing the use of 'mock Spanish' by White American English speakers. May (2023) correspondingly examined how discourses of linguistic racism are situated in everyday conversation and the media, highlighting the historical and ongoing marginalization and denigration of minoritized language varieties toward the Indigenous Māori language.

Scholars highlighted the role and influence of linguistic racism. Kroskrity (2020: 68) defines linguistic racism as constituting 'racist and racializing acts and/or projects that use linguistic resources as a means of discrimination and subordination'. May (2023: 652) pointed out that 'the perpetrators of linguistic racism are most often majority (often monolingual) language speakers', and victims of such racism are generally speakers of minoritized languages. Leonard (2023: 70) relatedly addressed that social justice can be promoted through 'language reclamation' because it allows marginalized groups to actively reclaim words or phrases that have previously oppressed or subjugated them. This process enables them to assert power and agency, reclaim their identity and dignity, and challenge negative stereotypes and unconscious biases.

The notion of 'languaging race' (Alim *et al.*, 2016: 7) also illustrates how to 'theoriz[e] race through the lens of language'. The idea involves speculating about race through language, examining how linguistic features, such as dialect, accent, lexicon and grammar, can be used to signify racial categories and perpetuate stereotypes. The project of 'racing language' and 'languaging race' by Alim, Reyes and Kroskrity (2020) aimed to examine how language is used to actively create, uphold and challenge racial identities by analyzing the ways words, phrases and speech patterns are used to categorize and stereotype individuals based on race. Rosa and Burdick (2017) suggested that it is essential to (re)language race because the way people currently talk about race often promotes and perpetuates stereotypes and power imbalances.

Because language is an under-examined yet crucial aspect of racial politics, inspecting 'the politics of race through the lens of language' (Alim & Smitherman, 2012: 3) is necessary to build a deeper understanding of how power dynamics, social hierarchies and racialized stereotypes are reinforced through everyday language within a sociopolitical confluence of racialization (Alim *et al.*, 2020; May, 2023; Rosa & Burdick, 2017).

The Emergence of Critical Language and Race Theory (LangCrit)

While Critical Race Theory (CRT) garnered increased attention in the fields of education, legal studies and social work, its integration into language studies has not yet developed to the same level of application (Crump, 2014). Alison Crump introduced a theoretical framework called Critical Language and Race Theory (LangCrit) in her 2014 article Introducing LangCrit: Critical Language and Race Theory. LangCrit is derived from and builds upon the foundation of CRT, which examines how race and racism have shaped legal systems, policies and social structures (see Chapter 7 for discussion about CRT). LangCrit is a framework that analyzes the complex relationship between language, race and identity within social and cultural contexts, challenging the idea that language and race are fixed. It asserts that these categories are not natural or inherent but are socially constructed and influenced by power structures.

LangCrit focuses explicitly on examining the intersection of language and race, specifically how language practices reinforce and perpetuate racism. A core tenet of LangCrit is its focus on the 'subject-as-heard' (i.e. linguistic identities) and the 'subject-as-seen' (i.e. racialized identities), which are significant in identifying how individuals are perceived and represented in society (Crump, 2014). This framework emphasizes how one's language use, including both visible and audible aspects such as accent, word choices and speech patterns, intersects and profoundly influences shaping an individual's social realities and opportunities. The idea that language boundaries are socially constructed and maintained, rather than natural or pre-determined, is a fundamental principle of LangCrit.

In her LangCrit framework, Crump (2014: 209) argued, 'power has come to be clustered around certain linguistic resources in certain spaces'. LangCrit is interested in investigating how power operates and is embedded in specific linguistic resources and particular social spaces. LangCrit scholars aim to uncover how race, racism and racialization intersect with language use, identity formation and perceptions of belonging within various social contexts. Crump's concept of LangCrit helps researchers and educators explore how language is used to construct racial identities, navigate social hierarchies and reinforce power relations. The LangCrit framework has become a vital component and a necessary addition to critical language studies because it explicitly examines how language practices are interwoven with power dynamics and racial hierarchies within broader social contexts.

Unpacking Raciolinguistic Ideologies: The Co-Naturalization of Race and Language

LangCrit shares significant common ground with raciolinguistics because both frameworks highlight the role of language in shaping racial identities and examine the intersections of language, race and power. Both fields are critical in nature, as they challenge traditional notions of race and language, and disrupt dominant ideologies and power structures. While LangCrit offers a broader framework for understanding the intersections of language, race and power within the sociopolitical and cultural contexts, raciolinguistics focuses specifically on language ideologies that naturalize racial categories and buttress racial hierarchies. Thus, raciolinguistics is considered a specific application of LangCrit, which examines the ways in which language shapes social inequalities and perpetuates racialized power dynamics within systems of oppression.

By claiming the intertwined relationship between race and language, Alim, Rickford and Ball (2016) claimed that the concept of race is (co)constructed, reconstructed and deconstructed through and by language. Scholars who have contemplated race throughout language studies employed a raciolinguistic approach (e.g. Alim *et al.*, 2016; Baker-Bell, 2020; Chaparro, 2019; Flores & Rosa, 2015; Rosa & Flores, 2017) to speculate how individuals' racial/ethnic/national identities impact lived experiences of their linguistic practices. In these studies, the researchers incorporated the concept of intersectionality (Crenshaw, 1989), which describes how different forms of inequality and oppression (e.g. racism, sexism and classism) create a complex web of discrimination, to inspect the interplay of language and race in current society. According to Kimberlé Crenshaw (1991: 1245), the focus of an intersectional approach is to underscore 'the need to account for multiple grounds of identity when considering how the social world is constructed'.

Using the lens of intersectionality helps us understand identity formations coalescing through language at the intersection of race, ethnicity, gender and/or socioeconomic class. The theory of raciolinguistics, viewed through the lens of intersectionality, transcends binary frameworks, such as the fixed notions of race as Whiteness versus non-Whiteness, by acknowledging the intricate and intersecting dimensions of race and language. Since one's ethnic or racial identity and language use can significantly impact and perpetuate social inclusion or exclusion (Rosa, 2018), raciolinguistic ideologies explain how specific linguistic practices are constructed as distinguishing markers of particular racial groups and as emblematic symbols of racial categories (Rosa & Flores, 2017). Because social identities do not exist or operate in isolation, raciolinguistic scholars explored how language shapes one's ideas about race and how the notion of race influences one's language use and speech perception (Alim *et al.*, 2016).

Babcock and Ke-Schutte (2023) explained raciolinguistics as a dynamic process rather than as a static entity. They endeavoured to advance a raciolinguistic perspective rather than considering it as a disciplinary configuration. The raciolinguistic intervention denies the colonial matrix of power that renders race and language as separate entities. According to Babcock and Ke-Schutte, the intervention 'refus[es] to treat race, language, and other regimes as merely epiphenomenal, immaterial, or atomistically individual in their materializations' (2023: 4). For Babcock and Ke-Schutte, the raciolinguistic perspective is not about the 'conjunction with a siloed approach' (2023: 6) to race and language, which simply adds discrete categories of each instead, it insists that the combined effects of social identities (i.e. race and language) are often intertwined, making it difficult to separate one from the other when people experience discrimination or privilege, even though each factor can be theoretically and experientially analyzed. In this regard, the concepts of 'languaging race' and 'racing language' (Alim *et al.*, 2016) provide a lucid explanation of how race and language should be understood as co-constitutive processes.

Flores and Rosa (2015) used the term 'raciolinguistic ideologies' to refer to the idea that 'conflate[s] certain racialized bodies with linguistic deficiency unrelated to any objective linguistic practices' (2015: 150). According to Flores and Rosa, raciolinguistic ideologies affect educational categorizations; they exemplified the three classifications – long-term English learners, heritage language learners and standard English learners – that stigmatize racialized populations as defective and subordinate because these linguistic categories are based on raciolinguistic ideologies that are produced by the White group's perceptions rather than racialized speakers' actual language performance. Since people's biases and stereotypes about race could shape their perception of speech and accentedness, language-minoritized students' linguistic practices are easily degraded and often viewed as flawed and incomplete according to their racial positioning (Flores & Rosa, 2015; Rosa & Flores, 2017). The lens of raciolinguistic ideologies considers the intersectional ways in which race and language constitute power dynamics in society.

Understanding Raciolinguistic Enregisterment from a Raciolinguistic Perspective

Rosa and Flores (2017: 622) theorized a raciolinguistic perspective that 'interrogates the historical and contemporary co-naturalization of language and race' to understand how colonial distinctions of Whiteness and non-Whiteness have been naturally established in society. Rosa and Flores explored five key components of a raciolinguistic perspective: (1) 'historical and contemporary colonial co-naturalizations of race and language', which indicates the process where language is interrelated to race, fabricating race through language and vice versa, (2) 'perceptions of racial and linguistic difference' that explains how people interpret and comprehend variations in both race and language, (3) 'regimentations of racial and linguistic categories' that denote the practice of classifying individuals into distinct racial and linguistic groups based on pre-determined criteria, (4) 'racial and linguistic intersections and assemblages' that specify the convoluted ways in which race and language intertwine and mutually influence each other and (5) 'contestations of racial and linguistic power formations' that explicate the challenges against systems where language perpetuates racial power dynamics across different social contexts.

Based on these five constituents of the raciolinguistic perspective, Rosa and Flores (2017: 631) countered scholars whose studies are rooted in 'distinctiveness approaches' that naturalize classifications of race and language. According to Rosa and Flores, examining the coexistence of race and language from a raciolinguistic perspective, rather than viewing them as empirical objects or distinct sets, allows us to understand language and race as intricately related categories. To describe this interrelation, Rosa (2018) coined the term 'raciolinguistic enregisterment', explaining that 'race and language are rendered mutually perceivable … [because] race is socially constructed through language … [and] language is socially constructed through race' (2018: 7).

Since raciolinguistic enregisterment explicates how specific linguistic variables are linked to particular racial groups, Rosa (2018: 8) explained that 'language practices and racial categories become iconic of one another', meaning that certain ways of speaking are associated with particular racial groups, often reinforcing negative stereotypes and reinforces racialized perceptions about language use. In other words, the way people speak can lead to assumptions about their race and imprecisely classify their racial identity, creating a form of discrimination called 'linguistic profiling' (Baugh, 2003), where people are potentially judged based on how they sound even though such associations are not always accurate. Thus, raciolinguistic enregisterment aims to reform and eradicate systems of domination rather than finding a way to improve racially minoritized speakers' linguistic skills (Rosa, 2018).

Important Role of Listening Subjects

Flores and Rosa (2015: 150) interrogated the concept of language standardization and linguistic subordination by claiming that, 'the discourses of appropriateness' are largely defined by speakers of the dominant culture (i.e. White speaking subjects). That is, what is considered appropriate language is often determined by the group holding the most power in a society, shaping the social norms that most people accept and follow in communication. By arguing that communication is a two-way street, Lippi-Green (1997) accentuated the listener's role in the communication process. According to Lippi-Green, listeners share equal responsibility with speakers, as their preconceived notions (e.g. existing beliefs and biases) can significantly influence how they interpret and perceive what is being said. Hence, listeners need to combat their implicit biases and stereotypes when interacting with individuals who do not speak the mainstream language.

Drawing from Inoue's (2003) notion of the 'listening subject', which highlights how listeners construct subjectivities about speakers based on race or ethnicity, Flores and Rosa (2015) developed the term 'white listening subject' as a specific theoretical concept to shift focus from the speaker to the listener, emphasizing how listeners can misconstrue the language practices of racialized speakers as flawed or deficient. Those White listening subjects regulate the meanings and interpretations of specific linguistic features that racialized people use, solely based on their perspectives, by applying a white norm rather than purely receiving the content of the speech or accepting the speaker's purpose or intended meaning.

Speakers' racialized position and the social implications associated with their racial identity shape how White listening subjects perceive and understand the speakers' language use and skills. The theoretical concept of white listening subject explains the reason why racialized people often encounter institutional and social exclusion. Since people's biases and stereotypes about race significantly influence how they perceive speech and accentedness, racialized people's linguistic practices are easily degraded based on their racial positioning (Rosa & Flores, 2017). Accordingly, racialized individuals are often labeled as either 'competent' or 'incapable' based on how their speech is perceived by the white listening subject, rather than on their discrete communicative competence in English. This dynamic frequently results in biased interpretations of their abilities, shaped by racialized language stereotypes associated with their accent or dialect (Flores & Rosa, 2015).

Current Research on Raciolinguistic Ideologies

Research to date has examined how racializing ideas have permeated speakers' linguistic practices in the US by focusing on Latinxs who use and learn Spanish as their heritage languages (e.g. Briceno *et al.*, 2018; Chaparro, 2019; Flores *et al.*, 2020) and African American Vernacular English (AAVE) speakers (e.g. Baker-Bell, 2020; Dyson & Smitherman, 2009; Khanna, 2016; Sung, 2018). Recently, there has been an increasing number of critical scholars working in regions beyond the traditional Western countries. By drawing attention to non-Western settings, myriad scholars (e.g. Babcock, 2022; Chandras, 2023; Garza, 2021; Lim *et al.*, 2021; Pak, 2021; Pak & Hiramoto, 2023; Roth-Gordon, 2017; Wirtz, 2014; Wong *et al.*, 2021) sought to investigate co-naturalizations of language and race by examining how a raciolinguistic perspective is intersectional and processual in social life.

For instance, Vincent Pak's (2021) study reported how antiracism was restructured as racism in Singapore, where members of the Indian community were publicly reprimanded for drawing attention to the government-sanctioned advertisement featuring a Chinese Singaporean actor in brownface to resemble an Indian Singaporean. As the findings showed that the state listening subject (Inoue, 2003) had significant power and substantial influence over the racialized speaking subject, the state listening subject was 'not only a percipient of linguistic practices but also an agent of rearticulation and racialization' (2003: 168). Pak addressed that although the theory of racial politics in the US would not be straightforwardly extrapolated to that of Singapore, the role of the state listening subject played a similar and central role in identifying the linguistic practices of racial minorities in Singapore. The racialization processes in Singapore, where marginalized groups are racialized alongside their linguistic practices (i.e. linguistic racism), suggests the need for a raciolinguistic perspective to undo taken-for-granted assumptions about language and race and to interrogate the naturalized relationship between race and language.

Similarly, Pak and Hiramoto (2023) examined Chinese privilege (i.e. 'a form of privilege accorded to those who can speak and understand the language [Chinese]') (2023: 54), which is prevalent in Singapore and is often regarded as a continuation of White privilege. Using Ahmed's (2004) notion of 'stickiness', Pak and Hiramoto coined the term 'sticky raciolinguistics' to explicate the inextricable co-naturalization of race and language in Singapore. They discussed how racialized power relations rooted in Whiteness and the system of white supremacy are reconstructed in postcolonial Singapore. Although the term 'Chinese privilege' is used to criticize or confess to racial advantages, it inadvertently reinforces existing racial categories. It perpetuates racialization by accepting a binary understanding of Chinese as a privileged group over other racial groups without thoroughly examining the complexities of race and privilege within the Chinese community. Like Whiteness in the US, Chineseness in Singapore becomes the default unmarked category associated with racial and linguistic privilege. Pak and Hiramoto described this as 'the reproductive semiotics of raciolinguistics [because] Chinese privilege is ultimately culpable in the reproduction of processes of racialization and racial categorization' (2023: 63). Their study insinuates how language contributes to sustaining racialized identities and inequalities by demonstrating how Chinese privilege reproduces racial categories and hierarchies.

Applying the theory of raciolinguistics to an Indian context, Chandras (2023) studied the identities and belonging of Banjara students by examining the complex and coalescing intersections of their race, socioeconomic class, language use and caste as postcolonial configurations, rather than looking at each element in isolation. By bringing an intersectional raciolinguistic perspective, Chandras revealed how language and language ideologies shape identity formation while also exposing the ways that race, in conjunction with caste, reproduce social segregation and socioeconomic disenfranchisement. This intersection often results in caste-based stigma and discrimination in Banjara students' identity construction. By exploring the impacts of the intersections of language use and race in India, where 'race and caste are mutually produced social hierarchies and unequal power structures' (2023: 7), Chandras's work contributed to the study of race and language by translating scholarship from the US and adapting it to the Indian context.

Research in the Western world paid little attention to Asian American language, racialization and education (Lo & Reyes, 2009). Yet, as discussed in the previous section, an increasing number of studies has recently focused on exploring the diverse experiences of Asian Americans across different ethnicities, examining issues such as intersectionality of racial and linguistic (in)justice (e.g. Babcock, 2022; Chandras, 2023; Garza, 2021; Lim *et al.*, 2021; Pak, 2021; Pak & Hiramoto, 2023; Wong *et al.*, 2021). Although recent scholarship has been carried out in countries situated on the continent of Asia by including individuals of Asian descent, more studies are still needed to investigate how Asian American students in the US encounter and disrupt raciolingustic ideologies while navigating a predominantly White society shaped by White privilege. Scholarship in Asian American studies in the past posited Asian Americans as perpetual foreigners due to their inherently foreign social and racial positioning (Lee *et al.*, 2009). Yet, racial positioning is also linked to linguistic ideologies (Rosa & Flores, 2017). Asian Americans are further perceived as 'linguistically White' (Yoo *et al.*, 2023) because they are more likely to be assimilated speakers of 'standard' American English and often do not preserve foreign accents from their heritage – Asian – languages.

Asian American scholars (e.g. Chung Allred, 2007; Chou, 2008; Kawai, 2005; Lee, 2001, 2009; Lee *et al.*, 2009; Lee & Kumashiro, 2005; Museus & Kiang, 2009; Ngo & Lee, 2007; Wu, 2014; Xu & Lee, 2013; Young, 2009; Zhang, 2010) have chiefly conceptualized a model minority myth that 'weaponize[s] the racial visibility of Asian Americans' (Yoo *et al.*, 2023: 131), which perpetuates white supremacy and ethnoracial hierarchies. Racial formations from model minority logic view Asian Americans as socially and linguistically close to whites. The (in)visibility of Asian bodies is both through their racial formations and linguistic practice, which leads to them being seen as either 'perpetual foreigners' or 'honorary Whites' (Tuan, 1998). Through the lens of raciolinguistic ideologies that consider the intersectional ways in which race and language constitute power dynamics in society, I explored how racial and linguistic inequalities from a raciolinguistic hierarchy impact multiethnic Asian American students' (re)construction of their identity by elucidating the enmeshed relationships between race, language and power in a multilingual/multicultural world (Lee, 2024, 2025).

Racial and Linguistic Anthropological Analysis of Asian American Students through the Lens of Raciolinguistics and Using Raciosemiotics

In my recent study (Lee, 2025), I utilized racialized semiotics data (i.e. raciosemiotics) (Smalls, 2020) of Asian American students to explore how their race, language and body are deeply intertwined and co-construct one another in the process of constructing their identities. Using Alim *et al.*'s (2016) sociolinguistics framework that focuses on the intersection of language and race and employing the lens of raciolinguistics (Flores & Rosa, 2015), I examined how the two focal fifth-grade students who were from multi-ethnic families (one male: Kenny and one female: Sunny) shaped and negotiated their racial and linguistic identities to seek whether and if so, how raciolinguistic hierarchies impacted the construction of their ethno-racial and linguistic identities. Both Kenny and Sunny were native English speakers as American citizens but racially identified as half Korean and half Vietnamese because each of their parents was from Korea and Vietnam. I employed an ethnographic case study approach to document and analyze the students' biographical narratives (i.e. from their writing samples and interview transcripts) that accompanied their lived experiences, including their resistance and resilience as Asian Americans. The two students' raciosemiotic artifacts that illuminate how they constructed and enriched their identities when confronting both ethno–racial and linguistic barriers are presented and discussed in the next section.

Intersectionality of race, language and power: Dealing with racial and linguistic barriers

Both Kenny and Sunny shared that they confronted both racial and linguistic obstacles. For instance, Sunny, a native English speaker, considered she was neither Korean nor Vietnamese because she was not fluent in both languages. She specified, 'I can't really say I am Korean or Vietnamese because I can't speak the languages perfectly' (see Figure 6.1 from Chapter 6 Stanza 2; lines 1–2). She also shared that people do not consider her White American due to her observable Asian physical characteristics. Likewise, Kenny recognized that his racial and linguistic identity provided him a sense of belonging neither to the American group because of his skin color ('not white enough') nor to the Korean group due to his limited Korean language proficiency ('not fluent enough') (see Figure 8.1 Stanza 2; lines 4 –5). Kenny then indicated, 'When people see me, I am an Asian kid. When people hear me, I am an American kid'. (Stanza 1; lines 1–2). Yet, Kenny drew himself thinking only in English in his self-portrait (see Figure 8.3). Both Kenny and Sunny acknowledged that they faced racial and linguistic barriers that prevented them from fully belonging to their ethnic and cultural groups because there is an incongruence between how people perceive them (i.e. Asians based on their phenotypic characteristics) versus how people hear them (i.e. native speakers of American English).

Encountering Racial Ideologies and Domination: Identifying the Significance of Racial Positioning. Although raciolinguistic ideologies were involved in shaping who she was for Sunny, meaning that both racial and linguistic features contributed heavily to her overall identity, racial

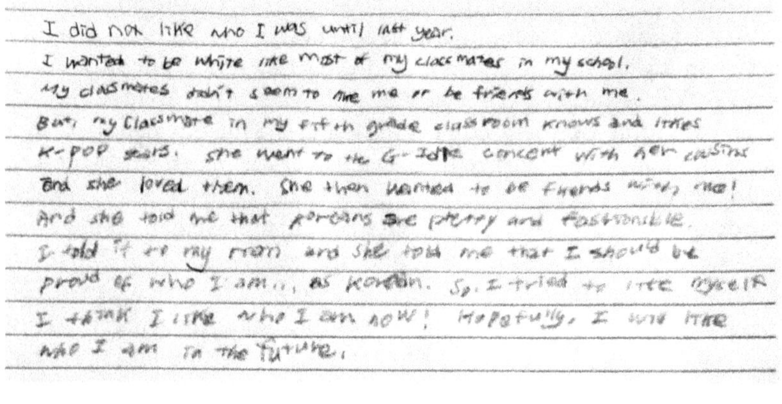

Figure 8.2 Sunny's autobiographical writing

American   thinking in English   Asian

SCHOOL   HOME

reading English

reading Korean comic books

listening English

listening to grandparents Speaking in Korean

Speaking English

speaking (short sentence) Korean

I love them so much

writing English

cooking Korean food

practicing Taekwondo

playing Basketball

traveling to Korea

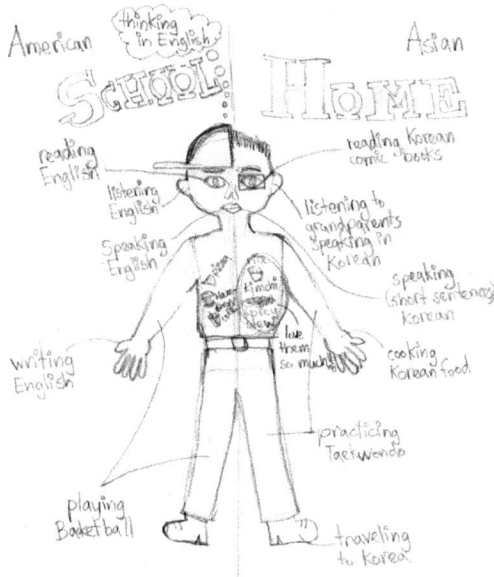

Figure 8.3 Kenny's self-portrait drawing

barriers seemed to be the most perceptible obstacles during her lifetime. Sunny identified and positioned herself as an ethnically other in her American school. Sunny understood that her racial positioning as Asian was a specific marker to determine that she was not considered enough to belong to the dominant group and society.

Experiencing Social Exclusion and Racial Segregation. Sunny stated that she experienced social exclusion from being marginalized by a peer group in her American school. In her autobiography, Sunny wrote, 'My classmates didn't seem to like me or be friends with me' (see Figure 8.2, line 3). During the interview, Sunny shared her honest thoughts about when she felt interpersonal rejection. Sunny stated that her phenotypic characteristics (i.e. Asian) led her deliberately to be excluded from her peer group, indicating her racial positioning played a pivotal role in belonging to the White peer group. She recalled:

There were four girls in my class. They looked cool and they were *popular*, so I wanted to be a part of that group, but I felt like they didn't like me. They seemed to be very close to one another already. I tried to approach them many times but couldn't fit into their group. I almost thought that they were so mean. The four girls are all White, by the way. I think they didn't include me because I looked different. Basically, I am not White. I think that's the reason why they didn't like me.

Sunny retrospectively regarded her biological traits (i.e. being non-White) as the salient marker that hindered her from joining the friend group she wanted to belong. As denoted in her responses, Sunny believed that her Asian racial identity hampered her building relationships with the so-called *popular* group because she was identified as racially and ethnically other. For Sunny, her race appeared as a barrier to her legitimate belonging in the peer group and her identification. As Sunny's racial identity acted as a significant way to build a sense of belonging and emotional connection within relationships, her experience led her to identify a racial hierarchy where White is considered higher than other racial groups.

Recognizing White Privilege and White Supremacy. Sunny not only experienced social exclusion and racial segregation but also acknowledged White supremacy while living in the US. Sunny wrote, in her poem (see Figure 6.1 from Chapter 6), that she desired to have the physical characteristics that are associated with White Americans, specifically lighter skin, blonde hair and large eyes. She believed that those features are considered the global beauty standard, which is deeply intertwined with the concept of White privilege, signifying societal advantages and benefits given to people perceived as White. Sunny then shared one of her friends' stories to corroborate her claim about White-skin privilege.

> My friend who I know from the church is mixed. She is half Asian and half White. Her dad is American, and her mom is Korean. But she just looks like White. I didn't know that she was half-Korean until she told me. We are both Asian-Americans, but we look different. I think she is lucky to be White because she doesn't have to go through all the challenges I deal with because I am 100% Asian. She looks the same or almost similar to other White girls in my school. That's how people see us: she [is] American, and I [am] Asian.

As shown, Sunny identified White-skin privilege as the societal privilege that benefits white people over non-white people in societies and protects white people against any form of discrimination. During the interview, Sunny addressed the benefits of being White while living in the US, such as not getting discriminated against and being perceived to be more popular and physically attractive among peers than other racial groups. Sunny also understood that the racial position of Asians within US society was often labeled as inherently deficient. Sunny considered that her friend, whose phenotypical features were close to whites, had more privilege than herself. She used the adjectives 'same' and 'almost similar' [to White people] when describing how her friend looked, but chose the word 'different' [from Whites] when illustrating her own appearance. Sunny's responses indicate that an individual's core identity is primarily based on their phenotypic traits.

Although both Sunny and her friend are native English speakers and learning Korean as their heritage language, her friend, who is half Korean and half Caucasian American, can be easily included in the majority group as she appears White. In contrast, Sunny, who is half Korean and half Vietnamese, is regarded as a racial minority because she does not look White. Sunny's subsequent statements ('That's how people see us. She [is] American, but I [am] Asian') during the interview further indicate how others' perception of identifying minority groups is fundamental because the dichotomy of 'looking like us' versus 'not looking like us' is based mainly on the racialized ideologies where Whiteness as the norm (Rosa, 2018).

Sunny asserted that racialized individuals' races can easily trigger people's positive or negative perceptions about their perceived identities. Sunny's story demonstrates that although White unmarked English could offset marginalized individuals' ethnic–racial stigma, 'their racially marked Otherness is never erased' (Kubota et al., 2023: 774). By identifying the existence of ethno–racial hierarchies and White privilege, Sunny recognized that she was categorized as Other due to her phenotypically racialized body, and she internalized how White people and their perceptions judge her racial identities. For Sunny, Whiteness, which is an unmarked and default racial category, provides both privilege and inequality (Babcock & Ke-Schutte, 2023). In other words, her social and racial positioning as Asian not only became a barrier when establishing a sense of her legitimate belonging to the dominant group but also could perpetuate the racial status quo and ingrained systems of racism (Flores, 2019).

Shifting Perspectives on Racial Identity Due to White People's Judgment. When comparing Sunny's autobiographical writing at the beginning and end (see Figure 8.2), it is evident that her viewpoints and perspectives have shifted. As discussed earlier, Sunny desired to be White. Yet, her autobiography explains that what she heard from her White classmate, who adored Korean celebrities and complimented Korean people, ultimately led Sunny to be confident in herself as Korean. Sunny shared during the interview:

> I never imagined that White people would think Koreans are pretty. So what my classmate told me was surprising because I always wanted to be White. But now I think being Asian is okay because White people like my classmate actually think that Koreans are pretty.

Sunny's testimonies demonstrate how the White peer's opinion or judgment played a major role in reshaping how she saw herself. Sunny admitted that her White classmate's compliments on Korean people led her to change her mindset and restructure her viewpoints. The White peer's positive perceptions of Korean ethnic identities appear to be a keen booster for Sunny to rethink her perception of being ethnically Korean by providing external validation that counters any internalized negative self-concept. Sunny's perspective transformation indicates that White people's views and perceptions still can easily determine who (or which racial/ethnic groups) are close enough to belong to the dominant group in society. As shown, Sunny's storytelling signifies the significant role of White people, who hold the most power in this racialized society.

Confronting Language Ideologies and Hierarchies: Understanding the Importance of Linguistic Abilities. Raciolinguistic ideologies were also deeply involved in establishing Kenny's identities since both race and language use have impacted Kenny's group memberships and social identities. Yet, unlike Sunny, Kenny viewed linguistic boundaries played a more crucial role than racial positioning in his life. Kenny shared multiple situations he had encountered to bolster his opinion about why people's language skills and linguistic identities are essential elements in establishing their group identity and solidarity.

Recognizing Language as a Marker to be Included in the Same Social and Cultural Groups. Kenny believed that language is a significant marker for identifying an individual's nationality and citizenship, which may differ from one's inherent ethnicity. Kenny explained that although his physical appearance identified him as Asian, his proficiency in the English language led him to identify himself as American. During the interview, Kenny stated:

> Although I like Asian, I am closer to American [than Asian]. My language proves this. I am fluent in English but not in Korean nor Vietnamese.... How you look is more important than having native-like proficiency at first because people judge you based on how you look. But once they know you, they will listen to you. So how you sound becomes more important [than how you look] to fit in. You can be friends with people who have different skin colors if they speak the same language, but it is very difficult to be close friends with a person who doesn't share the same language with you.

As exhibited, Kenny indicated that he was often initially perceived as Asian by others due to his racial phenotype before he was identified as a native speaker of American English. Kenny noted that one's perceived race is important initially, but language use and skills eventually become more salient factors in identifying one's group memberships and social affiliations. Kenny's biographical poem substantiates his argument that the linguistic boundary is more salient than the racial boundary. Kenny wrote, 'People think that I can speak perfect Korean because I look like Korean. But I say, "Sorry, I don't speak Korean well..."' (see Figure 8.1 Stanza 3; line 3) to people who thought he was a fluent Korean speaker only looking at his physical phenotype. He then stated, 'I am probably closer to American than Korean because I am fluent in English' (lines 4–5). Kenny's poem affirms that people who share the same language (despite their different races or physical appearances) can be closer than those who share the same racial or ethnic background but do not speak the same language. Kenny recognized his language skills as the most fundamental criterion in constructing his identity because he understood that linguistic ability in the shared language was the most perceptible factor in feeling solidarity and being accepted by others.

Kenny's belief that linguistic abilities are more important than racial background was reinforced when he shared his experiences in Korea. In his autobiography (see Figure 8.4), Kenny shared that he felt excluded when his relatives thought he was not 'genuine' (emphasis in original) Korean due to his limited proficiency in the language (Para 2; line 3). This experience directed him to realize that 'being fluent in Korean is important to be a real (emphasis in original) Korean' (Para 3; lines 1–2). Kenny explained during the interview that, 'although people assume that I am Korean by looking at how I look, they later figure out that I am not genuine Korean'. He highlighted the words 'real' and 'genuine' to describe the individual who perfectly speaks the shared language among the ethnic group. Kenny then pointed out that he could be called 'fasian', which refers to 'fake Asian' (people who physically appear to be of Asian descent but do not speak their heritage language). Kenny expressed a sense of isolation, felt rejected from his heritage culture and considered himself as not a 'true' member of a Korean ethnic/cultural group due to his American-accented Korean, which directed him to understand that individuals' (in)competence in their language skills is related to the notion of (il)legitimacy of their ethno-racial identities.

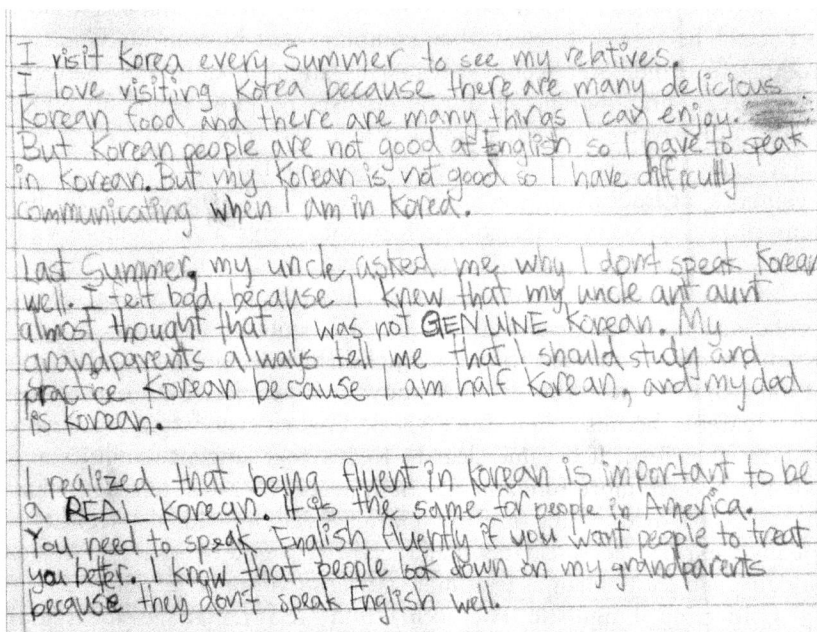

Figure 8.4 Kenny's autobiographical writing

Grasping the Importance of White Listeners' Perception. Kenny understood that racialized individuals' language practices are often judged or perceived based on their races or ethnicities. By acknowledging how others' perception plays a pivotal role in determining his linguistic abilities, Kenny comprehended that White people tend to pre-assume racially marginalized people's language skills based on their race. Yet, Kenny realized that if the racialized individuals possess discrete language skills in Standard English, White people are more likely to re-evaluate those speakers' language ability and linguistic identity. Kenny shared:

> When my new neighbors met my family for the first time, my grand-parents barely spoke English, so they automatically thought that I didn't speak English like my grandparents. But once they heard me, they seemed to be surprised. I saw their faces and that kind of reaction. They even asked me how I could be so good at English. Later, when the neighbors visited our house to ask something, they were looking for me although they had to talk about the issue with my grandparents because I am basically good at English. So, I became a translator for them. That's how I know being fluent in the language is important.

Kenny believed that race plays an important role in identifying racially minoritized people's linguistic skills as his neighbors predetermined his language abilities by merely hearing from his grandparents' limited English proficiency. But, as Kenny stated, his neighbors' judgments did not last long; as soon as they heard from Kenny and knew how proficient he was in English, they complimented him on his language competence and later Kenny became a language translator between his Korean grandparents and the English-speaking neighbors. This example illustrates how race can be a marker for White listeners' first impression of racialized people to judge their language abilities. The neighbors' attitudes and reactions, however, led Kenny to realize that minoritized speakers' linguistic performance plays a much more vital role than their race in identifying who they are or where they belong. In his autobiography, Kenny also explained the importance of having proficiency in the language of the society or country in which one resides. Kenny wrote, 'You need to speak English fluently [in America] if you want people to treat you better. I know that people look down on my grandparents because they don't speak English well.' (see Figure 8.4 Para 3; lines 3–5). It became clear to Kenny that language abilities and competence are more fundamental than perceived racial position when it comes to determining racially marginalized individuals' identities. Kenny's experience elucidates that racialized people who sound White are given an entitlement as legitimate citizens (Kubota *et al.*, 2023).

Criticizing Linguistic Hierarchization and Language Ideologies toward Non-Native Language Speakers. As Kenny believed that having language abilities is significant for racially minoritized individuals, he suggested that developing language proficiency is a way to narrow the gaps faced by racialized people due to their minority status. Kenny then shared his coping strategy during the interview by stating, 'I can be a better Korean if I study Korean harder and become good at speaking Korean'. Kenny understood that improving his Korean language skills would enable him to effortlessly belong to a Korean group. Yet, at the same time, Kenny acknowledged that he would not be considered an ethnic or cultural insider among the native Korean speakers. During the interview, Kenny further stated:

> I don't think I can be a *perfect* Korean [although I study Korean harder] because Korean people would know that I am not a *real* Korean. It is the same for my grandparents. Even though they practice English really hard, they can't be native English speakers because their heavy Korean accents make it difficult for Americans to understand when they say something in English. And, me, too. I sound awkward when I speak Korean because of my English accent. Korean people and even my grandparents often ask me to repeat what I said [in Korean]. I already know that I can't, I wish I could, but I can't be 100% *perfect* Korean.

Kenny's responses imply that although he could narrow his linguistic barrier by improving his Korean skills, he predicted that he would not be considered a native speaker of Korean because Korean listeners would detect his non-native renditions of Korean language sounds when he speaks. In other words, Kenny, who appears to be Korean, would always be perceived as linguistically other not because of his racial identity but due to his linguistic abilities by native Korean listeners. Kenny drew upon his critical consciousness, recognizing that his Korean skills are not based on how much he exercises and practices, but rather on listeners' (i.e. native Koreans) judgment and evaluations. Kenny reiterated the importance of listeners' perceptions, as they could determine speakers' language performance and competence based on native speakers' discernment. Kenny's experience in Korea – his limited Korean language skills hampered his ability to fit into the Korean group – led him to understand that his imperfect Korean accent intensified his position as an outsider despite his appearance, unlike Sunny, Kenny understood that his phenotype was not a primary factor influencing his sense of belonging; instead, his language abilities shaped his feelings of inclusion or exclusion.

Using the raciosemiotic framework, I discovered how the students' racialized identities are expressed and understood through their linguistic practices. Both students identified that raciolinguistic ideologies were embedded in their lived experiences and had shaped the course of their lives, but what each student considered the most detectable barrier in their lives was not the same. Sunny understood that one's racial identity was more important than language abilities in a sense of group position. In contrast, Kenny believed that an individual's language use was an essential indicator to identify where the person belongs to. Yet, both students identified the vital role of the White people, specifically their stated views on the Korean people (for Sunny) and their perception as the listening subjects (for Kenny).

Implications for Educational and Research Practice of Centering a Raciolinguistic Approach and Perspective

This chapter reinforces ideological challenges that racially marginalized groups face in the US educational system and establishes how raciolinguistic ideologies deeply operate in (re)shaping and negotiating racialized people's identities. By highlighting the intersectional ways in which race and language constitute power dynamics in society, the chapter demonstrates how multi-ethnic Asian American students confronted ethno-racial and linguistic barriers when participating in dynamic life events and discursive practices. As students understood that their physical appearance and language performance could accentuate their positions as Otherness, educators need to understand the centrality of co-naturalizations of language and race, as well as the interlaced connection between the two, to speculate on how individuals' racial, ethnic and national identities impact their lived experiences of linguistic practices or vice versa. This chapter demonstrated that raciolinguistic hierarchy impacted the multi–ethnic Asian American students' (re)construction and transformation of their identity by elucidating the enmeshed relationships between race, language and power in a racialized world.

Since mainstream school curriculum still largely provides discourses where Caucasian protagonists play a significant role in the White culture, asking mixed-ethnic or multi-racial students to share their stories with other student groups can offer different standpoints to challenge inaccurate stereotypes, prejudices and misconceptions about underrepresented groups. As the findings of the raciolinguistic study presented in this chapter show, students' discussions and reflections on their racial identity and linguistic practices can further inform educators and researchers about how they deal with and make sense of who they are within the raciolinguistic social and educational context. Educators ought to acknowledge each student's unique life experiences, varied discursive practices and individual thinking processes by allowing them to investigate and enrich their multi-layered, collective identities through relevant literacy practices. The discussion in this chapter underscores the pedagogical implications for educators of marginalized students that using racialized semiotics data (i.e. raciosemiotics) from students' biographical narratives (e.g. writing an autobiography, crafting a self-portrait creating an 'I Am' poem) can be a powerful analytical tool to understand the impact of language and race on the trajectories of their identity development. Literacy educators and researchers working with students with multiple identities are required to understand that encouraging students to create raciosemiotic artifacts by reflecting on their past and present experiences and allowing them to share their honest reactions and emotions verbally would provide them opportunities to explore, construct and negotiate their distinctive racial, linguistic and social identities.

References

Ahmed, S. (2004) Affective economies. *Social Text* 22 (2), 117–139.

Alim, S. and Smitherman, G. (2012) *Articulate While Black: Barack Obama, Language, and Race in the U.S.* Oxford University Press.

Alim, S., Reyes, A. and Kroskrity, P. (2020) The field of language and race: A linguistic anthropological approach to race, racism, and racialization. In S. Alim, A. Reyes and P. Kroskrity (eds) *The Oxford Handbook of Language and Race* (pp. 1–21). Oxford University Press.

Alim, S., Rickford, J.R. and Ball, A.F. (2016) *Raciolinguistics: How Language Shapes Our Ideas about Race.* Oxford University Press.

Angermuller, J. (2014) *Poststructuralist Discourse Analysis. Subjectivity in Enunciative Pragmatics.* Palgrave Macmillan.

Austin, J.L. (1962) *How to Do Things with Words.* Clarendon Press.

Babcock, J. (2022) Postracial policing, "Mother Tongue" sourcing, and images of Singlish standard. *Journal of Linguistic Anthropology* 32 (2), 326–344.

Babcock, J. and Ke-Schutte, J. (2023) Toward a "both-and" semiotics of intersectionality: Raciolinguistics beyond white settler-colonial situations. *Signs and Society* 11 (1), 1–21.

Baker-Bell, A. (2020) *Linguistic Justice.* Routledge.

Baugh, J. (2003) Linguistic profiling. In S. Makoni, G. Smitherman, A. Ball and A. Spears (eds) *Black Linguistics: Language, Society, and Politics in Africa and the America* (pp. 155–163). Routledge.

Beetz, J. and Schwab, V. (2017) *Material Discourse—Materialist Analysis: Approaches in Discourse Studies.* Lexington Books.

Blommaert, J. (2005) *Discourse: A Critical Introduction.* Cambridge University Press. https://doi.org/10.1017/CBO9780511610295.

Bourdieu, P. (1991) *Language and Symbolic Power.* Polity Press.

Brayboy, B.M., Castagno, A. and Maughan, E. (2007) Equality and justice for all? Examining race in education scholarship. *Review of Research in Education* 31, 159–194.

Caldera, A. and Babino, A. (2020) Moving toward culturally sustaining language instruction that resists white language supremacy. *The National Journal of Middle Grades Reform* 3, 9–15.

Chandras, J. (2023) (Out)Caste language ideologies: Intersectional raciolinguistic stigma and assimilation from denotified tribal students' perspectives in rural India. *Journal of Linguistic Anthropology* 33 (2), 161–183.

Chaparro, S.E. (2019) But mom! I'm not a Spanish boy: Raciolinguistic socialization in a two-way immersion bilingual program. *Linguistics and Education* 50, 1–12.

Chou, C.C. (2008) Critique on the notion of model minority: An alternative racism to Asian American? *Asian Ethnicity* 9 (3), 219–229.

Chun, E. (2011) Reading race beyond black and white. *Discourse & Society* 22 (4), 403–421. https://doi.org/10.1177/0957926510395833.

Chung Allred, N. (2007) Asian Americans and affirmative action: From yellow peril to model minority and back again. *Asian American Law Journal* 14 (1), 57–84.

Crenshaw, K. (1989) Demarginalizing the intersection of race and sex: A black feminist critique of antidiscrimination doctrine, feminist theory and antiracist politics. *University of Chicago Legal Forum* 8 (1), 139–167.

Crenshaw, K. (1991) Mapping the margins: Intersectionality, identity politics, and violence against women of color. *Stanford Law Review* 43 (6), 1241–1299. https://doi.org/10.2307/1229039.

Crump, A. (2014) Introducing LangCrit: Critical language and race theory. *Critical Inquiry in Language Studies* 11 (3), 207–224. https://doi.org/10.1080/15427587.2014.936243.

Dyson, A.H. and Smitherman, G. (2009) The right (write) start: African American language and the discourse of sounding right. *Teachers College Record* 111 (4), 973–998.

Errington, J. (2001) Ideology. In A. Duranti (ed.) *Key Terms in Language and Culture* (pp. 110–112). Blackwell.

Essed, P. (1991) *Understanding Everyday Racism: An Interdisciplinary Theory*. Sage.

Fairclough, N. (1989) *Language and Power*. Longman.

Fairclough, N. (1992) Discourse and text: Linguistic and intertextual analysis within discourse analysis. *Discourse and Society* 3, 193–217. https://doi.org/10.1177/0957926592003002004.

Fairclough, N. (2003) *Analysing Discourse: Textual Analysis for Social Research*. Routledge.

Flores, N. (2019) Translanguaging into raciolinguistic ideologies: A personal reflection on the legacy of Ofelia García. *Journal of Multilingual Education Research* 9 (5), 45–60.

Flores, N. and Rosa, J. (2015) Undoing appropriateness: Raciolinguistic ideologies and language diversity in education. *Harvard Educational Review* 85, 149–171.

Flores, N., Phoung, J. and Venegas, K. (2020) "Technically an EL": The Production of raciolinguistic categories in a dual language school. *TESOL Quarterly* 54 (3), 629–651.

Garza, J.Y. (2021) "Where all my bad girls at?": Cosmopolitan femininity through racialised appropriations in K-pop. *Gender and Language* 15 (1), 11–41.

Gee, J.P. (2007) *Social Linguistics and Literacies: Ideology in Discourses*. Routledge.

Goffman, E. (1974) *Frame Analysis: An Essay on the Organization of Experience*. Harvard University Press.

Halliday, M.A.K. (1975) *Learning How to Mean: Explorations in the Development of Language*. Edward Arnold.

Herzog, B. (2016) Discourse analysis as immanent critique: Possibilities and limits of normative critique in empirical discourse studies. *Discourse & Society* 27 (3), 278–292. https://doi.org/10.1177/0957926516630897.

Herzog, B. and Porfillio, L.A. (2022) Talking with racists: Insights from discourse and communication studies on the containment of far-right movements. *Humanity Social Science Communication* 9, 384. https://doi.org/10.1057/s41599-022-01406-y.

Hill, J. H. (2008) *The Everyday Language of White Racism*. Wiley Blackwell.

Inoue, M. (2003) The listening subject of Japanese modernity and his auditory double: Citing, sighting, and siting the modern Japanese woman. *Cultural Anthropology* 18, 156–193.

Irvine, J.T. (1989) When talk isn't cheap: Language and political economy. *American Ethnologist* 16 (2), 248–267. http://www.jstor.org/stable/645001.

Irvine, J.T. (1990) Registering affect: Heteroglossia in the linguistic expression of emotion. In C.A. Lutz and L. Abu-Lughod (eds) *Language and the Politics of Emotion* (pp. 126–161). Cambridge University Press.

Irvine, J.T. and Gal, S. (2000) Language ideology and linguistic differentiation. In P.V. Kroskrity (ed.) *Regimes of Language* (pp. 35–84). School of American Research Press.

Kawai, Y. (2005) Stereotyping Asian Americans: The dialectic of the model minority and the yellow peril. *Howard Journal of Communications* 16 (2), 109–130.

Khanna, N. (2016) "If you're half black, you're just black": Reflected appraisals and the persistence of the one-drop rule. *The Sociological Quarterly* 51 (1), 96–121.

Kroskrity, P.V. (2004) A companion to linguistic anthropology. In A. Duranti (ed.) *Language Ideologies* (pp. 496–517). Wiley-Blackwell.

Kroskrity, P.V. (2010) Language ideologies–Evolving perspectives. *Society and Language Use* 7 (3), 192–205.

Kroskrity, P.V. (2018) On recognizing persistence in the indigenous language ideologies of multilingualism in two native American communities. *Language and Communication* 62, 133–44.

Kroskrity, P.V. (2020) Theorizing linguistic racisms from a language ideological perspective. In H.S. Alim, A. Reyes and P.V. Kroskrity (eds) *The Oxford Handbook of Language and Race* (pp. 68–89). Oxford University Press.

Kroskrity, P.V. (2021) Language ideological assemblages within linguistic anthropology In A. Burkette and T. Warhol (eds) *Crossing Borders: Making Connections: Interdisciplinarity in Linguistics* (pp. 129–141). Mouton de Gruyter.

Kubota, R., Corella, M., Lim, K. and Sah, P. (2023) "Your English is so good": Linguistic experiences of racialized students and instructors of a Canadian university. *Ethnicities* 23 (5), 758–778.

Lee, C. (2024) Sanctioning a space for transnational literacy practices in a HL classroom. *International Multilingual Research Journal* 19 (1), 1–22. https://doi.org/10.1080/19313152.2024.2309695.

Lee, C. (2025) Challenging raciolinguistic ideologies: Asian American students' stories of resistance and resilience. *Asian Ethnicity*, 1–28. https://doi.org/10.1080/14631369.2025.2551703.

Lee, S.J. (2001) More than "model minorities" or "delinquents": A look at Hmong American high school students. *Harvard Educational Review* 71 (3), 505–528.

Lee, S.J. (2009) *Unraveling the "Model Minority" Stereotype: Listening to Asian American Youth* (2nd edn). Teachers College Press.

Lee, S.J. and Kumashiro, K.K. (2005) *A Report on the Status of Asian Americans and Pacific Islanders in Education: Beyond the "Model Minority" Stereotype*. National Education Association.

Lee, S., Wong, N.A. and Alvarez, A. (2009) The model minority and perpetual foreigner: Stereotypes of Asian Americans. In N. Tewari and A. Alvarez (eds) *Asian American Psychology: Current Perspectives* (pp. 69–84). Psychology Press.

Leonard, W. (2023) Refusing "endangered languages" narratives. *Daedalus* 152 (3), 69–83.

Lim, J.J., Chen, S.C. and Hiramoto, M. (2021) "You don't ask me to speak Mandarin, okay?": Ideologies of language and race among Chinese Singaporeans. *Language & Communication* 76, 100–110.

Lippi-Green, R. (1997) *English with an Accent: Language, Ideology, and Discrimination in the United States*. Psychology Press.

Lo, A. (2020) Race, language, and representations. *International Journal of the Sociology of Language* 263, 77–83.

Lo, A. and Reyes, A. (2009) Introduction: On yellow English and other perilous terms. In A. Reyes and A. Lo (eds) *Beyond Yellow English: Toward a Linguistic Anthropology of Asian Pacific America* (pp. 3–17). Oxford University Press.

May, S. (2023) Linguistic racism: Origins and implications. *Ethnicities* 23 (5), 651–661.

Museus, S.D. and Kiang, P.N. (2009) Deconstructing the model minority myth and how it contributes to the invisible minority reality in higher education research. *New Directions for Institutional Research* 142, 5–15. https://doi.org/10.1002/ir.292.

Ngo, B. and Lee, S.J. (2007) Complicating the image of model minority success: A review of Southeast Asian American education. *Review of Educational Research* 77, 415–453.

Pak, V. (2021) (De)Coupling race and language: The state listening subject and its rearticulation of antiracism as racism in Singapore. *Language in Society* 51 (1), 1–22.

Pak, V. and Hiramoto, M. (2023) Sticky raciolinguistics. *Signs and Society* 11 (1), 45–67.

Reisigl, M. and Wodak, R. (2001) *Discourse and Discrimination: Rhetorics of Racism and Antisemitism*. Routledge.

Rosa, J. (2018) *Looking like a Language, Sounding like a Race: Raciolinguistic Ideologies and the Learning of Latinidad*. Oxford University Press.

Rosa, J. and Flores, N. (2017) Unsettling language and race: Toward a raciolinguistic perspective. *Language in Society* 46, 621–647.

Rosa, J. and Burdick, C. (2017) Language ideologies. In O. García, N. Flores and M. Spotti (eds) *The Oxford Handbook of Language and Society*. Oxford University Press.

Roth-Gordon, J. (2017) *Race and the Brazilian Body: Blackness, Whiteness, and Everyday Language in Rio de Janeiro*. University of California Press. https://doi.org/10.1525/california/9780520293793.001.0001.

Rumsey, A. (1990) Wording, meaning, and linguistic ideology. *American Anthropologist* 92, 346–361. https://doi.org/10.1525/aa.1990.92.2.02a00060.

Schiffrin, D. (1995) Theory and method in discourse analysis: What context for what unit? *Language and Communication* 17 (2), 75–92.

Silverstein, M. (1979) Language structure and linguistic ideology. In C. Hofbauer, P. Clyne and W. Hanks (eds) *The Elements: A Parasession on Linguistic Units and Levels* (pp. 193–247). Chicago Linguistic Society.

Smalls, K.A. (2020) Race, SIGNS, and the body: Towards a theory of racial semiotics. In H.S. Alim, A. Reyes and P. Kroskrity (eds) *Oxford Handbook of Language and Race* (pp. 233–260). Oxford University Press.

Sung, K.K. (2018) Raciolinguistic ideology of antiblackness: Bilingual education, tracking, and the multiracial imaginary in urban schools. *International Journal of Qualitative Studies in Education* 31 (8), 667–683.

Tuan, M. (1998) *Forever Foreigners or Honorary Whites? The Asian Ethnic Experience Today*. Rutgers University Press.

Urciuoli, B. (2011) Discussion essay: Semiotic properties of racializing discourses. *Journal of Linguistic Anthropology* 21 (s1), E113–E122. https://doi.org/10.1111/j.1548-1395.2011.01100.x.

Valdes, G. (2023) Social justice challenges of "teaching" languages. *Daedalus* 152 (3), 52–68.

van Dijk, T.A. (1993) Principles of critical discourse analysis. *Discourse & Society* 4 (2), 249–283. https://doi.org/10.1177/0957926593004002006.

van Dijk, T.A. (2006) Discourse and manipulation. *Discourse & Society* 17 (3), 359–383. https://doi.org/10.1177/0957926506060250.

van Dijk, T.A. (2009) *Society and Discourse. How Social Contexts Influence Text and Talk*. Cambridge University Press. https://doi.org/10.1017/CBO9780511575273.

Van Dijk, T.A. (2011) *Discourse Studies*. Sage.

Wetherell, M. and Potter, J. (1992) *Mapping the Language of Racism: Discourse and the Legitimation of Exploitation*. Columbia University Press.

Wirtz, K. (2014) *Performing Afro-Cuba: Image, Voice, Spectacle in the Making of Race and History*. University of Chicago Press.

Wodak, R. (1996) *Disorders of Discourse*. Longman.

Wodak, R. and Richardson, J.E. (2013) Analysing Fascist discourse. European Fascism in talk and text. *Journal of Argumentation in Context* 2 (3), 352–358.

Wolfram, W., Hudley, A.C. and Valdés, G. (2023) Language & social justice in the United States: An introduction. *Daedalus* 152 (3), 5–17.

Wong, A.D., Su, H. and Hiramoto, M. (2021) Complicating raciolinguistics: Language, Chineseness, and the Sinophone. *Language & Communication* 76 (1), 131–135.

Wu, E.D. (2014) *The Color of Success: Asian Americans and the Origins of the Model Minority*. Princeton University Press.

Xu, J. and Lee, J.C. (2013) The marginalized "Model" minority: An empirical examination of the racial triangulation of Asian Americans. *Social Forces* 91 (4), 1363–1397.

Yoo, J., Lee, C., Cheng, A. and Anand, A. (2023) Asian American racialization & model minority logics in linguistics. *Daedalus* 152 (3), 130–146.

Young, A.V. (2009) Honorary whiteness. *Asian Ethnicity* 10 (2), 177–185.

Zhang, Q. (2010) Asian Americans beyond the model minority stereotype: The nerdy and the left out. *Journal of International and Intercultural Communication* 3 (1), 20–37.

9 A Call to Action for Educators

Applying the New Knowledge Gained

After social anthropologist Steven Vertovec (2007) coined the term 'superdiversity' to describe a level of diversity that is significantly more complex and multifaceted than previously understood, the concept of superdiversity has been adopted by a broad range of scholars and researchers across different disciplines (Blommaert, 2013; Creese & Blackledge, 2010). About a decade and a half after the term was introduced, our society has become ever more socially, culturally, politically and globally complicated and dynamic; thus, what Vertovec defined as superdiversity has undergone more radical changes. Beck (2011: 53) indeed claimed that 'we do not even have the language through which contemporary superdiversity in the world can be described, conceptualized, understood, explained and researched'. Blommaert *et al.* (2015: 1) defined superdiversity as 'diversity of diversity' because analyzing social dynamics requires multi-dimensional understanding and various intersecting elements beyond different ethnic or migrant groups (Song, 2023; Vertovec, 2017). Therefore, superdiversity signifies a society where cultural transformations and social changes are inevitable, and the level of variation surpasses traditional notions of diversity.

Responding to the current superdiverse global society, this book examines important philosophical concepts, theories and perspectives that contemporary educators need to understand when serving and supporting students from diverse racial, ethnic, linguistic, social and cultural backgrounds. Specifically, by introducing multilingualism and plurilingualism as new norms in US schools, Chapter 1 discussed the necessity of adapting teaching methods and implementing diverse instructional strategies in today's US schools, reflecting the ever-changing ethnic and racial backgrounds of school-aged students. Chapter 2 emphasized the importance of creating a transformative third space to facilitate historically minoritized students (i.e. heritage language learners who are children of immigrant parents) in developing their multi-layered identities by integrating their diverse linguistic/cultural experiences and dynamic discursive practices. Chapters 3 and 4 focused on the practical pedagogy and practices of translanguaging by illustrating teachers' translanguaging instructional pedagogy and bi/multi/plurilingual students' translanguaging performance, respectively. The chapters demonstrated how classroom teachers' strategically planned pedagogical translanguaging facilitated the learning, comprehension and participation of RCLD students by fostering more inclusive and ethical learning environments.

Chapter 5 highlighted the significance of enacting pedagogical interventions and innovations through culturally responsive instruction, demonstrating the benefits of incorporating multicultural literature (as an example of resource pedagogy) in facilitating students' cultural competence and understanding of justice and equity. By introducing the phenomena of transnationalism and transculturalism, Chapter 6 explained how transnational literacies can be used in literacy lessons to leverage students' dynamic border-crossing experiences and cultivate their sophisticated and multi-dimensional identities. Chapter 7 elucidated how teachers can utilize critical literacy instruction, using counter-narratives as social justice pedagogical resources, to help students challenge dominant perspectives and disrupt hegemony, stereotypes and racism. Lastly, Chapter 8 explained the significance of identifying raciolinguistic ideologies that define the enmeshed relationships between language and race and suggested using raciosemiotics for educators to fully understand students' ethno-racial and linguistic identity (re)/(de)construction.

All the chapters in this book have explored philosophical concepts of knowledge in relation to serving students in our increasingly diverse societies and have discovered instructional practices that educators can implement in their lessons. Each chapter provides in-depth analysis of the Asian American students' artifacts, documentations and testimonies that showcase how they engaged in translanguaging, transmodal and trans-semiotizing practices to create meaning and fully participate in interactions (Chapter 4), developed their critical thinking and consciousness by actively analyzing societal issues presented in socially and culturally conscious multicultural literature to dismantle injustice (Chapter 5), navigated their transnationalism and transculturalism in validating and negotiating their dynamic and fluid identities (Chapter 6), used their voices, stories, experiences and perspectives to challenge dominant hegemony and widespread stereotypes when encountering Asian American counter-narratives (Chapter 7) and constructed their ethno-racial and linguistic identities by creating raciosemiotic artifacts to challenge raciolinguistic ideologies (Chapter 8).

By synthesizing the messages from each chapter, I hope that educators will understand the importance of prioritizing the accommodation of diverse upbringings, languages, cultures and experiences within the classroom, which is crucial for ensuring equitable learning opportunities. To support students from a superdiverse world who represent a complex mix of identities and create a rich tapestry of perspectives, educators should prioritize building a supportive and inclusive classroom environment that actively celebrates and includes diverse cultural identities, unique perspectives and various learning resources and materials. Educators are also highly encouraged to promote a positive learning community by fostering a welcoming atmosphere and promoting a supportive culture where all students feel valued, respected and empowered to reach their full potential.

Although the respective chapters discuss different concepts, theories and perspectives, readers can synthesize key ideas from each chapter and apply the pedagogical implications to their teaching practices to enhance instructional quality and move toward differentiated instruction that meets every student's needs. By providing equitable opportunities that legitimize multi/plurilingual and multi/pluricultural mindsets, educators can help their students prepare for a diverse world and empower them to succeed.

References

Beck, J.S. (2011) *Cognitive Behavior Therapy: Basics and Beyond* (2nd edn). Guilford Press.

Blommaert, J. (2013) *Ethnography, Superdiversity and Linguistic Landscapes: Chronicles of Complexity*. Multilingual Matters.

Blommaert, J., Spotti, M. and Van Der Aa, J. (2015) Complexity, mobility, migration. *Tilburg Papers in Cultural Studies* 137, 349–363.

Creese, A. and Blackledge, A. (2010) Towards a sociolinguistics of superdiversity. *Zu einer soziolinguistik von superdiversität* 13 (4), 549–572. https://doi.org/10.1007/s11618-010-0159-y.

Song, M. (2023) "Superdiversity": It still packs a punch. *Ethnic and Racial Studies* 47 (8), 1670–1677. https://doi.org/10.1080/01419870.2023.2227693.

Vertovec, S. (2007) Super-diversity and its implications. *Ethnic and Racial Studies* 30 (6), 1024–1054. https://doi.org/10.1080/01419870701599465.

Vertovec, S. (2017) Talking around super-diversity. *Ethnic and Racial Studies* 42 (1), 125–139. https://doi.org/0.1080/01419870.2017.1406128.

Index

For Product Safety Concerns and Information please contact our EU Authorised Representative:

Easy Access System Europe

Mustamäe tee 50

10621 Tallinn

Estonia

gpsr.requests@easproject.com

www.ingramcontent.com/pod-product-compliance
Lightning Source LLC
Chambersburg PA
CBHW062021270326
41929CB00014B/2278